THE VOYAGEUR

THE VOYAGEUR

BY

GRACE LEE NUTE

ILLUSTRATIONS BY
CARL W. BERTSCH

Reprint Edition
MINNESOTA HISTORICAL SOCIETY
St. Paul, 1955

∞ The paper used in this publication meets the
minimum requirements of the American National
Standard for Information Sciences — Permanence for
Printed Library Materials.
ANSI   Z39.48-1984.

MINNESOTA HISTORICAL SOCIETY PRESS, St. Paul 55101

First published in 1931 by D. Appleton and Company
Reprinted in 1955 by the Minnesota Historical Society
First paperback printing, 1987, by the Minnesota Historical Society

International Standard Book Number: 0-87351-213-8
Manufactured in the United States of America
10 9 8 7 6 5 4 3 2

Library of Congress Cataloging-in-Publication Data
Nute, Grace Lee, 1895-
The voyageur.
Reprint. Originally published: New York: D. Appleton, c1931.
Bibliography: p.
Includes index.
1. French-Canadians. 2. Fur trade — Canada. 3. Canada
— Social life and customs. I. Title.
F1027.N96   1986   971'.004114   86-28468

"SAID ONE OF THESE MEN, LONG PAST SEVENTY YEARS OF AGE: 'I COULD CARRY, PADDLE, WALK AND SING WITH ANY MAN I EVER SAW. I HAVE BEEN TWENTY-FOUR YEARS A CANOE MAN, AND FORTY-ONE YEARS IN SERVICE; NO PORTAGE WAS EVER TOO LONG FOR ME. FIFTY SONGS COULD I SING. I HAVE SAVED THE LIVES OF TEN VOYAGEURS. HAVE HAD TWELVE WIVES AND SIX RUNNING DOGS. I SPENT ALL MY MONEY IN PLEASURE. WERE I YOUNG AGAIN, I SHOULD SPEND MY LIFE THE SAME WAY OVER. THERE IS NO LIFE SO HAPPY AS A VOYAGEUR'S LIFE!'"

PREFACE

It is time to write the story of the voyageur. His canoe has long since vanished from the northern waters; his red cap is seen no more, a bright spot against the blue of Lake Superior; his sprightly French conversation, punctuated with inimitable gesture, his exaggerated courtesy, his incurable romanticism, his songs, and his superstitions are gone.

In certain old books and in many unpublished manuscripts, however, he still lives. Read the diaries of Montreal fur-traders and the books of travelers on the St. Lawrence, the Saskatchewan, and the Great Lakes in the eighteenth and early nineteenth centuries. From their pages peals the laughter of a gay-hearted, irrepressible race; over night waters floats the plaintive song of canoeman, swelled periodically in the chorus by the voices of his lusty mates; portage path and campfire, foaming rapids and placid fir-fringed lake, shallow winding stream and broad expanse of inland sea, whitewalled cottage of Quebec hamlet and frowning pickets of Northwest post—become once more the voyageur's habitat; the French *régime* comes to its tragic close on the Plains of Abraham; the British rule lasts but a brief half-century in a large portion of the fur country; Washington supersedes London in the allegiance of many of the red children of the far western waters—still the

vii

voyageur places his wooden crosses by dangerous *sault* and treacherous eddy, sings of love in sunny Provence, and claims his dram on New Year's morning, undisturbed by wars, treaties, and the running of invisible boundary lines.

Though he is one of the most colorful figures in the history of a great continent, the voyageur remains unknown to all but a few. This little book seeks to do justice to his memory for the romance and color he has lent to American and Canadian history, and for the services he rendered in the exploration of the West.

My thanks are hereby offered to the many persons who have given me assistance and encouragement in the preparation of this study. I am especially indebted to several members of the staff of the Minnesota Historical Society, who have called my attention to data relating to the voyageurs; and to my sister, Virginia Beveridge, who typed the manuscript for me. Mr. Marius Barbeau, of the National Museum, Ottawa, has been both generous and very helpful in supplying me with the airs and words of "La belle Lisette" and "Voici le printemps," as well as with some material that does not appear in this volume. To Mr. J. Murray Gibbon I also wish to extend my thanks for his generosity in translating several songs especially for this volume. I am also grateful to Miss Constance A. Hamilton for permission to use her translation of "Voici le printemps," and to Mrs. William H. Drummond for permission to use her late husband's poem, "The Voyageur."

G. L. N.

CONTENTS

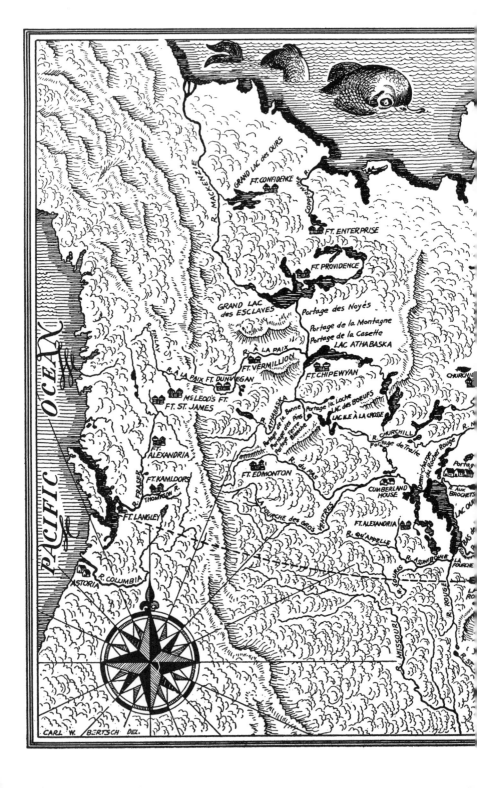

MAP
Showing the principal Water and Land Routes used by the
VOYAGEURS
in their pursuit of
TRADE and ADVENTURE

HUDSON BAY

JAMES BAY

K FACTORY

Peinturée
USE

QUÉBEC

LAC MÉGANE BLANC
HAUTEUR des TERRES
FT. WILLIAM
Grand Portage

LC SUPERIEUR

SAULT de STE. MARIE

Portage de l'Evielté
Décharge du Trou
Portage des Allumettes
GRAND CALUMET
SAULT des CHATS
Portage des Chaudières
LONG SAULT

GEORGIAN BAY
R. des FRANCAIS
LAC NIPISSING

R. des OTTAWAS

R. MATTAWAN

ST. LAURENT

MONTRÉAL

LA POINTE
FOND du LAC
R. BOIS BRULÉ   LA BAYÉ VERTE
Michillimakinac
Portage du Pais

LAC ONTARIO

LAC HURON

ATLANTIC OCEAN

R. MISSISSIPI
PRAIRIE du CHIEN
R. OUISCONSIN

LAC MICHIGAN

LAC ERIE

I

THE term *voyageur*, a French word meaning "traveler," was applied originally in Canadian history to all explorers, fur-traders, and travelers. It came in time to be restricted to the men who operated the canoes and batteaux of fur-traders, and who, if serving at all as traders, labored as subordinates to a clerk or proprietor. Even as late as 1807, however, the famous Beaver Club of Montreal, a group of prominent and, usually, successful fur-merchants or traders, balloted to determine whether its name should be changed to the Voyageur Club. Thus the term was somewhat vague, though always referring to men who had had actual experience in the fur trade among the Indians. In this book the term is restricted to French-Canadian canoemen.

The French *régime* was responsible for the rise of this unique group of men. From the days of earliest exploration until 1763 a large part of what is now Canada and much of the rest of the continent west of the Appalachian Mountains was French territory. In this vast region lived the several tribes of Indians with whom the French settlers about Quebec and Montreal were not slow to barter furs. Beaver, marten, fox, lynx, bear, otter, wolf, muskrat, and many other furs were obtained. Furs were in great demand in Europe and Asia, and both the English colonists along the Atlantic seaboard and the French

3

in New France supported themselves in large part by means of a very flourishing fur trade.

At first the Indians took their skins and furs down the St. Lawrence to Quebec and Montreal, whither annual fairs attracted them; but in the process of time ambitious traders intercepted the natives and purchased their furs in the interior, thus gaining an advantage over fellow traders. The enmity between the Iroquois and the Algonquin also tended to prevent the Indians from making their annual trips to the lower St. Lawrence, since the western tribes, who brought most of the furs, feared to pass down the river through enemy territory.

When traders began to enter the Indian country, the voyageur may be said to have been born. Farther and farther up the St. Lawrence, up the Ottawa River, into lakes Huron and Michigan, the traders ventured. Erie and Ontario were explored, and finally Lake Superior. From these lakes more venturesome traders entered the rivers emptying into them and reached the Ohio and Illinois countries and the region about the Mississippi. They even found the rivers emptying into Lake Superior from the west and marked out the route by way of Rainy Lake into Lake Winnipeg. When Canada was lost to the English in 1763, French posts were established far up the Saskatchewan, and French traders had seen the Rocky Mountains and knew of the "Oregon" River. On these trips westward the birch-bark canoe was almost the sole vehicle of transportation, and men from the hamlets on the lower St. Lawrence were the canoemen.

Naturally the French Government found it necessary as time went on to establish rules and regulations for this lucrative business. Licenses (*congés*) to enter the Indian country were required; certain articles were prohibited in the trade; and only a specified number of traders might be licensed in one year. A man with sufficient capital to purchase a season's outfit acquired a license and hired men of his neighborhood to take the goods in canoes to the point at which the trader wished to sell his wares to the Indians. After bartering knives, beads, wampum, blankets, vermilion, and numberless trinkets and other articles for furs worth infinitely more in monetary value, these subtraders returned to their proprietor with the results of their transactions. The French term for the proprietor was *bourgeois*, and for the subtrader *voyageur*. The latter in time became a general term covering the *mangeur de lard* ("pork-eater") and the *hivernant* ("winterer"). The former were the novices, the men who could be entrusted only with the management of the canoes and who for that reason returned home each season. The *hivernants* were experienced voyageurs who spent the winters at posts in the interior, exchanging trade goods for furs under the direction of a *commis*. The latter was a clerk who was training to become a *bourgeois* and who was frequently a son or a near relative of a *bourgeois*. These terms came into use in the French period, but they and the system described were retained by the British after 1763 and by the Americans after 1816, when the British abandoned their posts in the American Northwest. French remained the "official" language as long as the fur trade flourished. Some of the terms are still in use in the forts of the Hudson's Bay Company in northern and western Canada.

Because this system developed under the French *régime* and about Quebec and Montreal, the fur trade continued to its last breath to be dependent to a great degree for canoemen and winterers upon the French Canadians in the country about these two cities. Just as the sailing vessel could be managed best by men in whose families was the seafaring tradition, so the fur-trading expeditions into the Northwest proved most lucrative when carried out by men from Sorel, Three Rivers, L'Orignal, and other Quebec hamlets, where babes grew into manhood with the almost certain knowledge that they would some day paddle canoes for the Northwest Company, the Hudson's Bay Company, the American Fur Company, or a rival firm or trader. John Jacob Astor, the prince of American fur-traders and the organizer of the largest American fur company, is said to have remarked that he would rather have one voyageur than three American canoemen.

Though the voyageurs were usually unlettered men and unambitious as well, Fate has decreed that even their individual names should not be lost. When a trader made application for a license, he was required to state the names of all his men. Hundreds of these licenses are extant, especially in Montreal, Quebec, and Ottawa, and from them one learns to recognize whole families of voyageurs who were enrolled year after year in official records. Doubtless many of these visitors to the West in the seventeenth, eighteenth, and early nineteenth centuries will remain forever unknown, but hundreds of others are becoming better known year by year as these old records are investigated.[1]

The number of voyageurs in any given year is truly surprising. The West was not the unknown, uninhabited region that the imagination of writers has pictured. To dispel any doubt on this point one has only to refer to the lists of licenses already mentioned. In the year 1777, for example, 2,431 voyageurs are recorded in the licenses obtained at Montreal and Detroit. Add to this number the men already in the interior as *hivernants*, the employees of the Hudson's Bay Company, and the traders from the new states on the coast, and five thousand is a conservative estimate of the men who were sprinkled from Montreal to the Rocky Mountains, from Hudson Bay to the Gulf of Mexico.

Voyageurs formed a class as distinct in dress, customs, and traditions as sailors or lumberjacks. They had the further unifying characteristic of speaking a language which was not the native tongue either of their employers or of the people with whom they did business. They were termed voyageurs by all who had occasion to speak of them, and the word was used with the implication that a distinct and easily recognizable group of men was meant. Later writers have sometimes confused the terms *voyageur* and *coureur de bois*. The latter term was used in referring to illicit traders of the French *régime*, men who ventured into the wilderness without licenses. It is incorrect, therefore, to make it synonymous with *voyageur*. The only other term by which voyageurs were commonly known was *engagés*, a loose expression which might be translated as "employees."

In American and Canadian history these voyageurs played a significant rôle. The fur trade was for generations the chief industry of the continent. Unfortunately, no thoroughgoing history of the industry has ever been written, and so its significance has not been fully revealed. When such an account shall have been completed, it will become plain that several of the struggles between France and Great Britain were occasioned by a desire to reap the rich profits of the fur trade of the West; that the large fur-trading companies exercised powerful influence over English, French, and American statesmen; that England's manufacturers realized the importance of the Indian country as one of their chief markets; and that the control of the western fur-trading posts was one of the chief objects of the War of 1812 between Great Britain and the United States.[2] When these and other salient facts about the fur trade are made clear, the significance of the voyageurs will be seen, for without them the industry could hardly have flourished and attained the importance that it assumed. A peculiar set of circumstances produced a unique group of men.

Though the voyageur was the product of the French period, he attained his highest degree of individuality and usefulness in the years between 1763 and 1840, the period mainly to be considered in this volume. After Canada had been wrested from the French in 1763, British and American merchants took over the entire trade formerly conducted by the French, and great companies were soon formed with large capital and many resources. Since the employers of the voyageurs were, in the main, the three great fur-trading companies of the continent, it may be useful at this point to describe them briefly. The Hudson's Bay Company was chartered in 1670, largely as a result of the recommendations of two great French explorers, Pierre Esprit Radisson and his brother-in-law, Medard Chouart, Sieur des Groseilliers. It soon had posts at various places on the shore of Hudson Bay. Until the period of the American Revolution it "slept by the bay," having the Indians bring furs to its forts. Then the activity of Montreal traders in the interior forced the company to undertake a more strenuous policy and to erect forts in the interior. These traders from Canada, usually Scotch, had experienced a period of excessive competition from the time of the conquest till towards the end of the American Revolution. Then they began to pool their resources and profits and to be known as the Northwest Company. It was a loose organization, never a corporation like its great rival. Generally speaking, voyageurs were employees of the Northwest Company, or of a closely allied organization, the Southwest Company, for the Hudson's Bay Company, at least till about 1815, used Orkney men as their "servants." However, an American corporation soon developed which employed voyageurs in much the same manner as the Northwest Company. This was the American Fur Company of New York, chartered by John Jacob Astor in 1808. In 1821 excessive competition forced the two Canadian companies to coalesce and to assume the name of the one possessing charter rights. The American Fur Company was reorganized in 1834, but maintained its existence till it failed in 1842. After 1816 it took over most of the trade that the Northwest Company had been enjoying since the Revolution about the Great Lakes and in the region of the upper Mississippi and Missouri rivers.[3]

Licenses were no longer for the few, and an ever increasing number of voyageurs were required to man the numerous canoes to the interior. Posts dotted the wilderness along the Great Lakes and on practically every navigable river and lake in the area now embracing Michigan, Ohio, Indiana, Illinois, Wisconsin, Minnesota, Iowa, North and South Dakota, Montana, Idaho, Wyoming, Washington, Oregon, and all of western Canada. The writer has mapped the sites of the more important posts within the area of Minnesota and has located not less than 125.[4] At every fort were a number of voyageurs. They, with their traders, were thus the first white settlers of most of these areas. It was they, too, who did the actual exploring of the interior, for the great explorers, like Alexander Henry, Jonathan Carver, and Alexander Mackenzie, relied on their canoemen for knowledge of navigable streams, portages, wintering grounds, and other topographical features. Moreover, they or their descendants remained when the fur-trade era gave way to the period of actual settlement and thus supplied part of the stock from which the inhabitants of these regions are derived. They named the lakes and rivers, prepared the Indians for the incursion of the whites, and made it possible for missionaries to go among the tribes and convert and civilize them. They were humble, unassuming men, but this fact should not obscure their services and importance in American and Canadian history.

II
PORTRAIT OF THE VOYAGEUR

II

MY man dressed himself in the habit of a voyageur, that is, a short shirt, a red woolen cap, a pair of deer skin leggins which reach from the ancles a little above the knees, and are held up by a string secured to a belt about the waist, the aziōn ["breech cloth"] of the Indians, and a pair of deer skin moccasins without stockings on the feet. The thighs are left bare. This is the dress of voyageurs in summer and winter." [1] Add a few items which the worthy missionary, Sherman Hall, neglected to mention—a blue capote, the inevitable pipe, a gaudy sash, and a gay beaded bag or pouch hung from the sash—and you have the voyageur as he appeared speeding over lakes, advancing cautiously up narrow creeks, toiling over portages, cracking his whip over the heads of his dogs, laughing down rapids, fiddling in log forts, and singing wherever he was.

One would expect voyageurs to be men of heroic proportions, but usually they were not. The average voyageur was five feet six inches in height. Few were more than five feet eight inches. Had they been taller, they would have occupied too much of the precious space in a canoe already overcrowded with cargo. But though the voyageur was short, he was strong. He could paddle fifteen—yes, if necessary, eighteen—hours per day for weeks on end and joke beside the camp fire at the close of each day's toil. He could carry from 200 to 450 pounds of merchandise on his back over rocky portage trails at a pace which made unburdened travelers pant for breath in their endeavor not to be left behind. A distinguished traveler on the Great Lakes in 1826, Thomas L. McKenney, later of the United States Bureau of Indian Affairs, wrote how his men took the canoe out of the water, mended a breach in it, reloaded, cooked breakfast, shaved, washed, ate, and reëmbarked—all in *fifty-seven* minutes! "Some estimate may be formed from this," says McKenney, "of the celerity of the movements of these voyageurs. I can liken them to nothing but their own ponies. They are short, thick set, and active, and never tire. A Canadian, if born to be a labourer, deems himself to be very unfortunate if he should chance to grow over five feet five, or six inches;—and if he shall reach five feet ten or eleven, it forever excludes him from the privilege of becoming voyageur. There is no room for the legs of such people, in these canoes. But if he shall stop growing at about five feet four inches, and be gifted with a good voice, and lungs that never tire, he is considered as having been born under a most favourable star." [2]

One result of the voyageur's mode of life was the overdevelopment of arms and shoulders at the expense of other parts of the body. This fact is brought out in a description by Dr. John J. Bigsby, the secretary of the commission that marked out the international boundary between Canada and the United States according to the provisions of the Treaty of Ghent of 1814. His portraits of the canoemen of his party as he saw them first at

Lachine are probably more realistic than those of any other contemporary writer.[3]

"I was disappointed and not a little surprised at the appearance of the *voyageurs*. On Sundays, as they stand round the door of the village churches, they are proud dressy fellows in their parti-coloured sashes and ostrich-feathers; but here they were a motley set to the eye: but the truth was that all of them were picked men, with extra wages as serving in a light canoe.

"Some were well made, but all looked weak in the legs, and were of light weight. A Falstaff would have put his foot through the canoe to the 'yellow sands' beneath. The collection of faces among them chanced to be extraordinary, as they squatted, paddle in hand, in two rows, each on his slender bag of necessaries. By the bye, all their finery (and they love it) was left at home. One man's face, with a large Jewish nose, seemed to have been squeezed in a vice, or to have passed through a flattening machine. It was like a cheese-cutter,—all edge. Another had one nostril bitten off. He proved the buffoon of the party. He had the extraordinary faculty of untying the strings of his face, as it were, at pleasure, when his features fell into confusion—into a crazed chaos almost frightful; his eye, too, lost its usual significance; but no man's countenance . . . was fuller of fun and fancies than his, when he liked. A third man had his features wrenched to the right—exceedingly little, it is true; but the effect was remarkable. He had been slapped on the face by a grisly bear. Another was a short, paunchy old man, with vast features, but no forehead—the last man I should have selected; but he was a hard-working creature, usually called 'Passe-partout,' because he had been everywhere, and was famous for the weight of fish he could devour at a meal. . . . Except the younger men, their faces were short, thin, quick in their expression, and mapped out in furrows, like those of the sunday-less Parisians."

Now and again one found a giant among these dwarfs. Nicholas Garry, deputy-governor of the Hudson's Bay Company from 1822 to 1835, mentions as one of his voyageurs "a Man six Feet high and of herculean make, who was called in consequence 'La Petite Vierge.' " [4] Nicknames were common among these men. Frequently, too, as in the case of Garry's "little maiden," the nickname was in exact contradiction of some characteristic of the man. Stephen H. Long, an explorer in the valley of the Red River of the North in 1823, gives an example of this trait in describing how his men had no sooner seen his black man Andrew "than they immediately agreed among themselves to apply to him the term Wapishka . . . which means white." [5]

McKenney, in the letter already quoted, points out an essential characteristic of the voyageur—his pride of profession. He was class conscious; he considered himself favored by fortune to belong to his group; he took a happy pride in doing his work in such a way as to bring credit to his fellow workers; and he considered the toil and hardships of his chosen work incidental to the profession and was seldom known to pity himself. An example of this attitude is given by McKenney in describing a man on Lake Superior whose business it was at the time to catch fish. He was sixty-nine years of age and active as a boy, though radically diseased. "On his legs, and arms, and breast," writes McKenney, "are tatooed, the marks of superiority in his profession, which has been that of a voyageur, and it seems he excelled in carrying packages across the portages, both on account of their weight and the celerity of his movement. He is now sallow, and dropsical, but active as stated. On questioning him as to his former life, he said, with a slap of the hands, 'he had been the greatest man in the northwest.' It is questionable whether Bonaparte ever felt his superiority in all the departments of mind which so distinguished him, or in his achievements, to an extent of greater excitement, than does this poor man on Michael's island, in the animating and single belief in his supremacy as a *north-western voyageur*." [6]

The voyageurs gave proof of this joy and pride in their work by decking themselves and their canoes in color. "The voyageurs," again to quote McKenney, "are engaged, and on the spot, each with a red feather in his hat, and two others, in possession of the steersman, one for the bow, and the other for the stern of the canoe. These plumes in the canoe are intended to indicate that she has been tried, and found worthy." [7]

The young Chicago scientist, Robert Kennicott, who made a study of flora and fauna of the Canadian Northwest in the fifties and sixties, describing his guide as one of the best runners in America, remarks that he "seemed to feel much more pride in being a good voyageur than a famous runner." And to show how seriously these men took their work he relates that once on the voyage his canoe grazed a rock by accident. "Then, though not the least harm was done, and it was not altogether his fault, old Baptiste our guide was cross till the day after, when he recovered his good humor in the pleasure of running some difficult rapids." [8]

Whether in canoes or with dog trains the voyageurs were ever trying to outdo one another in speed and endurance. Kennicott relates how the agreeable change from working against the current to moving with it put his voyageurs in excellent humor: "the canoes were constantly contending for the lead, the relative cleverness of the bowsmen in cutting off bends in the river . . . causing much excitement and sport." Canoe racing was, indeed, one of the chief delights of voyageurs.[9]

With pride in their own ability went its usual concomitant, ridicule of lesser powers in others. To have the laugh on a greenhorn or to be able to taunt a fellow voyageur of weakness or slowness was to relish life thoroughly. "In an hour we were in still water," writes McKenney, "when our voyageurs, all wet . . . began to chatter again, and pass their jokes upon the bowsman, in whose face many a swell had broken in making this traverse." [10] With dog trains fear of this ridicule showed itself characteristically. Many a warming did Kennicott's dog No-gah get because he would not *mouche* ("go fast") when it was his spell ahead. When a sled could not keep up and take its proper place in the brigade at each spell, it was said to be *planted*, "which is considered something very disgraceful; and a good voyageur will push (i.e. help his dogs by pushing with a long pole always attached to the top of a loaded sled) till he is nearly knocked up, rather than be planted, even though his dogs are known to be weak, or his load extra heavy." [11] When the advance party with Kennicott arrived at Peel's River, they gave the dogs a *festin*, ate two suppers themselves, sat comfortably before the fire, and "boasted of our dogs; while the three unfortunate owners of poor trains lay in their windy camp that night and the next." When the laggards came up, the fortunate owners of good dogs laughed at them, much to their indignation. "Anyone who expects much sympathy for such trifling misery in this country," observes the author, "will be left to wipe his own eyes. If one gets frozen, starved, . . . he may expect ridicule, not condolence. . . . It is very comical, sometimes, to see the pains taken by the old voyageurs to cache a frost bite, or any fatigue." [12]

The boasting of which Kennicott makes mention was characteristic of the voyageurs. The speed of their dogs, the lines of their canoes, the heaviness of their burdens on portages, their skill in shooting rapids, and similar topics were points discussed soon and late before blazing camp fires. Pulling the long bow did not arise when the first Paul Bunyan story was told. For a century and more its counterparts had made animated many an encampment of gesticulating French-Canadian voyageurs. The difference lies in the fact that the hero of every voyageur's yarn was himself instead of a mythical giant embodying the same exaggerated traits and abilities as those of which he boasted.

One of the most interesting traits of the voyageur was his extreme courtesy. His Gallic ancestry was nowhere so evident as in the deferential ease with which

III

WITHOUT the birch-bark canoe the history of inland North America would have been altogether different
from that which is on record. Dugouts, batteaux, rafts,
and other clumsy craft could have replaced the canoe
in many instances and on many waterways; but dugouts
cannot be carried easily on men's shoulders over the
scores of portages which made tedious the explorers'
and traders' routes; batteaux and rafts cannot shoot
rapids skillfully; and a dozen other objections to such
water conveyances could be advanced to prove that the
canoe was the only practicable vehicle for a large part
of the fur-trader's frontier.

Disassociated from his canoe the voyageur can hardly
be imagined. As well separate him from his pipe! It
was his carriage by day, his house by night, the topic of
fully half his conversation, and the object of his pride.
His clothing, his food, his songs, his family life, his very
stature were all conditioned by a frail basket which he
could carry on his shoulders.

In what dim age the Algonquian tribes learned the
secret of making canoes from the rind of the yellow birch
tree is not known. Generations, perhaps even centuries,
witnessed the perfecting of the art, for it is no slight task
to build a vessel that weighs less than three hundred
pounds and yet can sustain the burden of five tons of

crew and freight. Moreover, no nails or other metal substances were used in its construction, all the building materials being found in the forests. And the reason for the use of the canoe by the Algonquian tribes and not by more southern bands was the fact that the canoe birch grows only in northern latitudes. One of the most potent arguments used by the British in their efforts before 1795 to retain control of the Lake of the Woods–Grand Portage water route was that birch-bark canoes were indispensable to British control of western Canada and that these were made by the Indians on the southern shore of Rainy Lake.[1]

This unique craft, this essentially native American product, has been described by numberless travelers. It varied in size according to the extent of the body of water on which it was to be used. Generally speaking, three types of canoes were in use among the white people of Canada and the United States. The "Montreal canoe," or *canot du maître*, which was thirty-five to forty feet long, was used on the Great Lakes and on large rivers like the St. Lawrence. The "North canoe," or *canot du nord*, about twenty-five feet in length and carrying only about three thousand pounds besides the crew, was used on smaller streams and lakes, particularly on those beyond Grand Portage—whence its name. Between these two in size was the *bâtard*, or "bastard canoe," which was propelled by ten men. Fourteen were usually required for the *canot du maître* and eight for a North canoe. A canoe about twenty feet long, called a "half canoe," was sometimes used; and Indian canoes, ten to fifteen feet, were sometimes termed "light canoes." Ordinarily, however, a "light canoe" was merely one dispatched without freight.[2] Either Indians or voyageurs were employed to build the canoes, in use in the fur trade. The rind of one birch tree was often sufficient to construct a canoe. *Wattape*, the fine root of some coniferous tree, usually the red spruce, was used in lieu of rope or thread to sew together the strips of bark. When a covering of sufficient size had thus been manufactured, it was placed over a framework of thin white-cedar boards shaped to form a structure twenty to forty feet long, four to six feet wide at the center, and narrowed to a point, or *pince*, at either end. Over the gunwales the bark was lashed with *wattape*, and four to nine narrow thwarts or bars were placed across the top at more or less regular intervals to hold the canoe in shape. In front of these thwarts and depending several inches from the gunwales were boards about four inches wide which served as seats for the voyageurs. The canoe was now ready for gumming. This substitute for calking was achieved by applying melted gum from pine trees with the aid of a torch; the process must be repeated daily or oftener throughout the voyage to keep the craft watertight.

Not all canoes were painted, but it was usual to depict a flag, a horse, an Indian head, or some similar object on the high prow and stern. One traveler describes his Lake Superior canoe thus: "The canoe would be an object of interest any where, even without paint; but now, ornamented as it is, it is really striking. . . . Around the sides, and upon a white ground, is a festoon of green and red paint. The rim is alternate green, red, and white. On each side of the bow, on a white ground, is the bust of an Indian chief, smoking, even larger than life. . . . In the bow is an enormous wooden pipe. . . . This is the canoe that was made at Fond du Lac; and on both sides, and against the swell of the middle, is painted in large letters, Fond Du Lac." [3]

Three sizes of paddles were used: the common paddle, about two feet long and three inches wide, which was used by the middlemen (*milieux*), or men in the center of the canoe; a longer kind, about five inches wide, which was used by the steersman (*gouvernail*), who stood in the stern; and a still larger paddle, which the bowsman or foreman (*avant de canot*, *devant*, or *ducent*) employed when running rapids or leaping small falls. These paddles were made of red-cedar wood and were very light. The blades were usually painted red and ornamented still further with some markings of black and green.

For other equipment the canoe carried an oilcloth which could be used both for covering the cargo and for improvising a sail when *la vieille*, or "old woman of the wind," was propitious. On such occasions a block was placed in the bottom of the canoe to receive the foot of a mast carrying a pole at right angles which served as a yard for the sail. The sail was trimmed by lines attached to the ends of the yard. Sometimes, instead of a single mast with its horizontal yard, two poles were erected at the center of the canoe between which the sail was hung.

Another essential article in the equipment of every well-stocked canoe was a large sponge capable of taking up two to four quarts of water. When the canoe sprang a leak, this sponge was used for bailing. A rope for cordelle, or towing purposes, sixty yards in length, also found a place in every canoe. When rapids were not of such magnitude as to require portaging the canoe, it could be towed by means of this rope.

"The proper crew of such a [North] canoe is eight men," writes Kennicott, "a *bowsman*, *steersman*, and six *middlemen*. The bowsman, who is the guide, sits alone in the bow; the six middlemen occupy three seats placed about five feet apart in the middle of the canoe; and the steersman stands in the stern, never sitting down while the canoe is in motion. . . . All, except the steersman, keep perfect stroke in paddling. . . . [They] paddle with great rapidity, making about forty strokes per minute, . . . dipping the paddle a foot or eighteen inches into the water and pulling with very considerable force. When it is considered that this is kept up, exclusive of several short resting spells of ten or fifteen minutes each, and of the stops for breakfast and dinner, from twelve to fifteen hours per day, some idea may be formed of the extreme powers of endurance possessed by these voyageurs." [4]

Another traveler betters Kennicott's statement, for he found by precise count that his voyageurs in a Montreal canoe made just a stroke a second.[5] Four to six miles per hour was the average speed of canoes propelled thus in calm water. When head winds or untoward weather of any sort were encountered, the voyageurs generally put ashore, for even though their strength was sufficient for the task, they knew that their frail bark could be broken in two by a wave of unusual size. Reading the many available diaries kept on such canoe trips, one finds again and again on almost every voyage the entry, "Wind bound—forced to remain at last night's encampment." The voyageurs' term for this state of affairs was *degradé*, and "degraded" soon became a part of the vocabulary of English-speaking travelers. On the other hand, if a favoring wind arose, the sail was hoisted and with wind and paddles eight to ten miles an hour could sometimes be attained.

While paddling, the voyageurs sang. Songs were chosen whose rhythm was such that the paddles could keep time to the music. Ordinarily the steersman chose the song and gave the pitch. Sometimes he sang the stanza and the others joined in the chorus. In the parlance of his fellows he was the *solo*. Voyageurs were chosen partly with respect to their vocal abilities, and the effect of six to fourteen of them in full song was quite impressive. Of course, they sang in French—of their canoes, of their country, of their life, of their loves, of their church— sentimental romances, old ballads, humorous jingles, lofty poems, and obscene versifications. Many of the songs were inheritances from the *trouvères* and *troubadours;* some were of the voyageurs' own composition. They lightened the work and were the natural expression of such an effervescent race of men as the French Canadians admittedly were.

Here is one of their songs in honor of the birch canoe, *"Mon canot d'écorce."* [6] It is an indigenous product, a voyageur's own composition, telling much of his attitude toward his canoe.

MON CANOT D'ÉCORCE

Dans mon ca-not d'é - cor - ce, as-sis à la frai-che' du temps, Où j'ai bra-vé tout' les tem - pê - tes, les grandes eaux du Saint Lau-rent; Car j'ai bra-vé tout' les tem - pê-tes les grands eaux du Saint Lau-rent. Mon ca-not est fait d'é - cor-ces fi - nes qu'on pleum' sur les bou-leaux blancs; Les cou-tur' sont fait' de ra - ci - nes, Les a - vi - rons de bois blanc.

Dans mon canot d'écorce, assis à la fraicheur du temps,
Où j'ai bravé toutes les tempêtes, les grandes eaux du Saint-
Laurent. (bis)

> Mon canot est fait d'écorces fines
> Qu'on pleume sur les bouleaux blancs;
> Les coutures sont faites de racines, ⎱ (bis)
> Les avirons de bois blanc. ⎰

> Je prends mon canot, je le lance
> A travers les rapides, les bouillons.
> Là, à grands pas il s'avance. ⎱ (bis)
> Il ne laisse j mais le courant. ⎰

C'est quand je viens sur le portage, je prends mon canot sur mon
dos.
Je le renverse dessus ma tête: c'est ma cabane pour la nuit. (bis)

THE VOYAGEUR

*J'ai parcouru le long des rives, tout le long du fleuve Saint-
    Laurent
J'ai connu les tribus sauvages et leurs langages différents.* (bis)

> *—Tu es mon compagnon de voyage!—
> Je veux mourir dans mon canot.
> Sur le tompeau, près du rivage,* ⎱ (bis)
> *Vous renverserez mon canot.* ⎰

*Le laboureur aime sa charrue, le chasseur son fusil, son chien;
Le musicien aime sa musique; moi, mon canot, c'est* [tout] *mon
    bien!* (bis)

TRANSLATION

MY BIRCH-BARK CANOE

In my birch-bark, canoeing, in the cool of evening I ride
Where I have braved every tempest St. Lawrence's rolling tide. (*repeat*)

> My canoe's of bark, light as a feather
> That is stripped from silvery birch;
> And the seams with roots sewn together, ⎱ (*repeat*)
> The paddles white made of birch. ⎰

> I take my canoe, send it chasing
> All the rapids and billows acrost;
> There so swiftly see it go racing, ⎱ (*repeat*)
> And it never the current has lost. ⎰

It's when I come on the portage, I take my canoe on my back.
Set it on my head topsy-turvy; it's my cabin too for the night. (*repeat*)

Along the river banks I've wandered, all along St. Lawrence's tide
I have known the savage races and the tongues that them divide. (*repeat*)

> —You are my voyageur companion!—
> I'll gladly die within my canoe.
> And on the grave beside the canyon ⎱ (*repeat*)
> You'll overturn my canoe. ⎰

His cart is beloved of the ploughman, the hunter loves his gun, his hound;
The musician is a music lover—to my canoe I'm bound. (*repeat*)

* By permission of J. Murray Gibbon.

30

The French of this song is very illiterate, and the tune appears to be a variant of an old English sea song or ballad. The French ballad writer may have picked it up at Quebec or Three Rivers where the lumbermen, after rafting their logs down to the seaport, helped to load the logs on the ships. Mr. Gibbon remarks that Ralph Connor gave him a song, which he picked up from a half-breed in the Northwest, in which the solo part was in French and the chorus an old sea-chanty called "Blow Ye Winds of Morning."

So frail were the bark canoes that, once in them, the voyageurs could hardly shift their positions for fear of breaking the gum. Thus they sat, hour after hour, in one posture without so much as moving their feet. Passengers unaccustomed to the tedium found the cramped position almost unendurable, especially for the first few days. Because of the brittleness of the gum a curious way of taking on and putting off passengers was customary. This was none other than a brief ride on the broad back of a voyageur. As contact with sand on the shore would be likely to break off bits of the gum, the canoe was anchored off shore. Before the momentum given by the last paddle stroke had been lost, every voyageur was out of the canoe with a swift, graceful spring. One held the bow and one the stern, and the others loaded their backs with freight or passengers as the case might be. Such novel transportation was rather startling even to male passengers; what, then, must have been the emotions of the missionary's little wife who was faced with a ride pickaback? She confessed her feelings in a letter to a relative: "When we came to a good place [to disem-

IV

To understand the voyageur completely one must accompany him on one of his trips from Montreal into the *pays d'en haut*, as he termed the Northwest. Thereby one learns his numberless little customs, his superstitions, his method of handling a canoe, and a thousand other phases of his mercurial nature.

Any year between 1770 and 1840, Montreal Island above the Lachine Rapids was the scene of much commotion on the May morning set for the departure of a brigade of canoes for the Northwest. During the winter months an agent of the fur company had been engaged in canvassing the hamlets and parishes round about for voyageurs. Experienced *engagés* were preferred, of course, but in every brigade there were certain to be *mangeurs de lard*, the butt of many a practical joke.

The region from which the voyageurs were drawn may be determined by the bonds given by the *bourgeois*, which included the names of voyageurs and the parishes from which they came.[1] In the years from 1774 to 1776 the following places were mentioned: Montreal, Laprairie, Lachine, Châteauguay, Sorel, Ile-Perrot, Pointe-Claire, St.-Philippe, Chambly, Boucherville, Ile-Jésus, Batiscan, St.-Laurent, Varrenes, Terrebonne, Lachenaie, Longueuil, St.-Ours, Yamaska, Trois Rivières, Contrecoeur, Berthier, Quebec, Vaudreuil, St.-Leonard,

Mascouche, L'Assomption, Ste.-Geneviève, St.-Pierre, St.-Joseph, Rivière du Loup, Pointe-aux-Trembles, St.-Michel, Lavaltrie, St.-Sulpice, Gentilly, Verchères, and St.-Denis. Thus the St. Lawrence from above Montreal to Quebec ran its majestic highway through a voyageur country. The Richelieu and St. Maurice rivers nourished a less numerous race of canoemen.

As soon as the agent had come to terms with his *engagé*, an *engagement* was signed. Many of these papers have come down to us and show the terms of the agreements. They were printed in French, with spaces left for the voyageur's name, his home, the wages he was to receive, and any special provisions. One to three years seems to have been the usual term for which the voyageur contracted to remain in the service. If he were a foreman or a steersman, he ordinarily received twelve hundred livres per annum,[2] but if he were a pork-eater, he got only four hundred livres. He agreed not to desert his master and not to give aid or encouragement to his master's rivals during the period of his engagement. At the bottom of the sheet one usually finds a cross instead of a signature, showing that a formal education was not one of the assets of these men.

Of course, such irresponsible persons as the voyageurs confessedly were often broke their engagements, and much of the confusion of the departure was due to the fact that Henri, Amable, Pierre, Hypolite, or some other renegade had failed to put in his appearance, though already supplied, as was the custom, with a third of his wages and his equipment. This equipment consisted usually of a blanket, a shirt, a pair of trousers, two handkerchiefs, several pounds of carrot tobacco (a carrot-shaped twist of tobacco weighing one to two pounds), and a few miscellaneous items for pork-eaters, and nearly twice the number of each item for winterers.

One of the chief agents of the American Fur Company found himself one day in May, 1817, in the usual situation of the person responsible for the voyageurs of a departing brigade. To his superior, John Jacob Astor, he wrote in his usual correct manner, but between the lines one can detect his exasperation: "All our Boats are off from Lachine in charge of Mr Matthews, but in consequence of a number of Engagés being still absent he has advanced only a short distance and remains on an Island waiting their arrival. I am in hopes this day will produce every one we expect . . . there are upwards of twenty five men missing [*sixty were engaged*], and of these I am sure at least a dozen will not come; indeed I shall consider ourselves lucky if we do not lose more than fifteen, of which number very few will have the honesty to return the money advanced them at the time they engaged." [3]

The agent, finding himself short of men, must prosecute the offenders and secure substitutes, a task not always easy to perform, especially during the periods of intense rivalry between fur companies. But worse could and frequently did happen: a voyageur could desert *en route*. Sad was his fate if he were recaptured. One of the missionaries to the Chippewa Indians relates how he prevented an angry *commis* from giving the regulation flogging to a deserter.

While the agent was filling up the quota of *engagés*,

the men themselves were down by the water's edge, gumming the canoes, making up packages, loading the canoes, bidding farewell to friends and families, and talking and weeping vociferously. Each package, or *pièce*, was made up to weigh ninety pounds, and two ears were left at the top by which the voyageur could lift it easily in the manner of a modern flour bag. Two of these *pièces* made an ordinary load for portaging, but emulation among the men in proof of unusual strength or endurance caused many an *engagé* to carry three or four. A member of a famous Negro-Indian family of voyageurs, the Bongas, is said to have had such strength that he could carry five. And the voyageurs before their camp fires told in awed tones of voyageurs who had carried eight. In such packages were arranged the blankets, scarlet cloths, strouds, calico, gartering, pins, beads, flour, pork, silver earbobs, and numberless other articles which were to be bartered in the interior for furs. Guns and ammunition were also packed into convenient packages; and intoxicating liquors and shot were packed usually in small kegs. When we read of such things as pigs and cookstoves being carried beyond Lake Superior in such brigades of canoes, we can but marvel at the ingenuity and perseverance of the fur-traders, and especially of their employees.

Having loaded each canoe with a cargo whose weight had been equalized by placing it on poles laid on the bottom of the canoe, the men and their clerks were ready to embark on their long and tedious journey. As many as thirty canoes or as few as two or three formed the brigade. Sometimes there was even a squadron of brigades. Flags were flying from sterns, feathers waving in caps, red oars flashing, and voices ringing out in a spirited canoe song as the shore receded.

But the voyageurs did not consider the journey begun as yet, for Ste. Anne's help and protection had not been implored. So the brigade proceeded up the river to where Ste. Anne's church, the chapel of the voyageurs, stood on the westernmost point of Montreal Island, the last place of worship that would be seen for months, perhaps for years. "This Church," writes Peter Pond, one of the earliest traders and explorers of the Northwest, in a perfect phonetic rendering of his own Connecticut dialect, "is Dedacated to St. Ann who Protects all Voigers. Heare is a small Box with a Hole in the top for ye Reseption of a Little Money for the Hole [holy] father or to say a small Mass for those Who Put a small Sum in the Box. Scars a Voiger but stops hear and Puts in his mite and By that Meanes they Suppose thay are Protected. . . . After the Saremony of Crossing them selves and Repeating a Short Prayer" they were ready to depart.[4] Even the Protestant clerks and *bourgeois* traveling with the brigade put coins in the box.

And now the hazardous expedition had begun. The route lay along the St. Lawrence to its confluence with the Ottawa and up that stream to the point where the Mattawa River joins it from the west. In this distance on *la grande rivière* there were eighteen portages. There were also approximately as many *décharges*. At these places the canoe and usually a part of the load were towed over the obstruction. To the numerous falls and rapids on their route the earlier voyageurs gave such curious names as *Les Chats* ("the cats"), *La Chaudière* ("the kettle"), *Les Allumettes* ("the matches"), and *Le Calumet* ("the peace pipe"). As early as the last quarter of the seventeenth century these names were already in use.

When the voyageurs passed from the St. Lawrence into the Ottawa and again when they entered the Mattawa, they performed one of the many rites that were traditional with them on their journeys. They pulled off their red caps and a man in each canoe uttered a prayer. A little later, when they left the Mattawa River, they performed another rite. Up to this point they had used "setting poles" as well as paddles wherever the current was too swift for the ordinary method of propelling the canoe. This system was called "tracking." At Lake Nipissing, however, they left the streams running east and entered one, French River, whose current was with them. For that reason they chose to express their joy of labor ended by going through a formal ceremony of throwing away their setting poles to the accompaniment of loud huzzas.

Another custom had already manifested itself on their trip. Near dangerous *saults* and rapids they had caught sight of tall wooden crosses on the banks. Whenever such a cross was passed, red caps came off and a prayer was uttered. For were not these crosses the rude but tender memorials of the voyageurs to mates who had perished at these spots, caught in the treacherous swirl and eddies of the stream? As many as thirty crosses on one bank are recorded by a clerk who entered the country in the summer of 1800.[5]

Soon after leaving Ste. Anne's all clerks or *bourgeois*

who had never before accompanied a brigade into the interior were given to understand that they would be "baptized" in the chilly waters of the river if they did not moisten the whistles of their men. Accordingly high wines (brandy) was produced, kegs were broached, and soon the red plumes in the Northmen's caps waved at more uncertain angles, and the sorrows of leaving home were forgotten.

On the second evening after the departure from Montreal, when the *campément* had been made in a pine-sheltered nook on the bank of the river, when *souper* had been eaten around the blazing fire, and whilst the smoke from many pipes lay like a cloud against the dark forest trees, the call for *la ronde* was issued. This dance was another customary part of the journey, and it was entered into heartily despite the moralizing tone of the verses.[6]

Two sacks were placed some ten feet apart in an open space, and on them two singers were seated facing each other, one an old man, the other a youth. Each carried an empty kettle under his arm. About these two the rest of the voyageurs formed a circle. The dance began with the singing of the first stanza by the young man, in his shirt sleeves, a feather in his cap, holding his head high and prancing about in a swaggering manner:

> *Ce sont les voyageurs*
> *Qui sont sur leur départ;*
> *Voyez-vous les bonn's gens*
> *Venir sur les remparts?*
> *Sur l'air du tra, lal-déra:*
> *Sur l'air du tra, lal-déra:*
> *Sur l'air du tra, déri-déra:*
>   *Lal-déra!*

41

When he had ended, the old voyageur, dressed in his big blue capote, wearing his *ceinture fléchée* (sash) and his *sac-à-feu* (beaded bag), and shaking his head wisely, sang in a staid manner a couplet of advice to the young people who were leaving for the *pays d'en haut:*

> *Mets d'la racine de patience*
> *Dans ton gousset;*
> *Car tu verras venir ton corps*
> *Joliment sec,*
> *A force de nager toujours*
> *Et de porter:*
> *Car on n'a pas souvent l'crédit*
> *D'se sentir reposer!*

And thereupon the voyageurs grasped hands and commenced to turn, dancing and singing the refrain, whilst the two singers beat on their kettles:

> *Lève ton pied, ma jolie bergère!*
> *Lève ton pied, légère!*
> *Lève ton pied, ma jolie bergère!*
> *Lève ton pied, légèrement!*

Three times they turned, repeating the strain. The remainder of the song runs as follows:

Young Man

> *Au revoir père et mère,*
> *Soeur, frère et toi Fanchon;*
> *Vous reverrez bientôt*
> *Votre cher Siméon!*
> *Sur l'air du tra, lal-déra:*
> *Sur l'air du tra, lal-déra:*
> *Sur l'air du tra, déri-déra:*
> *Lal-déra!*

VOYAGING

OLD MAN

Embarque-moi dans ton canot,
Prends ton paquet
Car tu vas laisser ton pays
Et tes parents,
C'est pour monter dans les rivières
Et dans les lacs
Toujours att'lé sur l'aviron,
Ainsi que sur les sacs!

CHORUS

*   *   *   *   *   *   *

YOUNG MAN

Ce sont les voyageurs
Qui sont de bons enfants;
Ah! qui ne mangent guère,
Mais qui boivent souvent!
Sur l'air du tra, lal-déra, etc.

OLD MAN

Si les maringouins t'piq' la tête,
D'leur aiguillon
Et t'étourdissent les oreilles,
De leurs chansons,
Endure-les, et prends patience
Afin d'apprendre
Qu'ainsi le diable te tourmente,
Pour avoir ta pauvre âme!

CHORUS

*   *   *   *   *   *   *

43

THE VOYAGEUR

YOUNG MAN

Quand on est en voyage,
Le saque sur le dos,
On s'écrie, camarade,
Camarade il fait chaud!
Sur l'air du tra, lal-déra, etc.

OLD MAN

Quand tu seras dans ces rapids,
Très dangereux,
Prends la Vierge pour ton bon guide
Fais-lui des voeux!
Et tu verras couler cette onde,
Avec vitesse,
Et prie bien du fond de ton coeur
Qu'elle coule sans cesse.

CHORUS

* * * * * * *

"We are voyageurs starting on our way," the young
man announces. "Don't you see the townsfolk watching
from the walls?" But the old man replies in admonition,
"Put some patience in your wallet, for you will get dry
from paddling constantly and from portaging, for rest
comes seldom." Then all sing a refrain from a familiar
song (*En roulant*), "Dance, pretty shepherdess, dance
lightly," etc. "Goodbye, Father and Mother," sings the
pork-eater, "you, too, Brother and Fanchon. You will
soon see your dear Simon again." But the old man is
relentless. "Embark in your canoe and take your pack,
for you are about to leave your country and your rela-

44

tives to go upstream and through lakes, always harnessed to your paddle and your pack." Nothing daunted, the young man breaks forth again, "We are voyageurs and good fellows. We seldom eat but we often drink." The old man then moralizes, "If the mosquitoes sting your head and deafen your ears with their buzzing, endure them patiently, for they will show you how the Devil will torment you in order to get your poor soul." This seems to chasten the tenderfoot, for he replies in serious vein, "When we are voyaging, pack on back, it will be, 'Comrade, how hot it is!' " As his parting bit of advice the Nor'wester preaches, "When you are in the worst rapids let Mary be your guide. Make your vow to Her and you will see the waves recede. And pray from the bottom of your heart that they may ever recede." Snatches from other *chansons* are recognizable.

Only two meals were eaten ordinarily, the breakfast and the evening meal. An hour was allowed, as a rule, for breakfast, but if portages were numerous or especially difficult, less time was permitted for the morning meal. Hard portages usually necessitated a third meal, for no human being could have labored more arduously than the voyageur on a difficult portage.

Nearly everyone who has written of canoe travel remarks on the laboriousness of portaging. One author describes a portage scene thus: "As soon as a canoe reaches a portage, a scene of bustle and activity takes place, which none can picture to themselves but such as have seen it. The goods are unloaded, and conveyed across, while the canoe is carried by the stern and bowsmen. As soon as they have reached the end of the portage, it is launched and reloaded without any loss of time. An obstruction of one hundred yards does not detain them more than twenty minutes. We had occasion, however, more than once, to regret their speed, which caused them to toss our baggage very unceremoniously, using it as they would packs of furs, which are so made up as not to be injured by this rough treatment. The whole care and attention of a voyageur seems to centre in his canoe, which he handles with an astonishing degree of dexterity and caution." [7]

The length of a portage was computed by voyageurs in a characteristic way. The canoe and goods were carried about a third of a mile and put down, or *posé*, two or more trips often being required to transport all the load to this point. Then, without resting, the men shouldered their burdens and went on to the next *posé*. And so on till all the *posés* had been passed. One long portage of forty-five miles in Wisconsin was divided into one hundred and twenty-two *poses*.[8]

Across these portages the men dogtrotted at a pace which kept passengers running. A missionary, William T. Boutwell, relates how he had merely a musket and two umbrellas upon his shoulder, and yet he could not keep in sight of the greater part of the voyageurs unless, as he says, "I *ran* faster than I chose." [9] So much lifting and carrying proved a strain to all but the toughest, and many a bruised foot and wrenched ankle were the result of nearly every portage. Hernia was very prevalent among voyageurs and not infrequently caused death. On the other hand, the voyageurs, though nearly amphibious, seldom had colds, and so, like the lumberjacks, they are good proof that exposure and wet feet bear no relation to respiratory infections.

For portaging, a sort of harness, called the "portage collar," was used. This consisted of a strap of leather about three inches wide, to which smaller straps were attached of sufficient length to tie around the packages. The straps were first tied around each end of a *pièce*, which was then swung upon the back, the lower part resting on the small of the back. The collar was then brought over the top of the head. The voyageur, taking a load, inclined a little forward, so that the load rested on the back and drew only gently on the collar on the head. After the first *pièce* was swung on the back, the second was taken up and laid on the top of it, reaching, if it was bulky, nearly to the top of the head. "I was surprised," adds the writer whose description of a portage harness has just been given, "to see with what ease these men, after they had suspended the first *pièce*, would raise up the second and place it on the top of it." [10]

The same observer was much impressed with the docility, strength, and good humor of the voyageurs in this "hard business" of portaging. "They appeared generally in good spirits, though some of them said it was hard business. One man in particular, I could not but feel a deep sympathy for. This was his first year in the country, and this probably the first time he had converted himself into a horse and baggage waggon to transport goods from the manufacturer to the far distant consumer. His back had become so heated and chafed by his loads, that several large boils had formed and which of themselves were very painful; yet his loads rested on them when he carried. He said in the morning when he first commenced his daily task, he could hardly endure the pain he suffered, notwithstanding he continued to carry his quota of goods with his companions." Very probably, when the missionary observer was not in his vicinity, the poor wretch expressed himself with many a *sacré* or even a *saccajé chien*, the favorite profanity of these men.

Sometimes it was not necessary to portage around an obstruction, but merely to remove some of the lading from the canoe. Such spots were termed *décharges*, which promptly became "discharges" in the English vocabulary of the clerk, proprietor, and passenger. To pass a *décharge* it was necessary to *cordelle*, that is, to tow the canoe by means of a rope (*cordelle*) or cable. Bad accidents happened occasionally when a towing rope broke and the canoe was precipitated down rapids or over falls, with loss or wetting of baggage and, not infrequently, loss of life. Often the current at the rapids was so violent that two or more men must accompany the canoe, wading waist deep in ice-cold water and over treacherous rocks. At the end no fire was made to dry the men's clothes, but all was hurry and away to the camping ground.

When the baggage became wet, or even damp, it was necessary to delay a day or even longer in order to dry the goods. Bales were unrolled, and blankets, cottons, clothes, and what not were hung on the bushes to dry. One traveler describes such a scene in delightful detail: "Left our encampment about 9 a.m. and proceeded to portage Coteau. Our private baggage was removed about one pose from the foot of the port[age]. The bales that

were in the canoe which broke upon the large stone in
the Rapids yesterday, were also brought up and opened.
Our encampment looks not a little like a clothier's establishment from the rolls of cloth, and pieces of stroud
nailed to the sides of trees and spread upon bushes. It
might, however, be mistaken for a laundress establishment in seeing the shirts, blankets, vests. &c. In addition
to the 5 bales that were drenched, was a box containing
sundries, such as knives, forks, siedlitz powders, sulphur,
starch, saltpeter, snuff, and numerous other articles, all
of which were soaked. Five or six of us have been employed the remainder of the day in hanging out and drying wet goods. I have labored in wringing shirts and
spreading clothes until I am quite tired. We shall not be
able to get half through today with this unpleasant
work." [11]

Sometimes, however, even the worm turns. A few in-
stances are recorded of mutiny among voyageurs. Duncan
M'Gillivray, a renowned trader and explorer of the
Saskatchewan plains, on his trip into the interior from
Grand Portage in 1794, records such an instance. At
Rainy Lake he found a strike in progress among the men
of a brigade already there. "A few discontented persons
in their Band, wishing to do as much mischief as possible
assembled their companions together several times on the
Voyage Outward & represented to them how much their
Interest suffered by the passive obedience to the will of
their masters, when their utility to the Company, might
insure them not only of better treatment, but of any other
conditions which they would prescribe with Spirit &
Resolution. . . . They all declared with one voice that

unless their wages would be augmented, and several other conditions equally unreasonable granted them they would immediately sett off to Montreal." Here, then, is material for students of labor history, and where one would least expect to find such an early instance of "walking delegates" and strikes. Of course the tractable voyageurs were unable to carry the strike to a successful conclusion. "Their minds were agitated with these scruples at the very time that they insisted on a compliance with their demands, and tho' they endeavoured carefully to conceal it, yet a timidity was observed in their behaviour which proved very fortunate for their Masters, who took such good advantage of it, that before night they prevailed on a few of the most timid to return to their duty, and the rest, being only ashamed to abandon their companions, soon followed the example." [12] It is refreshing and buoys up one's faith in human nature to read that "a few of the most resolute were obstinate enough to hold out . . . and were therefore sent down to Montreal in disgrace." Explorers like Fraser and Franklin found that there were limits even to voyageurs' endurance, and they were obliged to drive on their men where they refused to go.[13] Indeed, there was a prison at Fort William for "refractory voyageurs." [14]

We have seen that the voyageurs had their own method of measuring portages. They were not less original on the water. Here the *pipe* was the standard of measurement. This was the distance covered between respites, when the luxury of resting and smoking was indulged. The order *"Allumez"* was given by the guide when he deemed that the usual time between smokes had elapsed, and no second command was needed. Paddles were laid in the canoe, tired shoulders rested back on the thwarts or baggage, *sacs à feu* were opened, pipes were taken from *ceintures* and lighted, and jokes and stories were told for ten or fifteen minutes. The command to resume work given, the little craft moved on to the strains of another *chanson à l'aviron.*

Nightfall usually brought the toil of the voyageur to an end. A landing was made, the camp fire was lighted, the unloaded canoes were turned over on the shore, the clerk's tent was set up (in many brigades custom decreed that he must do this without aid from his men), the supper was cooked and eaten, and preparations were made for a night in the open. Though the clerk could indulge in such luxuries as tea, a voyageur's rations were almost invariably a quart of lyed corn [15] (dried peas were frequently used until Mackinac was reached) and an ounce or two of grease, pork, or bacon. From this last item, called *lard* in French, the class name, *mangeur de lard*, "pork-eater," was derived. The manner of cooking this monotonous but seemingly adequate diet was quite in keeping with the voyageur's other customs. "The men's practice in the culinary art was very simple, but good," writes a clerk in reminiscent mood. "The tin kettle, in which they cooked their food, would hold eight or ten gallons. It was hung over the fire, nearly full of water, then nine quarts of peas—one quart per man, the daily allowance—were put in; and when they were well bursted, two or three pounds of pork, cut into strips, for seasoning, were added, and all allowed to boil or simmer till daylight, when the cook added four biscuits, broken up, to the mess, and invited all hands to breakfast. The swelling of the peas and biscuit had now filled the kettle to the brim, so thick that a stick would stand upright in it. It looked inviting, and I begged for a plate full of it, and ate little else during the journey. The men now squatted in a circle, the kettle in their midst, and each one plying his wooden spoon or ladle from kettle to mouth, with almost electric speed, soon filled every cavity. Then the pipes were soon brought into full smoke." [16] This clerk became a trader of importance on the upper Mississippi.

It must not be supposed that the voyageurs did not add to their rations whatever berries, game, birds' eggs, or other "wild" items could be picked up in the day's "march." They were ever on the alert to catch a fish, turtle, or muskrat, to find a bird's nest full of eggs, to kill a deer or bear, or to locate a honey tree. A beaver's tail was considered an especially dainty morsel, and the story is that the voyageurs in the French period ate it even during Lent. To determine how far they were sinning, the matter was referred to the Sorbonne, and, no doubt because the aquatic habits of the beaver so closely resemble those of fishes, the privilege of eating the tail in Lent was permitted.[17]

Ingenuity came to their aid oftentimes when the voyageurs sought to add to their larder. One traveler describes the following scene as an illustration of their resourcefulness: "The Frenchmen here found a turtle, which they esteem as one of their luxuries. They were unsuccessful for a long time in getting its head from under its shell in order to kill it, when one of them put its tail to the fire, a second ready with two sticks, siezed its head as it thrust it from under its covering, and a third cut it off. So much for French wit." [18]

The same writer, however, had not such an exalted opinion of the cleanliness of the men, and his comment on that topic is worth noting: "It is perhaps difficult to determine which are the most squalid in their habits, the Indians, or some of the French voyageurs, who, as often as any way, recieve [*sic*] their rations in their pocket-handkerchief, or hat." [19]

Of the same opinion was the scientist Kennicott. He describes some of their culinary methods thus: "Near this lake Mr. Hubbard found the nest of a ruffed grouse containing five eggs. These our cook used in making our *galette*, thereby giving us quite a treat. This galette is the only form of bread used on a voyage, that is, when voyageurs are so fortunate as to have any flour at all. It is made in a very simple style:—the flour bag is opened, and a small hollow made in the flour, into which a little water is poured, and the dough is thus mixed in the bag; nothing is added, except, perhaps some dirt from the cook's *unwashed* hands, with which he kneads it into flat cakes, which are baked before the fire in a frying pan, or cooked in grease. . . . There is no denying that voyageurs are not apt to be very cleanly, either in their persons or in their cooking." And later he tells even more of the gustatory eccentricities of his voyageurs: "During the day I found the nest of a Canada goose. . . . It contained seven eggs. . . . Though the eggs mentioned had been incubated for some time, the voyageurs ate them. . . . It is very rarely that the voyageurs reject anything in the shape of fish or bird. A crow and pair of pigeon hawks, which I shot a few days before, were eaten, and I think they would eat eggs so nearly hatched that the chick could almost *peep*." [20]

Pemmican was used on voyages in the far interior. This was a kind of pressed buffalo meat, pounded fine, to which hot grease was added, and the whole left to form a mold in a bag of buffalo skin. When properly made, pemmican would remain edible for more than one season. Its small bulk and great nutritional value made it highly esteemed by all voyageurs. From it they made a dish called rubbaboo. "Rubbaboo," says Kennicott, "is a favorite dish with the northern voyageurs, when they can get it. It consists simply of pemmican made into a kind of soup by boiling in water. Flour is added when it can be obtained, and it is generally considered more palatable with a little sugar. Pemmican is supposed by the benighted world outside to consist only of pounded meat and grease; an egregious error; for, from experience on the subject, I am authorized to state that hair, sticks, bark, spruce leaves, stones, sand, etc., enter into its composition, often quite largely." [21]

Another writer, a native missionary, goes into the details not only of the manner of cooking rubbaboo, but also of the approved manner of eating it. Peter Jacobs' remarks are as follows: "The food that is generally prepared and eaten in these regions by voyageurs is what is called 'ahrubuhboo.' I do not know what the word itself means. I spell it as I hear it pronounced. All *pork eaters* from Canada do not know how to make it; I shall here tell my readers how I proceeded to make it; for it was this sort of food we had in the voyage. After I had got the wood in order, and made a good blazing fire, I took my kettle, went to the lake, and put in it about two quarts of water. While this was getting to boil over the fire I took a two-quart hand dish half full of water, and put into it some flour, and stirred it till it looked like *mush*. The pan was now full. As the water in the kettle was now boiling, I took my pan-dish, and put all that was in it in the kettle, where it became thinner. I then took a stick and stirred. This, of course, took some time to boil. When it boiled I kept stirring it in order to prevent the dregs of the flour-soup (if I may so call it) from sinking and sticking at the bottom of the kettle and burning. If it burned, the dinner would be spoiled. This frequently happens with bad and indolent cooks. I myself succeeded very well, as I was determined to be a good cook on this occasion. All depends upon the faithful continuance of stirring the flour-soup with a stick, until such a time as it is cooked. I carefully attended to this. When the flour-soup was quite cooked, I removed the kettle from the fire, and while my soup was boiling hot I jumped at my hatchet or tomahawk, and cut to pieces about a pound weight of *pemmican*, after which I threw this into the kettle. I stirred this quickly, so that the grease of the *pemmican* might be dissolved in the hot flour-soup. Thus ends the cooking. The time it takes to cook this is less than half an hour. It is very much like what is called in some countries *burgoo*. This 'ahrubuh-boo' is first-rate food for travelers in this country. At this time I poured it out in dishes for my men and myself, and made a good dinner out of it. Very often the men, when they are in a great hurry, instead of using dishes and spoons, pour out their 'ahrubuhboo' on the smooth hollow rocks, where it becomes cooler in a short time, and eat it; those who have no spoons generally eat it in the dog fashion, licking it up with their tongues." [22]

The nightly encampment was made about nine o'clock in the long twilight of the northern spring. McKenney, who became so deeply interested in the voyageur on his trip through Lake Superior in 1826, asked his men one evening at seven o'clock if they did not wish to go ashore for the night. "They answered," he relates, "they were fresh yet. They had been almost constantly paddling since 3 o'clock this morning. . . . 57,600 strokes with the paddle, and 'fresh yet!' No human beings, except the Canadian French, could stand this. Encamped . . . at half past nine o'clock, having come to-day *seventy-nine miles*." [23]

Encampments meant a tent and a sweet-smelling bed of fir boughs for *commis* or *bourgeois*. For the men, however, they connoted a canoe turned on its side as roof, the rocks of the shore as bed, and a single blanket as coverlet. Clerks often found these nights *à la belle étoile* full of romance and poetry, but the voyageurs were ordinarily too weary to observe the brilliance of the stars or to give heed to the soughing of winds in the pines or to the music of waves and *sault*. Despite myriads of mosquitoes, drenching thunder storms, blistering heat, or unseasonable cold they slept like the dead beneath their canoes.

One lone figure stood out darkly silhouetted against the blazing fire that he tended so assiduously. It was the cook, preparing food for the following day. Dr. Bigsby brings one of these men out from the general obscurity of their lives in the following story.

"The evening had been lowering, but afterwards became partially clear and starry. I left the tent at about eleven o'clock, and was much struck by the picture before and around me.

"Our men were asleep at the fire—all, save the cook on duty, who was feeding it with wood, and stirring the soup. The cool wind was shaking the birch trees, and the waves were whispering and rippling among the reefs below. . . .

"After a time I went and sat on a stone by the side of the cook, and watched his stirrings and tastings.

" 'Monsieur le Docteur,' said he breaking silence, 'these vile rocks and morasses remind me of a mishap of mine long ago in the Indian countries, which would have put an end to me, *"ici bas,"* had it not been for a tin-pot and a gull's nest—things very simple, Monsieur le Docteur.

" 'Our *bourgeois* took me and an Indian to look for a new beaver district on the Black River, which runs into the Mackenzie.

" 'Two days from the Fort, while crossing a pond, I saw a gull's nest, with four little gaping chicks in it, on a bare rock. I had lifted up my foot to kick the whole hatch into the water, according to our notion, that if you kill a bird, a deer, or what not, ten will come instead, when the *bourgeois* forbade me.

" 'Well, one day, three weeks afterwards our canoe capsized in a rapid, and we lost all—every thing, except a tin-pot, which stuck in one of its ribs. Of course we turned back, and lived on dead fish, green bilberries, now

57

and then a young bird, *tripe de roche*, and Labrador tea, which fortunately our pot enabled us to boil. . . .

" 'When we were near spent by many weary days' travel, the *bourgeois* told us that if we would work like gallant men, he would give us a meat-supper on the morrow's night. We wondered but somehow believed the *bon homme*.

" 'Sure enough, on the next evening, we reached a pond. I knew it immediately. Above a bare rock two old gulls hovered and sported in the air. Trusting the young birds had not flown, but fearing they had, we rushed to the nest and found four large plump pullets, which I certainly think, blessed be God, saved our lives. The next day we fell in with some friendly Indians.' " [24]

Dawn came, and before the first glimmerings of light the call of *"Alerte!"* or *"Lève, lève, nos gens"* ("Get up, get up, men") resounded through the camp. No time to hear the sweet songs of birds or to watch the silver sheen of mist rising from the water. All was bustle and confusion. Canoes were launched and loaded, and within fifteen minutes a *chanson* was struck up as the shore receded. Scant courtesy was shown to tardy risers, even though they were "dwellers in tents," for the tent poles were needed in the bottoms of the canoes to equalize the weight of the loads. It was always a race, therefore, between those in the tent and those outside, and the voyageurs considered it a tremendous joke to be able to pull down the tent and reveal a half-clad *bourgeois*.

Trois pipes, some twelve miles, of lusty paddling in the cool morning brought respite and breakfast. The canoes were moored offshore by long poles laid one end on the beach and one on the gunwale, the fire was lighted, and for the *commis*, *bourgeois*, or passenger a cloth was laid on the rocks. Should the traveler be a lady, as sometimes chanced, the never-failing *galanterie* of the voyageurs displayed itself in a little bunch of flowers before the plate, plucked from the numberless wild roses, red columbines, and other flowers that embroidered the clefts in the rocks of this north country in May and June. It was characteristic of this race of men who slept four hours a day in order to shorten their tedious journeys that they should spare time to gather wild roses to grace a lady passenger's breakfast table.

Perhaps they enjoyed, in their own mute way, the freshness and beauty of the scenes through which they passed. How could any human being remain untouched when such scenery as that described by Nicholas Garry presented itself:

"Our Dinner Table was a hard Rock, no Table Cloth could be cleaner and the surrounding Plants and beautiful Flowers sweetening the Board. Before us the Waterfall, wild romantic, bold. The River Winnipic here impeded by Mountainous Rocks appears to have found a Passage through the Rocks and these, as if still disputing the Power of Water, show their Heads, adding to the rude Wildness of the Scene, producing Whirlpools, Foam loud Noise and chrystal Whitness beautifully contrasted with the Black Pine . . . The Wildness of the Scene was added to by the melancholy white headed Eagle hovering over our Board." [25]

Thus the voyageurs spent their days in paddling, smoking, and singing, and their nights in making camp and sleeping, till Michillimackinac, near modern Mackinac, was reached. Just before reaching this, or any fort, the voyageurs, who were great dandies in their own way, must stop and, on a great rock or beach, literally *plume* themselves. For the *crowning* touch of their toilettes, destined to impress all beholders, was the colored feathers which Northmen, as distinguished from pork-eaters, had a right to wear. In such regalia and at top speed with ringing song they paddled vociferously to the landing.

At Mackinac a long halt was made, for *commis* and *bourgeois* must conduct negotiations with other traders, attend to supplies for their men in the big warehouses along the water front, and determine the destination and route of each of the canoes. It was here that the supply of Indian corn was shipped, to take the place of the peas eaten on the route thither from Montreal. From this point many routes diverged. Brigades for the lower Wisconsin and Illinois countries went south through Lake Michigan, but those for the region about Lake Superior and the "Northwest," that is, all of northern America beyond Grand Portage, took the hard route over the portage at the Sault de Sainte Marie and entered the greatest of the lakes.

At Mackinac and again at the Sault the voyageurs had respite while their masters attended to business matters. Gay were the sashes and plumes that were donned to win the favors of dusky maidens, and many the *piastres* spent for high wines, candles, and food. Carnival was the order both of day and of night, and he was an alert *commis* who could keep his men within bounds and round them up on the day of departure in condition to paddle his canoes. Here, as elsewhere when stops were made after arduous paddling and portaging, the men put on weight with amazing rapidity, so much so that one traveler in the far West after a three days' stop remarked, "Some of them became so much improved in looks that it was with difficulty we could recognize our voyageurs." [26]

Once again the long *marches* were resumed as the little hamlets on either side the rapids at the Sault faded from sight. Now the dangers of an immense stretch of water were added to the voyageurs' troubles. *Traverses* must be thought of, yes, prayed over. These crossings of wide stretches of water were hazardous in the extreme, mainly because of treacherous winds and storms which might arise suddenly while the canoes were far out from land. Ordinarily the men kept close, skirting the rocky northern coast or the picturesque southern shore of Lake Superior. But now and again a wide stretch of waters must be crossed. Auspicious weather might not be encountered for several days. Meantime the voyageurs lay in their encampments fretting to be thus delayed. Finally, when the command to move was given, every muscle was strained as the canoes were pushed with utmost speed across the dreaded expanse. Successful prediction of weather was naturally an acquired trait of this class of men whose life was a long struggle against the elements, and disasters in these crossings were not common; yet now and then a storm arose which left only a survivor or two and a wrecked canoe.

When the waves ran high on the lake, the voyageurs, with skill born of long experience, no longer plied their paddles incessantly, but suspended them just as a big wave was met. The object of this manœuver was to avoid sending the sharp nose of the canoe under the succeeding wave, which would have drenched them. When all precautions were unavailing and great waves swept over the canoe, it was necessary to bail with the large sponge kept for that purpose. Two quarts of water could be taken up at a time in this manner.

There were compensations, however, in traveling on Lake Superior. When the wind was soft and light and blowing from the proper quarter, sails were improvised from oil cloths or blankets, and the little vessels sped along while the voyageurs took their ease, smoking, singing, or sleeping. It was *La Vieille*, or "the old woman of the wind," who thus blessed the voyageurs with favoring breezes and lightened their toil; and so, sacrifices to her were always in order. The ritual consisted of throwing a little tobacco into the waters, or scattering a little water from the blades of the paddles, and uttering the formula, *"Souffle, souffle, la vieille"* ("Blow, blow, old woman"). This ceremony was doubtless borrowed from the Indians, whose customs were often appropriated by the voyageurs.[27]

A long spit of land on the southern shore, Keeweenaw Point, necessitated either a circuitous route around it or a portage. As early as Radisson's time the voyageurs had made their choice, for he recounts in the narrative of his first trip on the lake, about the year 1660, how he followed the portage route already well marked by the feet of the "commers and goers." [28] This epithet was sometimes used as the English equivalent of *mangeurs de lard*.

Did voyageurs then precede Radisson in the exploration of the Lake Superior country? So it would seem from this evidence produced by the great explorer himself.

Those who took this route along the southern shore of the lake were bound as a rule for either the northern Wisconsin or the Minnesota region. Two streams gave access to the interior, the Bois Brulé and St. Louis rivers. Both were famous highways into the fur country, and thousands of human feet packed the soil of the portages so firmly that even yet traces of the trails are discernible. When the voyageurs reached the Mississippi, they often met the traders who had entered by another route—*via* Green Bay, the Fox River and portage, and the Wisconsin River. And if they went far north, to the headwaters of the Mississippi, they often found *engagés* who had entered by still another way.

This last route was the most famous of all. It began at Grand Portage, the easternmost tip of soil in modern Minnesota, passed up the rivers and through the lakes that make the natural boundary between Canada and the United States in this region to the outlet of Rainy Lake, where an important fort had been located since the days of La Vérendrye; then through Lake of the Woods, down Winnipeg River to Lake Winnipeg, and up the Red River of the North and its tributaries to the headwaters of the Mississippi. At Lake Winnipeg the Red River traders parted company with the most hardy and venturesome of the Nor'westers, the men who passed up the Assiniboine and Saskatchewan rivers and on to the Rocky Mountains, the coast, and even to Great Bear Lake. Here, too, the menu changed. The corn of the pre-

ceding weeks was supplanted by pemmican, which thence-
forth was the chief article of diet.

Grand Portage, the gateway to this vast country until
shortly after 1800 (when Fort William was substituted),
was reached *via* the rocky northern shore of Lake Superior, where the winds were so violent that canoes were
often lost. It was a post of the first importance, being the
meeting point every June and July of hundreds of traders and voyageurs from interior posts. This was the destination of the Montreal canoes. Here the *mangeurs de
lard* turned back, having unloaded the cargo of manufactured goods from France or England and reloaded
with packs of furs and skins from the uttermost parts of
the wilderness. Here novices who wished to become experienced hands left the ranks of the pork-eaters and became *hivernants*. Here, too, the smaller canoes were procured for the shallower waters beyond Lake Superior.
And here life was so picturesque and unusual that Irving
found a place for a description of it in his *Astoria*.[29]

But even with all their endurance and speed the
voyageurs from the Athabasca country could not reach
Grand Portage during the short northern summers and
return before ice had choked the passages through rivers
and lakes. Accordingly, some of the Montreal men went
on to Rainy Lake, and at the fort there they met the far-
famed Athabasca men, delivered to them their annual
supplies, and reloaded the Montreal canoes with packs of
furs and skins. A special house, called the Athabasca
House, was erected within the stockade of the fort at
Rainy Lake to accommodate the travelers from the north.
Here, if the Athabasca men were delayed, the voyageurs

resorted to one of their rites for speeding the arrival of the expected brigade. This was the erection of crosses with one of the arms pointing in the direction from which the travelers were expected.[30]

The Athabasca men were the Gascons of the "voyaging" class. They looked down with pity mixed with scorn on the mere pork-eaters and even the winterers on the Fraser River and the Columbia were too inexperienced in their eyes to be treated seriously. Naturally the men of other regions resented their superior airs. Duncan M'Gillivray was an amused—even biased—onlooker in the competition which inevitably resulted from this attitude: He wrote of them: [31]

"The Athabasca Men piqued themselves on a Superiority they were supposed to have over the other bands of the North for expeditious marching, and rediculed our men *a la facon du Nord* for pretending to dispute a point that universally decided in *their* favor. Our people were well aware of the disadvantages they laboured under (being about ¼ Heavier loaded than their opponents) but they could not swallow the haughtiness and contempt with which they thought themselves treated, and tho' they could flatter themselves with no hopes of success from the event yet they resolved to dispute the Victory, with the greatest obstinacy that their opposers might not obtain it without the sweat of their brows. In consequence of this determination the two Bands instead of camping according to orders, entered the Lake at sunset, the one animated with the expectation of victory, and the other resolved, if possible, not to be vanquished. They pursued the Voyage with unremitting efforts without any considerable advantage on either side for 48 hours during which they did not once put ashore, 'till at length, being entirely overcome with labour and fatigue, they mutually agreed to camp where we found them, and cross the rest of the Lake together."

M'Gillivray understood the seriousness of this contest for the voyageurs. He goes on:

"Tho' this dispute will appear trifling to you, yet to shew you how much it interested the Parties concerned it will only be necessary to mention a circumstance, which clearly proves their emulation but will do no honor to their humanity. On the second night of the Contest one of our steersmen being overpowered with sleep fell out of the Stern of his Canoe which being under sail advanced a considerable distance before the people could recover from the confusion that this accident occasioned; in the mean time the poor fellow almost sinking with the weight of his cloathes cried out to 2 Canoes that happened to pass within a few yards of him to save his life *pour l'amour de dieu;* but neither the love of God or of the blessed Virgin, whom he powerfully called to his assistance, had the least influence on his hard hearted Countrymen who paddled along with the greatest unconcern, and he must have certainly perished if his own Canoe had not returned time enough to prevent it."

Grand Portage was left with regrets for the end of rest and conviviality. The carrying place there was nine miles in length, and the voyageurs earned six *livres* extra for every *pièce* carried over the bitterly toilsome way. Now the current was against the voyageurs until the height of land was reached near Rainy Lake. On this eminence, whence water flowed northward to Hudson Bay, east to the Atlantic, and south to the Gulf of Mexico, the voyageurs halted for another of their many ceremonies. Here every novice, be he *bourgeois*, clerk, or pork-eater, must be made a Northwester. The ceremony consisted of sprinkling the candidate with a cedar branch dipped in water. He then gave certain promises, among others, never to allow anyone to pass that way without initiation into the ranks of Nor'westers, and never to kiss a voyageur's wife without her consent. The rites were completed with a dozen gunshots fired in rapid succession and a treat of high wines by the new members.[32]

Another custom practiced in this region was the construction of a lob stick. It was customary to make one of these Maypoles in honor of any gentleman who might be a passenger in a canoe. A tall pine, standing out on a point in the lake, was climbed by one of the voyageurs, who, with an ax, cut off all the branches except a tuft at the top, thus rendering it very conspicuous. The name of the passenger was then carved on the trunk, and ever after the spot was called after him. As the crew paddled off, the lob stick was saluted with three cheers and the discharge of guns, the honored passenger, of course, being expected to acknowledge the compliment by a treat at the first opportunity.[33]

On the route from Rainy Lake to Lake Winnipeg, as earlier on the French River, the voyageurs had ample opportunity to display their skill in shooting rapids. The thrill of such dangerous sport appealed powerfully to these French Canadians. To the uninitiated it seemed incredible that such frail structures as bark canoes could remain intact among such rocks and seething waters. It was very exciting to travelers to see how easily and perfectly the voyageurs managed their canoes on the rapids —the bowsman and steersman using their long paddles with wonderful celerity and effect, often turning sharp angles while shooting down bad runs at full speed. The guide very rarely spoke to the steersman, giving his orders merely by a nod of the head or leaving the other to find the course by observing his motions, to every one of which a good steersman responded instantly. "During our first day among the rapids old Baptiste, the guide, was constantly in great glee," writes Kennicott, "and always laughed when entering a bad rapid." [34] To avoid concealed rocks the most perfect skill and coolness, as well as great strength, were required of the guide. To strike a rock while shooting down a rapid with great velocity would almost certainly break or upset a canoe, and in the dashing water any other than a practiced eye and ear would fail to distinguish the hidden boulders. Any attempt at checking the velocity of the canoe when in such danger would be worse than useless, and it was never made; on the contrary, the men all paddled as hard as possible when running a rapid. "When on bad rapids," says the same writer, "I repeatedly saw our guide turn our canoe aside in less than a second, by a stroke of his big paddle, when detecting a sunken rock within two or three feet of the bow, and that, too, when he knew that within several seconds after he must pass in dangerous proximity to other rocks. . . . Still I think he would have dreaded the disgrace attending an accident on a rapid more than the personal danger."

In this stretch many rapids were interdicted to the voyageurs of the Northwest and Hudson's Bay companies because of the great danger to life and property; but voyageurs were not famous for obedience when proprietors and clerks were absent, and so they were often run. Nicholas Garry, who passed that way in 1821, tells in his diary how his crew disobeyed orders: "A few minutes paddling brought us to the Portage de Petite Roche which is a dangerous Rapid but the Water being high we run it, which was great Folly as it is seldom run and we certainly touched. . . . At 2 we embarked, at 5 we arrived at the Portage de l'Isle. This is a very dangerous Rapid, and so many fatal Accidents have attended the Sauting of it that it has been interdicted to the Servants of both Companies. Our Men forgetting Orders and wishing to avoid the Trouble of carrying the Canoe run it and we escaped, though an Absolution of Sin in a severe Ducking would not have justified this Rashness. . . . In half an Hour we arrived at a Décharge but our Steersman preferred running it and we had a narrow escape having just touched. A harder Knock would have broken our Canoe." [35]

When such a blow was sustained and the canoe injured, a sickening sensation was experienced, which one traveler describes as "your Feeling when under the Hands of an unskilful Dentist." [36] Sometimes the danger was not alone to one canoe but to all those following in the brigade. Garry, who had escaped so many accidents, at length had his experience: "entered the Hill River which is full of Rapids and Cataracts the water so low that we struck at every Moment and at last about two o'clock when going down a Rapid we struck upon a rock and broke our Canoe. Our Situation was very perilous. Our Canoe immediately began to fill and Mr McGillivray who was following us close was bearing down upon us, and had he struck us both Canoes would have been knocked to pieces and all of us thrown into the violent Rapid below us. By the great Skill of the Steersman and a wonderful Effort he brought the Canoe alongside and we remained on the Rock. . . . We found four Feet of Bark had been knocked to Pieces. . . . If we had been alone many of us must have perished or if we had escaped a watery Grave we should have been exposed to Starvation and a miserable Death. The Day was fortunately very fine and dry and with several fires we soon dried our Papers, Linen, Beds, &c., for everything was wetted. Our Encampment had a singular Appearance, the Trees covered with our Linen, Sheets, Beds, &c., and the Earth covered with Papers." [37] Wettings were especially detrimental to packs of fur.

When such a hole had been made in the canoe, it was necessary to cut away all the injured bark and patch with new. In such a case as Garry's it might have been impossible to get a piece sufficiently large, for such a wound was larger than the usual patches kept rolled in the front of every canoe. Here Garry pays his tribute to the voyageur: "It now became necessary to consider how we should get on but the Canadian Voyageur soon finds a Remedy and our Men were immediately occupied in repairing the Hole. The Woods furnished the material. Bark from the Birch Tree Wattape from the Root of the Pine, Splints made from the Cedar Tree and the Cross-bars. In the Evening all was ready to start in the Morning." [38]

Even the voyageur had nerves, however. The next day, when another dangerous rapid was reached, the hero of the previous occasion found himself so unnerved that he gave up his post at the most dangerous point. "We escaped in Safety," remarks Garry, "having struck against a flat Rock, in going down, which almost upset us." [39] One day, however, sufficed to restore the guide's confidence in himself. "At 4," continues the same author, "we arrived at the last Rapid before the Rock Depôt, a most dangerous Rapid, where we were nearly lost. Our old Guide, who had before resumed his Situation and Courage, and who had conducted us through many dangerous Rapids, with admirable Skill, was now at the Bows, and directing the Canoe. At once, when in the most dangerous Part, his Pole broke. Two Seconds would have dashed us over the Rocks into the deep Rapid, when the most of us, if not All, must have perished. With an admirable Presence of Mind, he took another Pole and in a Second guided us through the Channel." Garry then goes on to reflect, "How singularly the Mind of Man is framed, how unnerved at one Moment, the next showing Heroism and Presence of Mind, and never has there been a greater proof of this, than in our Guide, at this perilous Moment, and when he gave up the Steering."

Beyond Grand Portage the method of portaging was slightly different from what it had been earlier in the route. After the canoe had been emptied, instead of being turned over and carried upturned by four men at the ends and two in the center, it was now left in its normal position and carried by two men.[40] This change was due to the smallness of the North canoes. Here, too, it was sometimes necessary to use the bedding in carrying the canoe over steep rocks. The beds were placed in the recesses of the rocks as steps or supporting places for the canoe. The bow of the canoe was placed on the bedding as it was lifted from step to step up the rock; in very much the same manner it was let down as carefully on the other side.

With such difficulties and dangers as those described, it is small wonder that orders were not carried out as precisely as some of the clerks in distant posts could have desired. Gabriel Franchere, the famous Astorian and later a clerk of the American Fur Company at Sault Ste. Marie, was able to understand, as many less experienced clerks would not have been able to do, why his brigade from Montreal in the spring of 1837 was so long in arriving and why so many articles were missing. Indeed, there is more than an accent of censure in his letter for the stupidity of superiors in New York who so little realized the burdens of the voyageur. He writes: "The reason of their long passage was owing to an accident which occurred on the Otawa River. They broke one canoe, drowned 1 man, had to run back to Fort Colonge for other canoes and provisions which they procured from Mr. Sicought [Siveright?], and thereby lost 8 men by desertion. Of the articles sent up, all the portage collars were lost, 65 prs shoe-packs, 8 side leather and 6 stoves; that is they brought sundry stove plates here, but only one of the smallest kind was complete. It is to be regretted that such heavy articles should be sent by Grand

River & in such weak vessels as a bark canoe. However, I suppose you followed instructions from New York. It will teach us a lesson for the future." [41]

Do not imagine that these long trips were accomplished in the company of only one's own canoemates. On a certain trip in the early twenties, to mention only one instance to the contrary, the voyageurs in one light canoe encountered five groups of canoes, some forty or so in all, between Montreal and Lake Huron. The parties not only met or passed one another on the water, but at times they camped together. Then the leaders needed to exercise their utmost control, for quarreling was likely to result. An artist with an eye for the picturesque has left us a word sketch of one of these encounters at an encampment: "Here we found waiting for the morn seven loaded canoes and eighty *voyageurs* belonging to the Hudson's Bay Company. . . . It was an uncouth scene. There was a semi-circle of canoes turned over on the grass to sleep under, with blazing fires near them, surrounded by sinister-looking long-haired men, in blanket coats, and ostrich feathers in their hats, smoking and cooking, and feeding the fires. I particularly noticed one large square man, squat on the wet ground, with a bit of looking-glass in his hand, intently watching his wife, as she carefully combed out his long jetty hair. . . ." [42]

The long hair to which the traveler refers was a protection against the hosts of mosquitoes which beset all who *voyaged*. It was an object of great pride, and voyageurs bestowed much time and energy in dressing it. In truth, voyageurs were great dandies in their own fashion. They were even known to wash their garments occasionally.

73

They dried them with just that difference of method which characterized everything they did—they spread them on the sands to dry, even when bushes were available.

Even though they did not subscribe to the tenet that cleanliness is next to godliness, the voyageurs usually took excellent care of their few articles of wearing apparel. If rain overtook a canoe, the passengers vanished under oilcloths or tarpaulins. The voyageurs pulled off their garments to keep them dry, while the cold rain coursed down their powerful, naked backs. Of course, this precaution was fully as much in the interest of comfort later on as in desire to preserve the garments themselves.

By early autumn most of the brigades had reached their destinations, sometimes a large important fort, like that at Rainy Lake, sometimes an insignificant wintering post on an inland lake. But wherever the voyageur went in the fur country, his life was very much like that of every other voyageur. Hence, though details might differ in such widely separated posts as Mackinac and Astoria, the everyday routine was very similar. It is possible therefore to describe this fort life accurately in a general way.

V

FORT LIFE

C. BERTSCH

V

THE first duty of voyageurs on reaching their wintering ground was to erect a fort, unless, of course, the post was already established and supplied with buildings. A consultation was frequently held with the chief Indians as to the best site. When this was determined, a clearing was made, trees were cut and hewed in proper lengths, and a storehouse and "shop" were erected. Next came the clerk's house, then a house for the men, and finally a high stockade, the *fort* in local parlance. The day on which the great gate was hung and locked for the first time marked the completion of the post in the eyes of the men. Other buildings, such as a roothouse or a magazine, might be added, and a flagstaff was always put up in the enclosure. Often a well was dug within the stockade. Chimneys of mud and sticks or mud and stones were put up at the ends of the dwellings, and roofs were thatched with boughs held down by poles or sticks. Nails were expensive and heavy to bring into the interior, and so the logs were held in place in a unique way. Grooves were cut in logs set upright at each corner of the foundation. Down these grooves were slipped the ends of the wall logs, which were cut to fit exactly between the uprights. Thus one log lay in place above another, all being held in position by the vertical logs.[1] A certain kind of white clay served admirably in place of plaster and whitewash and gave a neat appearance to the interiors. A puncheon floor was laid, bunks were constructed against the walls, rough tables and stools were made, and a window or two was filled with oiled deerskin in lieu of glass. Such a cabin, filled with the odors of game roasting on a blazing grate which flung fantastic shadows over guns, knives, and snowshoes on the walls, was not an unhomelike place, and it was the prototype of many a pioneer's home as the frontier moved westward.

From a diary kept during the winter of 1804-05 on a branch of the St. Croix River, within the present boundaries of Minnesota, something of an idea of the time required for building a fort may be drawn.[2] Three, possibly four, buildings were erected in three weeks. Four chimneys are mentioned; these required four days. The "masonry" of them, however, to use the clerk's term, was completed in two days. A few weeks later one of them caught fire and had to be repaired. The "covering" of the houses apparently took two days. The "flooring" of both houses and the plastering of the clerk's residence consumed five days. Three weeks after the first tree was felled the clerk wrote in his journal, "This evening entered my dwelling House." It must have been unfinished within, however, for two evenings later he recorded, "Men finished my Bed Room." At this point All Saints' Day with its "enchanting Weather" caused a temporary halt. The usual dole of rum, one gallon in this case, was made, and the voyageurs "did no Work of course." On Sunday, November 4, twenty-six days after work was begun, the clerk recorded, "My Men entered their dwellings." The cutting of the stockade was begun

on the seventh of November, and by the thirteenth the
"Men began raising the Stockades." This was evidently
a long process, for it was not till the twentieth that the
clerk could enter in his diary that "the Doors of the Fort
were fixd & Shut this Evening." All this time, apparently, the *commis* was doling out a dram morning and
evening to each voyageur, for at the very outset he recorded: "men perform'd a great Days Work gave them
each a Dram morning & Evening & promised to do the
same till our Buildings are Compleated provided the[y]
exert themselves."

The site of a fort was chosen with several requirements in mind. It must be near Indian villages; it must
be readily accessible from the highways of trade; usually
it must be on a stream or lake well stocked with fish, the
staple diet of the wintering fur-traders; and wood for
building and fuel purposes must be at hand. In the region
beyond the Mississippi the feeding grounds of the buffalo were also taken into account, both because of food
and robes which could be obtained from them and for the
additional reason that buffalo "chips" could serve as
fuel.

Once settled in their fort, the men must prepare for
the long winter. Seines were set in the water just before
the ice "took" on the lake or river. Whitefish and trout
were taken in the bigger lakes, and tollibees, sturgeon,
pike, and other varieties in the smaller lakes and rivers.
The method of preserving the winter's supply of fish was
the same throughout the wilderness. Each fish was pierced
with the point of a knife about two inches from the tail
and strung on a twisted willow branch. Groups of ten

were thus made and hung heads down in a shady place. If they did not undergo too much warm weather before they froze, the fish were excellent all winter; otherwise a strong, rank taste developed. Approximately four fish per person was reckoned the daily ration. Hence, many hundreds were required in the course of a winter for a fort of a dozen or fifteen persons. The following entry in a clerk's diary may be taken as a good fish story, but so it stands on the yellowed pages: "Took a Pike of 37^{lb} Weight in our Net the largest I ever yet saw." [3]

Wild rice was another staple item in the larder of every fort in the regions where this plant grew. It was usually called "oats" by the traders and was bought by the sack from squaws, who gathered it in the lakes and marshes in the late summer. In the spring maple sugar was also bought by the *makuk* (a birch-bark vessel) from the squaws. At Connor's fort in the St. Croix valley five kegs of sugar were secured in one season, four of which were cached under the fireplace in the clerk's house for the next year's use.

In the buffalo country the traders' chief reliance was on the "cows," as the female buffaloes were almost invariably called. These were hunted in the fall and spring. A part of the meat was preserved by drying or "jerking" in summer and by freezing in winter. Much of the remainder was made into pemmican. At Archibald Norman McLeod's fort at Alexandria, on the Assiniboine River in modern Saskatchewan, there were stored away in March, 1801, the meat of about eighty-five buffalo cows, sixty-two bags of pemmican weighing ninety pounds each, and nine kegs of grease, each of seventy pounds. It must be added, however, that this fort was a depot for supplying the western brigades of canoes with pemmican and grease.[4]

In the autumn the clerk chose as hunter for his fort an Indian who was reliable and a good marksman. It was the business of this man to keep the fort supplied with fresh meat or wild fowl. It was everyone's business, however, to assist in this work whenever other duties did not prevent. Thus Connor records at various times during the winter of 1804-05: "At Sun rise the Men that went for Meat came back"; "the 2 Men that went Yesterday with Mr Seraphin to Lodges arrived before day light with the Meat of 6 Deers"; "This afternoon Desève arrived with 2 Beavers & the Meat from Pierro &co"; "This evening my Men came home with the Meat of 5 Deers." [5]

Yet with all these precautions the forts at times were as bare as Mother Hubbard's cupboard, and starvation was by no means unknown. The following are typical entries from the diaries of clerks: "We have now thirty people in the fort, and have not a supply of provisions for two days"; "During the last three days we have subsisted on tallow and dried cherries"; "I really begin to fear we shall starve this winter, at any rate we'll be oblidged to make use of the little dry provisions the Indians may bring to the Fort, & G—d alone knows whether we'll be able to scrape together what will make a little Pimican to bring us all to the Point." [6]

Two meals a day, breakfast and the evening meal, were customary everywhere in the fur country. The voyageurs were prodigious eaters, for, says Harmon, "a

Canadian, with his belly full of fat meat, is never otherwise" than happy.[7] To supplement this rather meager diet, most of the clerks at posts of any size planted gardens, where potatoes, turnips, beans, peas, and other vegetables were raised. At a time when the world believed that these hyperborean regions (the adjective was often used in contemporary references) were capable of producing only icicles and furs, the traders were producing one thousand bushels of potatoes at Leech Lake, near the source of the Mississippi River, and six hundred bushels of potatoes, besides barley and peas, at Sandy Lake a little farther south.[8] Nor were vegetables the only products of these pioneer farms. There were horses at Leech Lake in 1807; cows which had been driven overland were not uncommon on the Red River of the North in the twenties; and even the humble hen and pig could be heard within the stockades of some forts. An interesting reminiscent article written by an erstwhile missionary to the Chippewa Indians of the St. Croix valley in western Wisconsin appeared in the New York *Evangelist* in 1860 under the title, "Stray Leaves from an Old Man's Portfolio." [9] Here is told with a humor which one does not expect the story of how pigs were driven into the region in 1834. Doubtless the same ludicrous methods of transportation—canoes on the lakes and chase through the forests—were used in introducing the swine that were found earlier at Leech and Sandy lakes. Dogs, of course, were numerous at every post.

One suspects that these gardens and animals were raised not alone for food, but with some such motive as prompts the modern city dweller to plant his sterile back yard to vegetables which he could buy infinitely cheaper in the markets. Harmon, more articulate than most traders, hints at the underlying reason: "We are preparing a piece of ground for a garden, the cultivation of which, will be an amusement; and the produce of it, we hope, will add to our comforts." Then, without pause, he adds as his next sentence, "Mr Goedike plays the violin, and will occasionally cheer our spirits, with an air." [10] How easily a few words like these two sentences, especially their juxtaposition, produce the homesick atmosphere of those little, isolated posts of the "western waters."

The voyageurs, however, had their own ways of cheer, which the clerks and *bourgeois* wisely countenanced. Christmas and the New Year were celebrated with vastly more acclaim and spontaneity than in most civilized countries, and there were many other gala days which no voyageur ever passed up without the celebration prescribed in the *pays d'en haut*. Harmon's first Christmas in the interior came as somewhat of a shock to him, accustomed to the proprieties of the New England mode of celebration, for he says, "This day being Christmas, our people have spent it as usual in drinking and fighting." [11] Kennicott, however, was alive to the picturesqueness of this class of men and more in sympathy with their methods of self-expression. Consequently his remarks on a Christmas celebration in the Northwest are more detailed and full of interest. "The day after Christmas, Flett gave a Christmas ball. . . . The dancing was, I may say without vulgarity, decidedly 'stunning.' I should hardly call it graceful. The figures, if they may be called

such, were only Scotch reels of four, and jigs; and . . .
the main point to which the dancers' efforts seemed to
tend, was to get the largest amount of exercise out of
every muscle in the frame. . . . The music consisted of
a very bad performance of one vile, unvarying tune, upon
a worse old fiddle, accompanied by a brilliant accompaniment upon a large tin pan." [12]

Perhaps one may ask of the dusky partners of the men
in these gala affairs. Sir John Franklin, the Arctic explorer, recorded their conduct with some interest. He
noted at a dance in a northern post how fond of dancing
the half-breed women were, though a stranger would
imagine the contrary on observing their apparent want
of animation. On such occasions, he said, they affected a
sobriety of demeanor which was the very opposite to
their general character.[13] Another traveler found worthy
of even more detailed description the female portion of
an assembly which celebrated a certain Christmas with
a dance in a far northwestern post. The great hall was
lit up by means of a number of tallow candles, stuck in
tin sconces round the walls. The men, in their Sunday
jackets and capotes, sat on benches and chairs. Around
the stove, which had been removed to one side to leave
space for the dancers, a strange group was collected.
"Squatting down on the floor, in every ungraceful attitude imaginable, sat about a dozen Indian women,
dressed in printed calico gowns, the chief peculiarity of
which was the immense size of the baloon-shaped sleeves,
and the extreme scantiness, both in length and width, of
the skirts. Coloured handkerchiefs covered their heads,
and ornamented moccasins decorated their feet; besides

which, each one wore a blanket in the form of a shawl, which they put off before standing up to dance. They were chatting and talking to each other with great volubility, occasionally casting a glance behind them, where at least half a dozen infants stood bolt upright in their tight-laced cradles." [14]

On both Christmas and New Year's the men were given a *régale* with which to have a feast; in other words, they were served with flour to make cakes or puddings and with rum, usually a half pint. Perhaps no finer picture of the celebration of New Year's Day is afforded than in James McKenzie's amused and tolerant account: "Great preparations going on here this night for to-morrow, which is New Year's Day. Dusablon, with hands which have not seen a drop of water since last New Year's Day, made a large kettle full of *boulettes* of fish, each as big and as ill-shaped as his own head. Lambert made fish cakes, *alias 'pêtes,'* boiled for an hour with dried meat. Masquaro made the fire, drew water and cleaned shoes, &c. Mr. Wentzel and I were continually running from the shop to the *hangard*, from the *hangard* to the garret, from thence to the kitchen; in short, every body in the house had a finger in the pie and were as busy all night as *une queue de veau.* This morning before day break, the men, according to custom, fired two broadsides in honor of the New Year, and then came in to be rewarded with rum, as usual. Some of them could hardly stand alone before they went away. . . . After dinner, at which every body helped themselves so plentifully that nothing remained to the dogs, they had a bowl of punch. The expenses of this day with fourteen men and women are: 6½ fathoms spencer twist [tobacco], 7 flagons rum, 1 ditto wine, 1 ham, a skin's worth of dried meat, about 40 white fish, flour, sugar, &c. Felix Labrie, whose beard, from *chagrin* for his brother's death, is as long as my pen, was the first that began to drink and sing, and the last who gave up that farce. He is a gentleman who stands upon no ceremony; he was not backwards in taking along with him to his own house the punch which remained in the bowl, and, there, drink it." [15]

Many of the *bourgeois* and clerks in the interior were Scotch, and the voyageurs, with their typical Gallic courtesy, never failed to remember St. Andrew's day. Of course, their pure goodwill was mixed with the alloy of self-interest, for the customary presentation of a St. Andrew's cross was always rewarded with a quart or so of high wines in the morning and in the evening with another gift of wine or rum. Dancing was the entertainment of the evening. In the year 1800 at Archibald Norman McLeod's post on the upper waters of the Assiniboine they danced "till three oClock in the morning to Frise's singing." [16]

As the descriptions already quoted will show, the orchestras for these balls were not uniform. Music oozed from every pore of the voyageur, and when a fiddle was not handy, substitutes could always be found. In fact, musical instruments were far from uncommon in the interior, even excepting tin pans from the category. Many of the voyageurs carried fiddles with them to their wintering posts, and even on their winter jaunts from post to post. The arrival of such a man at a post where no

musical talent was boasted was always the signal for a
ball, which not infrequently lasted all night.

These accounts of festivals and balls must not be taken
to indicate that the life at a fur post was a round of
pleasure. The duties of the men were legion, even if
their main task be excepted, which was, of course, the
procuring of furs from the Indians. Before describing
these trips afield, however, let us observe the everyday
life in a typical fort. The diaries kept scrupulously by
the clerks afford the best material. In them one reads of
daily chores, of arrivals of Indians, of hunting and fishing, of illnesses, of deaths, and even of marriages. It must
be explained, however, that marriages were "according
to the custom of the country"; that is, they were rather
informal and often temporary, judged by civilized stand-
ards. It would be too much to suppose that the hundreds
of voyageurs who passed their young manhood in the Indian country lived ascetic lives. On the contrary, they
made alliances with Indian girls, much to the gratifica-
tion of the girls' parents, who received gifts of considerable value in return. Harmon, whose scorn for such
unions was intense on his arrival but who later succumbed
to the inevitable, describes such a wedding: "This evening, Mons. Mayotte took a woman of this country for a
wife, or rather concubine. All the ceremonies attending
such an event, are the following. When a person is desirous of taking one of the daughters of the Natives, as a
companion, he makes a present to the parents of the
damsel, of such articles as he supposes will be most ac-
ceptable; and, among them, rum is indispensable; for of
that all the savages are fond, to excess. Should the parents

accept the articles offered, the girl remains at the fort with her suitor, and is clothed in the Canadian fashion. The greater part of these young women, as I am informed, are better pleased to remain with the white people, than with their own relations. Should the couple, newly joined, not agree, they are at liberty, at any time, to separate; but no part of the property, given to the parents of the girl, will be refunded. . . . Payet, one of my interpreters has taken one of the daughters of the Natives for a wife; and to her parents he gave in rum, dry goods, &c. to the value of two hundred dollars." [17]

Thus the forts were occupied not only by traders, but by their wives and children. The Indian women seem to have been very adaptable and to have been not only willing drudges but good mothers. Harmon, in fact, became so attached to his *femme* that he took her back to civilization with him in his later years. History does not record her reactions to her new surroundings. In general, however, the alliances were more or less temporary, though the children took their father's name and as a rule were acknowledged and cared for by him. Garry tells the following laughable tale of a half-breed boy who thought he knew who his father was: "A very nice Canadian Boy, moitié noir et moitié blanc, presented himself at our Tent and enquired for Mr. McGillivray. The elder Mr. McGillivray answered. After a short Preface the Boy said, 'Monsieur, vous êtes mon Père.' Mr. McGillivray, 'Comment, Coquin,' and his Look with it I shall never forget, and it set his Brother and Myself laughing in such a manner that I thought we should never have ceased. However the Laugh was a good deal turned against Mr.

Simon McGillivray on the Boy stating that Simon was
his name. However after a few more Questions the poor
enfant trouvé was dismissed without finding his Père. I
could not but admire the Ruse de Guerre of the old voyageur Mr. McGillivray turning the Tables on his Brother
who was not less expert in Expedient, as he took me aside
afterwards saying it was an odd Adventure but added 'I
see how it is,—it is my nephew Simon's Son.' So the poor
Boy must go to the Athapascan for a Father and when he
arrives the Nephew will be as ready in throwing the
charge from his Shoulders. The Mr. McGillivrays in-
tend enquiring out the History of the Boy." [18]

From these unions with Indian women developed the
large class called indiscriminately half-breeds, *métis*, *bois
brulés*, which formed such a large percentage of all
American and Canadian frontier settlements. Many of
their descendants are men and women of distinction and
social standing in the modern cities that have developed
from old posts, such as Detroit, Milwaukee, St. Paul,
Winnipeg, and St. Louis.

With such a personnel, therefore, the fort was a busy
place. The *commis* or resident *bourgeois* directed the work
of all his numerous dependents and planned the winter's
campaign for furs. A typical entry in such a *bourgeois'*
journal may, perhaps, give the flavor of the setting better
than any attempt at paraphrase. Such an entry is Mc-
Leod's for Tuesday, November 25, 1800: "A very mild
day, the most of the Snow melted today I sent E. Ducharm for the Red Deer that the hunters kill'd Sunday
La Rose & H. Ducharm I sent to look for Birch to make
chairs, Vallé went to get wood for a Sledge, Roy took a

Doze of Physic, I scolded Girardin, for some stupid observation of his, to Mr Harmon & Collin. he is making me a pair of Deer skin trowsers. old Parant, is busy making a Slay to haul the fire wood home with, Danis is making a Couple of window Shutters."

A little later in the winter of 1801 McLeod's diary shows some other interesting occupations of the men: "Monday 2^d [February, 1801] Sent off, Roy, Giradin, Dannis, & Plante with 120 sk[in]s value of Goods, Rum, &c. to trade with the Indians   Tuesday 3^d.   A very boisterous day. Blows prodigiously. Some of the men at work making horse sledges, others melting or Boiling back fat to put in the Pimican. All the women at work sewing Bags to put the Pimican into. Roy, Giradin &. E. Ducharm came home with the last of the meat & brought home the Lodge & now we have finished hauling meat, for this Season. We have now about eighty five Buffaloe Cows in the Meat house Collin very busy making kegs to put Grease into, old Parrant, making nails for the Sledges, &. Plante hanging up the meat &. tongues he put in salt ten days ago, today. Wednesday 4th I got the last Pounded meat we got made into Pimican, vizt 30 bags of 90^{lb} so that we have now 62 Bags of that Species of provisions &. of the above weight. I likewise got nine kegs filled with Grease, or Tallow rather each keg nett 70^{lb}. . . . the men &. women danced till twelve oClock at night."

Kane, a Canadian artist, with an eye for the picturesque, wrote in his memoirs of a winter sojourn at the fort at Edmonton a sketch of the ordinary life of the place. The fort, says he, presented "a most pleasing picture of cheerful activity." He describes the occupations of both voyageurs and squaws, and then goes on: "The evenings are spent round their large fires in eternal gossiping and smoking. The sole musician of the establishment, a fiddler, is now in great requisition amongst the French part of the inmates who give full vent to their national vivacity, whilst the more sedate Indian looks on with solemn enjoyment." [19]

The men were not often sick, but when illness did occur, the clerk must assume the rôle of physician or surgeon. Cox, an Astorian and a trader on the Pacific Coast, says of the men that they enjoyed good health and, with the exception of occasional attacks of rheumatism, were seldom afflicted with disease. "The principal trading establishments," he says, "are supplied with well-assorted medicine chests, containing books of directions, lancets, &c. An assortment of the more simple medicines is made up for each out-post; and as each clerk must learn how to bleed, we generally manage, between low diet, salts, castor-oil, opodeldoc, friar's balsam, and phlebotomy, to preserve their health unimpaired, and cure any common accident." [20] Several doctors were traders at one time or another in the interior, and their professional skill made them great assets to their whole regions. Thus, Dr. John Munro was at Grand Portage in 1797. Dr. John McLoughlin was at the same post in the early twenties; about 1806 he had spent a winter on Vermilion Lake, close to Rainy Lake fort, and in 1808 he was on Sturgeon Lake in the Nipigon Department; in the year 1823-24 he was at Rainy Lake post. Dr. Charles W. W. Borup traded in Michigan in the later twenties, and in the thirties he was the trader at Yellow Lake in western Wisconsin and, later, the manager of the very important post at La Pointe, on the south shore of Lake Superior. Dr. Bell was a rival of the American Fur Company's man on Leech Lake near the source of the Mississippi in 1833. All of these men are known to have rendered medical service to the voyageurs and to the Indians.[21]

Communication between forts and with the Indians of a vast outlying area was not as uncommon as might be supposed. Voyageurs and clerks became almost as expert as Indians in their ability to cover ground rapidly. They adopted not only the Indian's canoe, but also his snowshoes, his dog trains, and his ponies as well. One gets the notion from reading the diaries of such men as McLeod, Harmon, Malhiot, and McDonell that scarcely a day passed without the arrival of Indians, other voyageurs, or clerks from neighboring posts.[22]

Indians were by far the most numerous guests, but they were seldom allowed within the stockade except in small groups, and then only on business. The fear of them was great, even though they appeared friendly. When they succeeded in getting the clerk to issue fire water to them, they became so quarrelsome and committed murder so easily that they became very unwelcome guests. Connor writes, as the culmination of a long series of entries on the turbulence of his Indians in the St. Croix valley: "Yesterday Evening the Indians began their usual Custom of Stabbing no less than 7 got wounded: 2 of them I believe are Mortally so. they are still Drunk." [23]

Several times in the course of a winter it was usually

necessary to send groups of voyageurs to distant bands to collect either furs or food. Such trips were usually made by *traîneaux de glace*, or long, toboggan-shaped sleds, drawn by dogs, sometimes by horses. Such a trip was termed a *dérouine* by the traders and voyageurs.

The dogs used to draw the trains were of the well-known Eskimo or huskie stock, though teams of fierce wolf dogs were sometimes employed, so wild that only their master and his guide could control them. The dogs of one team of this kind in the far north had to be chained up every night and kept in a stockade like wild animals in the summer. Finally they had to be shot, after they had attacked an Indian who had entered their stockaded yard. It was customary to put these dogs in "pensions" for the summer. Garry mentions such a dog hotel on the lower Red River in 1821. It contained "at least 100 Dogs" and was kept by a man who received two dollars per day for each dog. He had chosen "an excellent Fishing Place" in order to provide food, but from the fact that some twenty dogs followed Garry's canoe for some distance in the hope of getting food, he concluded that the poor beasts were not deriving the full benefit of the two dollars.[24]

The dogs were driven in tandem style in the forest regions, but on the prairies each animal pulled on his own traces. They were decked out with gaudy saddle cloths, fringed and embroidered in the most fantastic manner, with innumerable small bells and feathers. Many of the voyageur's hard-earned *piastres* were squandered on the trappings of his train of dogs. Usually four dogs constituted a train, pulling five or six hundred pounds and traveling forty to seventy miles per day. Their sleds were made of two oak boards securely fastened by cross pieces and planed thin at one end. By a process of steaming this end was rolled to enable the dogs to pull it more easily over rough country. These sleds were about ten feet long and sixteen to eighteen inches wide. The guide usually preceded the leading train, and on him rested the responsibility for keeping to the route.

The dogs, accustomed to fend for themselves about the fort, were hard to catch when wanted for a trip. The artist Kane relates how he was awakened one morning in a western fort by a yelling and screaming which made him rush from his room in great alarm. "There," says he, "I saw the women harnessing the dogs. Such a scene! The women were like so many furies with big sticks, thrashing away at the poor animals, who rolled and yelled in agony and terror, until each team was yoked up and started off." [25]

Much has been written of the unerring instincts of these guides, but from reading contemporary diaries one is forced to the conclusion that they were by no means infallible. In fact, the instances of voyageurs lost on the prairies and in the woods are legion. One of David Thompson's companions on a trip from the Assiniboine to the Mandan villages on the Missouri in 1797 owed his life to a chance discovery by his associates.[26] The clerk at the great fort on Rainy River recorded in his diary for the winter of 1804-05 how some of his voyageurs, sent on a *dérouine*, were lost and had to return to the post.[27] The wonder is that more were not lost.

On the road the dogs were fed but once daily. After

the encampment had been made, chunks of poor pemmican or two frozen whitefish for each dog were laid by
the blazing fire to thaw. In their nervous eagerness to get
these the dogs often fell to fighting amongst themselves,
one team setting upon another. Seldom did the dogs of a
train set upon one another, for there seemed to be an
esprit de corps among those which pulled together. Unless
watched, the dogs would eat anything of animal origin,
including their own harness and their master's snowshoes. After eating, the dogs were allowed to settle themselves in the snow to shiver through the long winter
night. Only dogs of such hardy stock and such woolly
coats could endure this life. Even they often suffered
from rough ice and stubble. Their paws would become
sore, and then they were unfit for service. For such emerg-
encies their masters carried many sets of little leather
shoes which were pulled on like gloves and tied with
thongs of deerskin. The dogs often became very fond of
these accessories and would whine piteously for them.
Frequently they would lie on their backs pawing the air
to attract their master's attention to their feet in the hope
of having their shoes put on.[28]

Often the men rode, but usually they followed on
snowshoes. "Riding and running" was the expression used
for swift traveling by dog train. Then only a light burden
was carried, and the voyageur himself rode until so
chilled that he must jump off and run for a time to get
warm again.

If the thermometer registered between ten degrees below zero and ten above, five hundred pounds of baggage
could be drawn by three dogs. At that temperature the

friction that hindered the dogs in colder weather was absent. On the other hand, neither dogs nor men could travel well if the mercury mounted to more than ten degrees above zero.

The voyageur had his own method of reckoning distance by dog sled just as he coined his own phrases for computing the length of portages and stretches of water. Every five miles or so a halt was made to rest the dogs and to allow the men to smoke. These stops were termed "spells" or "pipes," and the voyageurs spoke of a day's journey as of so many spells or pipes. On a well-known road the spelling places were the same spots on every journey.

Customs developed in this kind of travel just as in canoeing, and the voyageur built up his own vocabulary. Thus, to "*mouche*" meant for a dog to increase his speed. "To spell ahead" referred to the custom that decreed that each train must take its turn in leading the procession of sleds. As the first *traîneau* had to beat the track for those following, the foremost dogs tired most easily. Consequently, after a period of spelling ahead the foremost train went to the rear of the procession, just as the leading gander in a flock of wild fowl is often seen to drop to the rear, presumably to get respite from the friction of the leader's position.

To "give track" was another expression used by these men. "Not to 'give track' is another disgrace," says Kennicott. "When the dogs of one sled keep so close to the one in advance that the foregoer's traces slacken, the sled ahead is said not to *give* track." [29] To call a dog the voyageur cried, "*Mon chien, vien ici.*" To stop was "*wo*" porary description of a journey through the region just south of Lake Superior makes the whole process clear: "We generally stopped for the night about sundown. In the winter, it is of the first importance, to find a place for encamping where there is the best fuel for a fire. The second item of encampment, is the balsam tree, the branches of which are generally used for the foundation of a bed. On stopping for the night, the collars are stripped from the necks of the dogs—one man plies the axe in chopping wood for the night, cutting it from eight to ten feet long; another carries it on his shoulders to the camp; another, if there is a third, with a snow shoe, clears away the snow for a place for a bed and a fire, and a sufficient distance around for the baggage and dogs. We then break off the twigs of the balsam to prepare for a bed: or if these cannot be obtained, we search for dry grass or rushes. Sometimes pine boughs, and even little bushes a half inch in diameter are used, when nothing better can be obtained. When the foundation of our bed is laid, a fire is kindled, and one hangs on a kettle of snow or water for cooking our supper. We now gather before a cheerful fire, pull off our leggins and moccasons, and hang them by the fire to dry, putting on dry socks and moccasons. The cook urges forward the supper, which when ready is eaten with a keen relish. Supper ended, and dogs fed, preparations are made for lying down. Having spread our skins and blankets upon our foundation of boughs, with a bag of rice or meal, or our folded coats for a pillow, we . . . lie down, all in one bed, with all our clothes on except our coats; and even them, and caps and mittens too, sometimes. We lie at right angles with the fire, and put our feet as near it as we can and not burn them. When the weather is very cold, we are obliged to get up two or three times during the night, and renew our fire. When the wind blows cold we stick up bushes, or branches of the balsam, to break off the force of it. Traveling under the circumstances we do, it is impossible to carry bedding enough to make us comfortable in extreme cold weather—we consequently occasionally suffer much during the night." [30]

In the western mountains a "regular" winter encampment meant one made where the snow was very deep. Green logs eighteen or twenty feet in length were necessary for the hearth, for the snow melted to the depth of six to ten feet even beneath these poles. The length of the logs prevented them from falling into the well formed by the heat of the fire. The green logs seldom burned through in a night. Incautious voyageurs, however, sometimes rolled in their sleep into the pit, much to the amusement of their companions. The depth of the snow in these regions could be easily gauged by the height of the stumps of trees cut for previous encampments. In the summer or in open winters these stumps rose fifteen to twenty feet above the trail, though their tops were on the snow level when the voyageurs' axes were put to them. Around the fires made from these trees the old voyageurs amused themselves by telling the pork-eaters that the Indians in those parts were giants from thirty to forty feet in height and that fact accounted for the trees being cut off at such an unusual height.[31]

For respite on these, as also on canoe trips, the mer sang, played cards, threw quoits, and boasted to one another. "All their chat is about horses, dogs, canoes, women and strong men, who can fight a good battle," wrote Harmon.[32] Boasting was as much a part of their make-up as it is of most grown-up children. They boasted of all their deeds, relatives, possessions, masters, friends, canoes, and dogs; and when they summed up all these, they announced to an admiring world that they were "North-westers," or merely *"Je suis un homme,"* and as such they could "live hard, lie hard, sleep hard, eat dogs." It was commonly remarked of them: *"les voyageurs n'avaient jamais vu de petits loups"* ("voyageurs never see little wolves").

Winter finally passed. All the labors of the season were to be seen finally in the packs of furs and kegs of grease, castoreum, and sugar that lay waiting for news to come that the streams and lakes were free of ice. The first duck or goose was sighted and the news sent hither and yon. Most of the squaws moved to their sugar bushes for their sugar-making. A few, accompanied by voyageurs, went to the woods to "raise" birch bark for canoe-mending or to gather gum. The canoes were brought out, mended, and gummed, and all was made ready for departure. On a bright May morning the canoes were packed and manned, a few men were left in charge of the fort, and the others paddled blithely off, singing in anticipation of the balls, wines, and *camaraderie* of Grand Portage.

VI

FAINTLY as tolls the evening chime
Our voices keep tune and our oars keep time.
Soon as the woods on shore look dim,
We'll sing at St. Ann's our parting hymn,
Row, brothers, row, the stream runs fast,
The rapids are near and the daylight's past.

Why should we yet our sail unfurl?
There is not a breath the blue wave to curl,
But, when the wind blows off the shore,
Oh, sweetly we'll rest our weary oar.
Blow, breezes, blow, the stream runs fast,
The rapids are near and the daylight's past.

Utawas' tide! this trembling moon
Shall see us float over thy surges soon.
Saint of this green isle! hear our prayers,
Oh, grant us cool heavens and favoring airs.
Blow, breezes, blow, the stream runs fast,
The rapids are near and the daylight's past.

THOMAS MOORE

Moore tells us in a letter appended to this poem, written in 1804, that it was adapted to the music of a song
his voyageurs sang to him on a trip that he made from
Kingston to Montreal. "The original words of the air,"
he writes, "to which I adapted these stanzas, begin:

> 'Dans mon chemin j'ai rencontré
> Deux cavaliers très bien montés.'"

103

Moore was not the first—nor the last—to enshrine in verse the appeal of the voyageurs' songs, but probably this poem has done more than any other bit of writing to preserve the memory of an almost forgotten class of men. Scores of writers have recorded the impressions made on them by the haunting melody of these folk songs, but unfortunately only a few took pains to record either the words or the airs. Consequently, a century later, we are obliged in the main to hear the voyageurs of our imaginations singing the folk songs that were current among *all* Canadians. Probably it is true that sooner or later the rocks of the Ottawa and the pines of the *pays d'en haut* heard most of the airs that the *habitants* of the little hamlets on the lower St. Lawrence were accustomed to sing; nevertheless, we should like to know the favorites —the songs that had special appeal to this special group of Canadians.

Some clues are given now and again, though usually in a garbled French which defies analysis. It is certain that *"A la claire fontaine"* was the general favorite. It was sung from coast to coast, not only in canoes, but wherever the voyageur was found. Kennicott, for example, tells of singing it in the snowbound Northwest; atop his *traîneau à lisse* (dog train), he gave a yell, which, he says, "started my dogs off on a gallop, and [I] rode down the mountain singing *La Claire Fontaine* and other voyaging songs, to encourage my dogs, for dogs, and horses, seem to like singing." [1] Just why this song should have been the universal favorite of voyageurs is hard to say. Certainly the subject matter bore no relation to any phase of their existence, and the rhythm and lilt are not so

pronounced and catchy as those of many other *chansons*.
The music and words are as follows:

A LA CLAIRE FONTAINE

A la clai-re fon-tai-ne M'en al-lant pro-me-ner,

J'ai trou-vé l'eau si bel-le Que je m'y suis bai-gné.

Lui ya long-temps que je t'aime, Jamais je ne t'oublierai.

A la claire fontaine
M'en allant promener,
J'ai trouvé l'eau si belle
Que je m'y suis baigné.
  Lui ya longtemps que je t'aime,
  Jamais je ne t'oublierai.

J'ai trouvé l'eau si belle
Que je m'y suis baigné;
Sous les feuilles d'un chêne
Je me suis fait sécher.
  Lui ya longtemps, etc.

Sous les feuilles d'un chêne
Je me suis fait sécher;
Sur la plus haute branche
Le rossignol chantait.
  Lui ya longtemps, etc.

Sur la plus haute branche
Le rossignol chantait.
Chante, rossignol, chante,
Toi qui as le cœur gai.
  Lui ya longtemps, etc.

THE VOYAGEUR

Chante, rossignol, chante,
Toi qui a le cœur gai;
Tu as le cœur à rire,
Moi je l'ai-t-à-pleurer.
    Lui ya longtemps, etc.

Tu as le cœur à rire,
Moi je l'ai-t-à-pleurer:
J'ai perdu ma maîtresse
Sans l'avoir mérité.
    Lui ya longtemps, etc.

J'ai perdu ma maîtresse
Sans l'avoir mérité,
Pour un bouquet de roses
Que je lui refusai.
    Lui ya longtemps, etc.

Pour un bouquet de roses
Que je lui refusai.
Je voudrais que la rose
Fût encore au rosier.
    Lui ya longtemps, etc.

Je voudrais que la rose
Fût encore au rosier,
Et moi et ma maîtresse
Dans les mêm's amitiés.
    Lui ya longtemps que je t'aime,
    Jamais je ne t'oublierai.

TRANSLATION *

AT THE CLEAR RUNNING FOUNTAIN

At the clear running fountain
    Sauntering by one day,
I found it so compelling
    I bathed without delay.
        Your love long since overcame me,
        Ever in my heart you'll stay.

VOYAGEUR SONGS

I found it so compelling
I bathed without delay;
Under an oak tree's umbrage
I dried the damp away.
    Your love, *etc.*

Under an oak tree's umbrage
I dried the damp away.
There where the highest branch is,
    Sir Nightingale sang hey!
    Your love, *etc.*

There where the highest branch is,
    Sir Nightingale sang hey!
Sing, Nightingale, keep singing,
    You sing with heart so gay.
    Your love, *etc.*

Sing, Nightingale, keep singing,
    You sing with heart so gay.
You have the heart a-ringing;
    My heart—ah! lack-a-day!
    Your love, *etc.*

You have the heart a-ringing;
    My heart—ah! lack-a-day!
I lost my lovely lady
In such a blameless way.
    Your love, *etc.*

I lost my lovely lady
In such a blameless way.
For one bouquet of roses
    Which I must say her nay.
    Your love, *etc.*

For one bouquet of roses
    Which I must say her nay—
I wish that now the roses
    Bloomed on their tree today.
    Your love, *etc.*

I wish that now the roses
    Bloomed on their tree today,
And I and she, the lady,
    Were friends the same old way!
    Your love long since overcame me,
    Ever in my heart you'll stay.

* From *Canadian Folk Songs: Old and New,* by J. Murray Gibbon, by permission of the publishers, J. M. Dent & Sons, Ltd., London, Toronto and Vancouver, and E. P. Dutton & Company, New York.

In another version the final wish of the singer is,

> *Et que le rosier même*
> *Fût à la mer jeté.*

"and that the tree itself were thrown into the sea."

Another *chanson* commonly sung by the voyageurs was that to which Moore refers. There were many variations of it. In his letter Moore mentions the refrain, which differs considerably from the commonly accepted form in *"J'ai trop grand' peur des loups."* James Lanman in an article on the fur trade published in *Hunt's Merchants' Magazine* gives still a third rendering.[2] The music and the French form as given by Ernest Gagnon follows:[3]

J'AI TROP GRAND' PEUR DES LOUPS

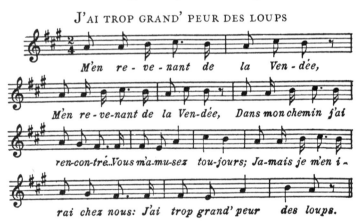

M'en re-ve-nant de la Ven-dée,

M'en re-ve-nant de la Ven-dée, Dans mon chemin j'ai

ren-con-tré..Vous m'a-mu-sez tou-jours; Ja-mais je m'en i-

rai chez nous: J'ai trop grand' peur des loups.

> *M'en revenant de la Vendée,* (bis)
> *Dans mon chemin j'ai rencontré. . . .*
> *Vous m'amusez toujours;*
> *Jamais je m'en irai chez nous:*
> *J'ai trop grand' peur des loups.*

> *Dans mon chemin j'ai rencontré* (bis)
> *Trois cavaliers fort bien montés.*
> *Vous m'amusez, etc.*

Trois cavaliers fort bien montés, (bis)
Deux à cheval et l'autre à pied.
   Vous m'amusez, etc.

Deux à cheval et l'autre à pied; (bis)
Celui d'à pied m'a demandé. . . .
   Vous m'amusez, etc.

Celui d'à pied m'a demandé: (bis)
—Où irons-nous ce soir coucher?
   Vous m'amusez, etc.

Où irons-nous ce soir coucher? (bis)
—Chez nous, monsieur, si vous voulez.
   Vous m'amusez, etc.

—Chez nous, monsieur, si vous voulez; (bis)
Vous y trouv'rez un bon souper.
   Vous m'amusez, etc.

Vous y trouv'rez un bon souper, (bis)
Et de bons lits pour vous coucher.
   Vous m'amusez, etc.

Et de bons lits pour vous coucher, (bis)
Les cavaliers ont accepté.
   Vous m'amusez toujours:
Jamais je m'en irai chez nous:
   J'ai trop grand' peur des loups.

TRANSLATION *

They Have Me Scared, Those Wolves

On my return from la Vendée, (*repeat*)
Coming along met on my way. . . .
   You make me laugh, you do;
Never shall I bid home adieu:
   They have me scared, those wolves.

Coming along met on my way (*repeat*)
Three cavaliers in fine array.
   You make me laugh, *etc.*

Three cavaliers in fine array, (*repeat*)
One of them walked the footpath way.
   You make me laugh, *etc.*

One of them walked the footpath way; (*repeat*)
He that was walking made me say. . . .
   You make me laugh, *etc.*

He that was walking made me say: (*repeat*)
—Where shall we sleep tonight, I pray?
   You make me laugh, *etc.*

Where shall we sleep tonight, I pray? (*repeat*)
—If you so wish, with us you may.
   You make me laugh, *etc.*

—If you so wish, with us you may; (*repeat*)
Supper you'll like when done our way.
   You make me laugh, *etc.*

Supper you'll like when done our way, (*repeat*)
Cosy the beds for you we lay.
   You make me laugh, *etc.*

Cosy the beds for you we lay, (*repeat*)
And they accepted without delay.
   You make me laugh, you do;
   Never shall I bid home adieu:
   They have me scared, those wolves.

  * By permission of J. Murray Gibbon.

Lanman mentions also another boat song which he heard sung by the voyageurs. His version is not complete, and so the fuller form, as found in Mr. Marius Barbeau's collection of folk songs, is given here.[4]

Voici le printemps

Voi ci le-prin-temps, les amours se renou-vel-lent, Et tous les amants vont

charger de maîtresse. Le bon vin m'en-dort—, l'amour m'y réveil-le.

Voici le printemps, les amours se renouvellent,
Et tous les amants vont changer de maîtresse.
Le bon vin m'endort, l'amour m'y réveille.

Changera qui voudra, moi je garde la mienne.
Elle a les yeux doux, et la bouche vermeille.
Le bon vin, etc.

Ah! qu'il serait doux d'être aimé de la belle;
Encore bien plus doux d'avoir un baiser d'elle.
Le bon vin, etc.

Encore bien plus doux d'avoir un baiser d'elle,
Le long d'un ruisseau, d'une claire fontaine.
Le bon vin, etc.

TRANSLATION *

IN THE GAY SPRING TIME

See the Spring is here,
Our loves we are a-waking,
And lovers all now
New mistresses are taking.
  Good old wine makes me doze,
  But love keeps me a-waking.

And all lovers now
New mistresses are taking,
Let all those change who may,
I keep to my old mistress.
  Good old wine, *etc.*

Let all those change who may,
I keep to my old mistress,
So soft are her eyes
And so tender are her kisses.
  Good old wine, *etc.*

* By permission of Constance A. Hamilton.

Bela Hubbard, a fur-trader who was well acquainted with the voyageurs about Mackinac, Detroit, and Chicago in the thirties of last century, gives the words of two songs.[5] One of them is the well known *"Frit à l'huile,"* but with so many variations from the ordinary form that it may be well to give it as he wrote it down.

THE VOYAGEUR

FRIT À L'HUILE

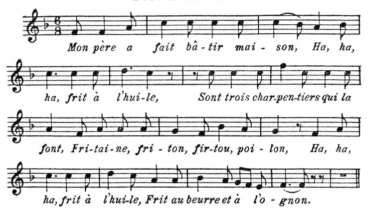

Mon père a fait bâtir maison, Ha, ha,
ha, frit à l'huile, Sont trois charpentiers qui la
font, Fri-tai-ne, fri-ton, fir-tou, poi-lon, Ha, ha,
ha, frit à l'hui-le, Frit au beurre et à l'o-gnon.

Mon père a fait bâtir maison,
Ha, ha, ha, frit à l'huile,
Sont trois charpentiers qui la font,
Fritaine, friton, firtou, poilon,
Ha, ha, ha, frit à l'huile,
Frit au beurre à l'ognon.

Sont trois charpentiers qui la font,
Ha, ha, ha, frit à l'huile.
Qu'apportes-tu dans ton giron?
Fritaine, etc.

Qu'apportes-tu dans ton giron?
Ha, ha, ha, frit à l'huile,
C'est un pâté de trois pigeons,
Fritaine, etc.

C'est un pâté de trois pigeons,
Ha, ha, ha, frit à l'huile,
Assieds-toi et le mangeons,
Fritaine, friton, firtou, poilon,
Ha, ha, ha, frit à l'huile,
Frit au beurre et à l'ognon.

The full song as given by Gagnon is much longer and tells how the youngest of the three carpenters who have built a house for the singer's father is her favorite, and how he and she sat down to eat the pigeon pie that she had in her skirt, he with such a bound that it frightened the fishes and made the sea and the rocks tremble.

The other song given by Hubbard is called *"La jeune Sophie."* His version differs somewhat from Mr. Barbeau's *"La belle Lisette,"* which was obtained from M. François Saint-Laurent, a folk-singer of Ste.-Anne des Monts. Hubbard and his printer failed to coöperate in the matter of French spelling and diction, and so the more correct version is given here.[6]

La belle Lisette

La bel - le Li-set-te Chan-tait l'au-tre jour. La Chan-tait l'au-tre jour. Les é - chos ré-pè-tent:"Qui n'a pas d'a - mour, Qui n'a pas d'a-mour N'a pas de beaux jours. Qui..?"

> La belle Lisette
> Chantait l'autre jour. } (bis)
> La belle Lisette
> Chantait l'autre jour.
> Les échos répétent:
> "Qui n'a pas d'amour,
> Qui n'a pas d'amour
> N'a pas de beaux jours." } (bis)

113

Son berger l'appelle, } (bis)
Le berger Colin.
Le berger Colin.
Veillent à la chandelle,
La main dans la main } (bis)
Du soir au matin.

"Si gente, si belle,} (bis)
Dedans tes atours,
O ma tourterelle!
Répétons toujours,
Répétons toujours } (bis)
Nos serments d'amour.

"Unissons ensemble } (bis)
Ton cœur et le mien!
Ton cœur et le mien."
"Ne puis m'en défendre,
O berger charmant,
O berger charmant, } (bis)
A toi je me vends!"

Pretty Lisette (or Betty) was singing recently, according to this song. The echo sang back, "Who has no lover knows naught of happiness." Her shepherd, Colin, calls her. Hand in hand they watch the night out. "So sweet, so beautiful in your fine clothes, O my turtle dove! Let us renew our pledges of love. Let us join your heart and mine." "I can not resist, O charming shepherd. To you I give myself."

Dr. John J. Bigsby, who accompanied the British commissioners on their trip through the boundary waters in the early twenties, secured from one of his voyageurs the following variation of the old slumber song of Cambrésis, *"Une perdriole."* [7] It is substantially like Gagnon's ver-

114

sion, and, as in his, each day adds a new gift to the previous donations of the lover. This fact accounts for the addition of a bar to the music of each succeeding stanza and for the change in the second word in each stanza, successive ordinal numbers being used to represent the days of May as they come. Gagnon's music for the first stanza is as follows; the words are Bigsby's:

UNE PERDRIOLE

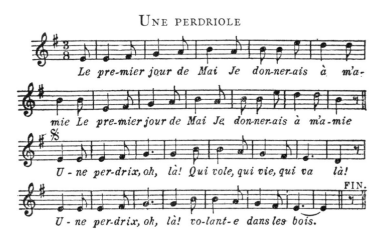

Le pre-mier jour de Mai Je don-ner-ais à m'a-mie Le pre-mier jour de Mai Je don-ner-ais à m'a-mie U - ne per-drix, oh, là! Qui vole, qui vie, qui va là! U - ne per-drix, oh, là! vo-lant-e dans les bois.

TRANSLATION *

THE OP'NING DAY OF MAY

The op'ning day of May,
What shall I give my dear one?
One, a little partridge, who comes, who goes a-flying,
One a little partridge a-flying in the wood.

* By permission of J. Murray Gibbon.

Only three days are accounted for in Bigsby's version:

Le premier jour de Mai
Je donnerais à m'amie
Une perdrix, oh, là! qui vole, qui vie, qui va là!
Une perdrix, oh, là! volante dans les bois.

115

Le deuxième jour de Mai
Je donnerais à m'amie
Deux tourterelles, une perdrix, oh, là! qui vole, qui
    vie, qui va là!
Une perdrix, etc.

Le troisième jour de Mai
Je donnerais à m'amie
Trois rats de bois, deux tourterelles, une perdrix, etc.

Gagnon, however, gives the accumulation of gifts on the tenth,[8] remarking that nothing is to prevent the singer from improvising after the tenth day, even as far as the thirty-first of May. If then the child is not asleep, it is useless to think of paregoric or laudanum, for nothing will close his eyes.

Dix veaux bien gras,
Neuf chevaux avec leurs selles,
Huit moutons avec leur laine,
Sept vach's à lait,
Six chiens courant,
Cinq lapins grattant la terre,
Quatr' canards volant en l'aire,
Trois rats des bois,
Deux tourterelles,
Une perdriole, etc.

Ten fatted calves,
Nine apparelled saddle horses,
Eight fat sheep with woolly fleeces,
Seven milking cows,
Six running dogs,
Five young hares that scrape the earth up,
Four wild ducks a-wing in air,
Three woodland rats,
Two turtle dove birds,
One a little partridge, *etc.*

The music for the second and third donations is the same:

The gifts for the fourth and fifth days are also sung to similar notes:

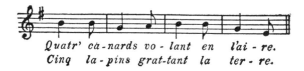

The notes of the sixth and seventh couplets are likewise similar:

The notes of the ninth are a repetition of those of the eighth:

The music of the tenth day goes back in form to that of the second. Each new bar of music is inserted after the repetition of the opening clause, so that the gift for the new day is always given first in the series of donations.

117

McKenney recounts how "the bowsman pushed the canoe into the current, and a chaunt was struck up, called the 'White Rose.' " [9] Many other travelers make mention of it, among them Robert Ballantyne in his *Hudson's Bay*, published at the middle of the century, which tells of six years spent in the North during the forties. He characterizes it as "the lively air of 'Rose Blanche,' sung by the men as we swept round point after point and curve after curve of the noble river." [10] Garry in 1821 took down the words, which differ slightly from Mr. Gibbon's version given here. Gibbon's, in turn, differs from Gagnon's version.[11]

J'AI CUEILLI LA BELLE ROSE

J'ai cueil-li la bel-le ro - se, J'ai cueil-li la bel-le ro - se, Qui pen-dait au ro-sier blanc, La bel-le ro - se, Qui pen-dait au ro-sier blanc, La bel-le ros' du ro-sier blanc.

> J'ai cueilli la belle rose,
> J'ai cueilli la belle rose
> Qui pendait au rosier blanc,
>   La belle rose,
> Qui pendait au rosier blanc,
>   La belle ros' du rosier blanc.

Je l'ai cueilli' feuille à feuille (bis)
Mis dans mon tablier blanc,
  La belle rose,
Mis dans mon tablier blanc
  La belle ros' du rosier blanc.

Je l'ai porté' chez mon père, (bis)
Entre Paris et Rouen,
  La belle rose,
Entre Paris et Rouen,
  La belle ros' du rosier blanc.

Mr. Gibbon has used "*Qui pendait au rosier blanc*" as the fifth line in every stanza after the third. Gagnon, however, continues the scheme of the first three stanzas, that is, the fifth line a repetition of the third in every stanza.

Je n'ai pas trouvé personne (bis)
Que le rossignol chantant,
  La belle rose,
Qui pendait au rosier blanc,
  La belle ros' du rosier blanc.

Qui me dit dans son langage: (bis)
Mari'-toi, car il est temps,
  La belle rose,
Qui pendait, etc.

Comment veux-tu que j'm'y marie? (bis)
Mon père en est pas content.
  La belle rose,
Qui pendait, etc.

Ni mon père ni ma mère, (bis)
Ni aucun de mes parents.
  La belle rose,
Qui pendait, etc.

119

THE VOYAGEUR

Je m'en irai en service, (bis)
En service pour un an.
  La belle rose,
Qui pendait, etc.

Combien gagnez-vous, la belle, (bis)
Combien gagnez-vous par an?
  La belle rose,
Qui pendait, etc.

Je gagne bien cinq cents livres, (bis)
Cinq cents livr's en argent blanc.
  La belle rose,
Qui pendait, etc.

Venez avec nous, la belle, (bis)
Nous vous en donn'rons six cents.
  La belle rose,
Qui pendait au rosier blanc,
  La belle ros' du rosier blanc.

TRANSLATION *

I Have Culled That Lovely Rosebud

I have cull'd that lovely rosebud,
I have culled that lovely rosebud
  Hanging on the white rose-plant,
    That lovely rosebud,
  Hanging on the white rose-plant,
  That lovely rose from white rose-plant.

I have cull'd petal by petal, (*repeat*)
Fill'd my apron with its scent,
    That lovely rosebud,
  Fill'd my apron with its scent,
  That lovely rose from white rose-plant.

I have brought it home to father, (*repeat*)
From Rouen to Paris went.
    That lovely rosebud,
  From Rouen to Paris went,
  That lovely rose from white rose-plant.

I found none—no, not a person (*repeat*)
Save the thrush who sung his chant.
    That lovely rosebud,
   Hanging on the white rose-plant,
    That lovely rose from white rose-plant.

Who informed me in his own tongue: (*repeat*)
"Marry now, ere time prevent."
    That lovely rosebud,
    Hanging, *etc.*

"Why your will that I should marry? (*repeat*)
Father would not be content."
    That lovely rosebud,
    Hanging, *etc.*

"Neither father nor my mother, (*repeat*)
Nor my kin would give consent."
    That lovely rosebud,
    Hanging, *etc.*

"I will now go into service, (*repeat*)
Service till a year is spent."
    That lovely rosebud,
    Hanging, *etc.*

"What the wage you gain, fair lady? (*repeat*)
What the wage per year you want?"
    That lovely rosebud,
    Hanging, *etc.*

"I gain quite five hundred shillings, (*repeat*)
Shillings silver-white I meant."
    That lovely rosebud,
    Hanging, *etc.*

"Come with us, and we, fair lady, (*repeat*)
Will six hundred then present."
    That lovely rosebud,
   Hanging on the white rose-plant,
    That lovely rose from white rose-plant.

* From *Canadian Folk Songs: Old and New,* by J. Murray Gibbon, by permission of the publishers, J. M. Dent & Sons, Ltd., London, Toronto and Vancouver, and E. P. Dutton & Company, New York.

Garry's version lacks the final stanza which makes the interrogator offer the girl a hundred shillings more than she will earn by going into service as she threatens to do.[12] Presumably she accepts.

Garry gives the words of two other songs and mentions many. Thus, he writes in his diary on September 6, 1821: "In the Morning the Voyageur sings 'Bon Jour, Jolie Bergère,' &c. 'Brave Capitaine,' 'Vin blanc,' 'Champagne,' &c., at Dinner. 'A terre, à terre' in the Evening at the Encampment." The words for one of the three songs given in full below are but slightly different from Gagnon's version.[13]

QUAND J'ÉTAIS CHEZ MON PÈRE

Quand j'é-tais chez mon pè-re, Quand j'é-tais chez mon pè-re, Pe-tite Je-anne — ton don-dai-ne, don. Pe-tite Je-anne — ton don-dai-ne.

Quand j'étais chez mon père, (bis)
  Petite Jeanneton,
    Dondaine, don,
  Petite Jeanneton,
    Dondaine.

M'envoi' t-à la fontaine, (bis)
  Pour pêcher du poisson,
    Dondaine, don, etc.

122

La fontaine est profonde, (bis)
J'me suis coulée au fond,
Dondaine, don, etc.

Par ici-t-il y passe (bis)
Trois cavaliers barons,
Dondaine, don, etc.

—Que donneriez-vous, belle, (bis)
Qui vous tir'rait du fond?
Dondaine, don, etc.

—Tirez, tirez, dit-elle, (bis)
Après ça, nous verrons . . .
Dondaine, don, etc.

Quand la bell' fut tirée, (bis)
S'en fut à la maison,
Dondaine, don, etc.

S'assit sur la fenêtre, (bis)
Compose une chanson,
Dondaine, don, etc.

—Ce n'est pas ça la belle, (bis)
Que nous vous demandons,
Dondaine, don, etc.

C'est votre cœur en gage, (bis)
Savoir si nous l'aurons,
Dondaine, don, etc.

—Mon petit cœur en gage, (bis)
N'est pas pour un baron,
Dondaine, don, etc.

Ma mère me le garde, (bis)
Pour mon joli mignon,
Dondaine, don,
Pour mon joli mignon,
Dondaine.

THE VOYAGEUR

WHEN I WAS HOME WITH MY FATHER

When I was home with my father, (*repeat*)
Little wee Jeanneton,
  Ding a ding dong,
Little wee Jeanneton,
  Dong dain-a.

Off to the spring he sent me, (*repeat*)
So am a-fishing gone,
  Ding a ding dong, *etc.*

Deep in the spring a-sunken, (*repeat*)
Tumbled the whole way down,
  Ding a ding dong, *etc.*

There by the way came passing (*repeat*)
Three knights of proud renown,
  Ding a ding dong, *etc.*

"What would you give him, fair one, (*repeat*)
Who pulls you out anon?"
  Ding a ding dong, *etc.*

"Pull out, pull out," her answer, (*repeat*)
"We'll see when all is done."
  Ding a ding dong, *etc.*

When the girl out was lifted, (*repeat*)
Straight to the house was gone,
  Ding a ding dong, *etc.*

Sat down beside the window, (*repeat*)
There she composed a song,
  Ding a ding dong, *etc.*

"It is not that, my fair one, (*repeat*)
Which we from you would dun,"
  Ding a ding dong, *etc.*

"It is your heart in guerdon, (*repeat*)
Say, shall we have our own?"
  Ding a ding dong, *etc.*

"My little heart in guerdon (*repeat*)
Is for no baron grown."
Ding a ding dong, *etc.*

"My mother keeps it for me, (*repeat*)
Sweetheart shall win alone."
   Ding a ding dong,
"Sweetheart shall win alone."
   Dong dain-a.

* By permission of J. Murray Gibbon.

Probably Garry's "Bonjour, jolie bergère" was "*La bergère muette*." The salutation comes in the second stanza.[14]

LA BERGÈRE MUETTE

Ecoutez la complainte,
  Petits et grands,
D'une bergère muette
  Qui, dans ses champs,
Gardait ses brebi-ettes,
  Le long d'un pré.
Jésus, par sa bonté,
  L'a fait parler.

125

Un jour, la sainte Vierge } (bis)
   Lui apparut.
"Bonjour, joli'bergère,
   Grande Isabeau.
Voudrais-tu me donner
   Un des agneaux?"

—"Ah non, certes!" dit-elle, } (bis)
   "Sont pas à moi.
A mon père, à ma mère
   J'en parlerai.
A mon père, à ma mère
   Je leur dirai."

Ell' s'en est retournée } (bis)
   Bien promptement.
"Mon père, y-at une dame
   Dans mon troupeau.
Grand Dieu! ell' me demande
   Un des agneaux."

Son père, aussi sa mère, } (bis)
   Fur' bien surpris
D'entendre la muette
   Parler ainsi.
A Dieu firent prière
   Qu'il ait merci.

"Va lui dire, ô bergère, } (bis)
   Dans ton troupeau,
Qu'ils sont à son service,
   Grands et petits,
Que tous sont pour lui plaire,
   Jusqu'aux plus beaux."

La bergère, elle est morte } (bis)
   Avant trois jours.
Ell' tenait une lettre
   Dedans sa main,
Ecrite du grand maître,
   Dieu souverain.

Son père, aussi sa mère, } (bis)
 N'ont jamais lu.
A fallu que l'arch'vêque
 Y soit venu
Parler à la muette,
 Grande Isabeau.

"Ouvre ta main, bergère, } (bis)
 Ouvre ta main,
De la part du grand maître,
 Dieu souverain!"
A bien lu la lettre,
 A bien compris.

Qu'en chante la complainte } (bis)
 Le vendredi
Gagne les indulgences, } (bis)
 Le paradis.

TRANSLATION *

THE DUMB SHEPHERDESS

Hark ye to the complaint,
 Grown and little,
Of a dumb shepherdess,
 Who in her fields
Did guard her little sheep
 Along the mead!
'Twas Jesus, out of goodness,
 Made her speak.

One day the holy Maid } (repeat)
 To her appeared.
"Good day, sweet shepherdess,
 Big Isabeau!
And would you give to me
 One of the lambs?"

"Ah, no indeed," she said, } (repeat)
 "They are not mine.
To father, to my mother,
 I'll speak of it;
To father, to my mother,
 I'll tell of it."

127

She came back to her home ⎱ *(repeat)*
   Straightaway. ⎰
"My father, there's a lady
   In my flock.
O God! she asks of me
   One of the lambs."

Her father, mother too, ⎱ *(repeat)*
   They were amazed ⎰
To hear the speechless maiden
   Speaking thus;
To God they made a prayer
   For his mercy.

"Go tell her, shepherdess, ⎱ *(repeat)*
   In thy flock, ⎰
That they are at her pleasure,
   Big and little,
That all are for her pleasing,
   Even the best."

The shepherdess was dead ⎱ *(repeat)*
   Before three days. ⎰
A letter she was holding
   In her hand,
Writ by the sovereign master,
   Mighty God.

Her father, mother too, ⎱ *(repeat)*
   They could not read. ⎰
It had to be the bishop
   Came to them
To speak to the dumb maid,
   Big Isabeau.

"Open, shepherdess, ⎱ *(repeat)*
   Open thy hand, ⎰
For the sake of the sovereign master,
   Mighty God!"
And well he read the letter
   And understood:

"Whoever sings on Friday ⎱ *(repeat)*
   This complaint, ⎰
Is freed of sinful taint, ⎱ *(repeat)*
   Gains Paradise." ⎰

* From *Folk Songs of French Canada*, by Marius Barbeau and Edward Sapir, by permission of the publishers, Yale University Press.

Another of the songs that Garry quotes from his voyageurs is a variation of the well-known "A-Rolling My Ball." Garry's men sang *"Ye, ye ment"* in place of *"En roulant ma boule"* in the second line of every stanza, *"Tous du long de la Rivière"* in the fourth line, and *"Légèrement ma Bergère Légèrement, ye ment"* in place of the last two lines.[15]

EN ROULANT MA BOULE

En roulant ma boule roulant,
    En roulant ma boule.
En roulant me boule roulant,
    En roulant ma boule.

Derrièr' chez nous, ya-t-un étang,
    En roulant ma boule.
Derrièr' chez nous, y'-t-un étang,
    En roulant ma boule.
Trois beaux canards s'en vont baignant,
Rouli, roulant, ma boule roulant,
En roulant ma boule roulant,
    En roulant ma boule.

Trois beaux canards s'en vont baignant, } (bis)
   En roulant ma boule.
Le fils du roi s'en va chassant,
Rouli, etc.

Le fils du roi s'en va chassant, } (bis)
   En roulant ma boule.
Avec son grand fusil d'argent,
Rouli, etc.

Avec son grand fusil d'argent, } (bis)
   En roulant ma boule.
Visa le noir, tua le blanc,
Rouli, etc.

Visa le noir, tua le blanc, } (bis)
   En roulant ma boule.
O fils du roi, tu es méchant!
Rouli, etc.

O fils du roi, tu es méchant! } (bis)
   En roulant ma boule.
D'avoir tué mon canard blanc,
Rouli, etc.

D'avoir tué mon canard blanc, } (bis)
   En roulant ma boule.
Par dessous l'aile il perd son sang,
Rouli, etc.

Par dessous l'aile il perd son sang, } (bis)
   En roulant ma boule.
Par les yeux lui sort'nt des diamants,
Rouli, etc.

Par les yeux lui sort'nt des diamants, } (bis)
   En roulant ma boule,
Et par le bec l'or et l'argent,
Rouli, etc.

Et par le bec l'or et l'argent, } (bis)
   En roulant ma boule.
Toutes ses plum's s'en vont au vent,
Rouli, etc.

Toutes ses plum's s'en vont au vent, } (bis)
   En roulant ma boule.
Trois dam's s'en vont les ramassant,
Rouli, etc.

Trois dam's s'en vont les ramassant, } (bis)
   En roulant ma boule.
C'est pour en faire un lit de camp,
Rouli, etc.

C'est pour en faire un lit de camp, } (bis)
   En roulant ma boule.
Pour y coucher tous les passants.
Rouli, roulant, ma boule roulant,
   En roulant ma boule roulant,
   En roulant ma boule.

TRANSLATION *

A-ROLLING MY BALL

On, roll on, my ball I roll on,
  On, roll on my ball, on!
  On, roll on, my ball I roll on,
  On, roll on my ball, on!

'Way back at home there is a pond,
  On, roll on my ball, on!
'Way back at home there is a pond,
  On, roll on my ball, on!
Three bonnie ducks go swimming 'round,
  Roll on, my ball, my ball I roll on.
    On, roll on, my ball I roll on,
    On, roll on my ball, on!

Three bonnie ducks go swimming 'round, } *(repeat)*
On, roll on my ball, on!
The prince goes off a-hunting bound,
  Roll on, *etc.*

131

THE VOYAGEUR

The prince goes off a-hunting bound, } *(repeat)*
On, roll on my ball, on!
His gun so big with silver crown'd,
   Roll on, *etc.*

His gun so big with silver crown'd, } *(repeat)*
On, roll on my ball, on!
The black he saw, the white he down'd
   Roll on, *etc.*

The black he saw, the white he down'd, } *(repeat)*
On, roll on my ball, on!
O prince, that was a wicked wound!
   Roll on, *etc.*

O prince, that was a wicked wound, } *(repeat)*
On, roll on my ball, on!
To kill the white duck that I own'd,
   Roll on, *etc.*

To kill the white duck that I own'd, } *(repeat)*
On, roll on my ball, on!
Each eye becomes a diamond,
   Roll on, *etc.*

Each eye becomes a diamond, } *(repeat)*
On, roll on my ball, on!
Silver and gold her beak surround,
   Roll on, *etc.*

Silver and gold her beak surround, } *(repeat)*
On, roll on my ball, on!
Beneath her wings a bloody wound,
   Roll on, *etc.*

Beneath her wings a bloody wound, } *(repeat)*
On, roll on my ball, on!
The feathers in the wind fly 'round,
   Roll on, *etc.*

The feathers in the wind fly 'round, } *(repeat)*
On, roll on my ball, on!
Three dames to pick them up are bound,
   Roll on, *etc.*

Three dames to pick them up are bound, } *(repeat)*
On, roll on my ball, on!
They make a camp bed on the ground,
   Roll on, *etc.*

They make a camp bed on the ground, } *(repeat)*
On, roll on my ball, on!
That passers-by may slumber sound,
  Roll on, my ball, my ball I roll on,
  On, roll on, my ball I roll on,
  On, roll on my ball, on!

* From *Canadian Folk Songs: Old and New,* by J. Murray Gibbon,
by permission of the publishers, J. M. Dent & Sons, Ltd., London, Toronto
and Vancouver, and E. P. Dutton & Company, New York.

One suspects that Garry had in mind one song only
when he wrote, "The Voyageur sings. . . . 'Brave
Capitaine,' 'Vin blanc,' 'Champagne,' &c., at Dinner,"
though he wrote it as though there were three. The text
of the following song includes most of the words he
quotes: [16]

NOUS ÉTIONS TROIS CAPITAINES

Les reprises en chœur.

Nous e - tions trois ca-pi - tai - nes,

Nous é - tions trois ca-pi - tai - nes De la

guer-re re-ve - nant, Bra-ve, bra - ve, De la

guer-re re - ve - nant Bra-ve - ment.

Nous étions trois capitaines (bis)
De la guerre revenant,
  Brave, brave,
De la guerre revenant
  Bravement.

THE VOYAGEUR

Nous entrâm's dans une auberge: (bis)
—Hôtesse, as-tu du vin blanc?
Brave, brave,
Hôtesse, as-tu du vin blanc?
Bravement.

Oui, vraiment, nous dit l'hôtesse; (bis)
J'en ai du rouge et du blanc,
Brave, brave,
J'en ai du rouge et du blanc,
Bravement.

Hôtess', tire-nous chopine, (bis)
Chopinette de vin blanc,
Brave, brave,
Chopinette de vin blanc,
Bravement.

Quand le chopine fut bue, (bis)
Nous tirâm's trois écus blancs,
Brave, brave,
Nous tirâm's trois écus blancs,
Bravement.

—Grand merci! nous dit l'hôtesse, (bis)
Revenez-y donc souvent,
Brave, brave,
Revenez-y donc souvent,
Bravement.

TRANSLATION *

WE WERE THREE YOUNG TROOP COMMANDERS

We were three young troop commanders (*repeat*)
From the war returning home,
  Bravely, bravely, [*or* brawly]
From the war returning home,
  Bravely done.

In we went into a tavern: (*repeat*)
"White wine, hostess! have you some?"
  Bravely, bravely,
"White wine, hostess! have you some?"
  Bravely done.

"Yes, indeed," the hostess told us; (*repeat*)
"Both of red and white have some,"
  Bravely, bravely,
"Both of red and white have some,"
  Bravely done.

"Hostess, draw us now a flagon, (*repeat*)
With a flask of white wine come,"
  Bravely, bravely,
"With a flask of white wine come,"
  Bravely done.

When the flagons all were emptied, (*repeat*)
With three florins paid the sum,
  Bravely, bravely,
With three florins paid the sum,
  Bravely done.

"Many thanks," remarked the hostess, (*repeat*)
"Come again and often come,"
  Bravely, bravely,
"Come again and often come,"
  Bravely done.

* By permission of J. Murray Gibbon.

One of the most observant of the many travelers in the interior was Mrs. Jameson. Her favorite among the many songs that her voyageurs sang on discovering her fondness for their *chansons à l'aviron* was one which is still sung by tiny maidens spinning their tops along the steep, narrow sidewalks of Quebec. "After dinner," she writes, "the men dashed off with great animation, singing my favourite ditty,

'*Si mon moine voulait danser,*
Un beau cheval lui donnerai!' " [17]

It has a jolly tune, and our translator has been successful in rendering the pun on the word *moine*, which ordinarily means "monk" but which has an added meaning of "top" in Canada. A slightly different version of these two lines is ordinarily given in anthologies of French-Canadian songs. The following is probably the standard version: [18]

AH! SI MON MOINE VOULAIT DANSER

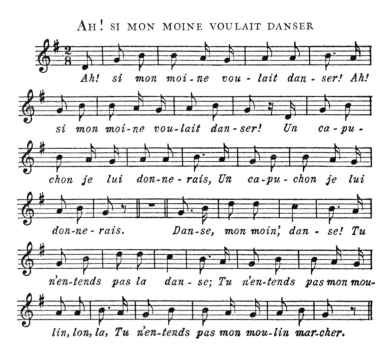

Ah! si mon moine voulait danser!
Ah! si mon moine voulait danser!
Un capuchon je lui donnerais,
Un capuchon je lui donnerais.

136

Danse, mon moin', danse!
Tu n'entends pas la danse,
Tu n'entends pas mon moulin, lon, la,
Tu n'entends pas mon moulin marcher.

Ah! si mon moine voulait danser! (bis)
Un ceinturon je lui donnerais. (bis)
    Danse, etc.

Ah! si mon moine voulait danser! (bis)
Un chapelet je lui donnerais. (bis)
    Danse, etc.

Ah! si mon moine voulait danser! (bis)
Un froc de bur' je lui donnerais. (bis)
    Danse, etc.

Ah! si mon moine voulait danser! (bis)
Un beau psautier je lui donnerais. (bis)
    Danse, etc.

S'il n'avait fait vœu de pauvreté! (bis)
Bien d'autres chos' je lui donnerais. (bis)
    Danse, mon moin', danse!
    Tu n'entends pas la danse,
Tu n'entends pas mon moulin, lon, la,
Tu n'entends pas mon moulin marcher.

TRANSLATION *

If My Old Top Were a Dancing Man

If my old top were a dancing man!
If my old top were a dancing man!
A cowl to fit I would give him then,
A cowl to fit I would give him then.
    Dance, old top, then, dance in!
    Oh! you don't care for dancing,
    Oh! you don't care for my mill, la, la!
    Oh! you don't care how my mill runs on.

137

If my old top were a dancing man! (*repeat*)
A sash to fit I would give him then. (*repeat*)
Dance, *etc.*

If my old top were a dancing man! (*repeat*)
A cap to fit I would give him then. (*repeat*)
Dance, *etc.*

If my old top were a dancing man! (*repeat*)
A gown of serge I would give him then. (*repeat*)
Dance, *etc.*

If my old top were a dancing man! (*repeat*)
A psalter fine I would give him then. (*repeat*)
Dance, *etc.*

Had he not vowed he would poor remain, (*repeat*)
A lot more things I would give him then. (*repeat*)
Dance, old top, then, dance in!
Oh! you don't care for dancing,
Oh! you don't care for my mill, la, la!
Oh! you don't care how my mill runs on.

* From *Canadian Folk Songs: Old and New,* by J. Murray Gibbon, by permission of the publishers, J. M. Dent & Sons, Ltd., London, Toronto and Vancouver, and E. P. Dutton & Company, New York.

Mrs. Jameson mentions other favorites: "This peculiar singing has often been described: it is very animated on the water and in the open air, but not very harmonious. They all sing in unison, raising their voices and marking the time with their paddles. One always led, but in these there was a diversity of taste and skill. If I wished to hear 'En roulant ma boule, roulette,' I applied to Le Duc. Jacques excelled in 'La belle rose blanche,' and Lewis was great in 'Trois canards s'en vont baignant.'" [19]

F. A. H. La Rue, who made a special study of these songs, declares that " 'La belle Françoise,' is the song *par excellence* of our boatmen." There are several versions, but the one that he describes is as follows.[20] Only six stanzas are sung as a rule.

LA BELLE FRANÇOISE

C'est la bel-le Fran-çoise, lon, gai, C'est la bel-le Fran-
çoi - se Qui veut s'y ma-ri-er, ma lu-ron, lu-ret - te,
Qui veut s'y ma-ri-er, ma lu - ron, lu - ré.

C'est la belle Françoise, lon, gai,
C'est la belle Françoise
Qui veut s'y marier, ma luron, lurette,
Qui veut s'y marier, ma luron, luré.

Son amant va la voire, lon, gai,
Son amant va la voire
Bien tard, après souper, ma luron, lurette,
Bien tard, après souper, ma luron, luré.

Il la trouva seulette, lon, gai,
Il la trouva seulette
Sur son lit, qui pleurait, ma luron, lurette.
Sur son lit, qui pleurait, ma luron, luré.

—Ah! qu' a' vous donc, la belle, lon, gai,
Ah! qu' a' vous donc, la belle,
Qu' a' vous à tant pleurer? ma luron, lurette,
Qu' a' vous à tant pleurer? ma luron, luré.

THE VOYAGEUR

—*On m'a dit, hier au soire, lon, gai,*
On m'a dit, hier au soire
Qu'à la guerr' vous alliez, ma luron, lurette
Qu'à la guerr' vous alliez, ma luron, luré.

—*Ceux qui vous l'ont dit, belle, lon gai,*
Ceux qui vous l'ont dit, belle,
Ont dit la vérité, ma luron, lurette,
Ont dit la vérité, ma luron, luré.

Venez m'y reconduire, lon, gai,
Venez m'y reconduire
Jusqu'au pied du rocher, ma luron, lurette,
Jusqu'au pied du rocher, ma luron, luré.

Adieu, belle Françoise, lon, gai,
Adieu, belle Françoise!
Je vous épouserai, ma luron, lurette,
Je vous épouserai, ma luron, luré.

Au retour de la guerre, lon, gai,
Au retour de la guerre,
Si j'y suis respecté, ma luron, lurette,
Si j'y suis respecté, ma luron, luré.

TRANSLATION *

BEHOLD THE FAIR FRANÇOISE

Behold the fair Françoise, ah! lon, gai,
Behold the fair Françoise, ah!
She would wed if she may, maluron, lurette,
She would wed if she may, maluron, luré.

Her love comes late a-calling, lon, gai,
Her love comes late a-calling.
Supper long cleared away, maluron, lurette,
Supper long cleared away, maluron, luré.

He found her all so lonely, lon, gai,
He found her all so lonely.
In bed weeping she lay, maluron, lurette,
In bed weeping she lay, maluron, luré.

"What ails you, then, my fair one, lon, gai?
What ails you, then, my fair one?
Why do you weep this way, maluron, lurette?
Why do you weep this way, maluron, luré."

"They told me yestereven, lon, gai,
They told me yestereven,
Off to the war you're away, maluron, lurette,
Off to the war you're away, maluron, luré."

"Who told you that, my fair one, lon, gai,
Who told you that, my fair one,
Told but truth as they say, maluron, lurette,
Told but truth as they say, maluron, luré."

* By permission of J. Murray Gibbon.

The full song carries on the conversation between the
lovers to the point where Frances' lover begs her to accompany him to the foot of the cliff, where he bids her adieu
and promises to marry her on his return from the war.

La Rue took down from the mouths of voyageurs
themselves seven songs which he characterized as the
ones most in vogue at the time he was writing. It is obvious that many of them are parodies of older songs.
Gagnon says of the first that it is "very remarkable" and
that he regrets he does not know the air.[21]

C'EST DANS LA VILLE DE BYTOWN

C'est dans la ville de Bytown
Mon capitain' je rencontrai;
Il a tiré son écritoire
Du papier pour m'engager.
Hélas! j'ai eu la promptitude,
Hélas! Je me suis engagé.

141

M'y promenant dedans la ville,
Ma maîtresse j'ai rencontrée.
Et qu'a'vous donc jolie maîtresse,
Et qu'a'vous donc tant à pleurer?
Et tout le monde dedans la ville
Dis'nt que vous êtes engagé.

Ceux qui vous ont dit ça, la belle,
Vous ont bien dit la vérité;
Mais nous irons dans l'écurie,
Nous trouverons chevaux sellés;
Mais les brides sont sur les selles,
Nos amours il faut nous quitter.

Quand vous serez dedans ces îles,
Mon cher amant, vous m'oublierez;
Mais si vous fait's un long voyage,
Pensez-vous bien de m'épouser?
En attendant de vos nouvelles,
Mon cher amant je languirai.

Pour t'épouser, charmante belle,
Tu ne m'en as jamais parlé;
Mais tu y as fait difficile,
Le plus souvent tu m'as r'fusé.
A présent j'en ai t'une autre
Qui y est bien plus à mon gré.

This dialogue between a voyageur and his mistress in the outpost of Bytown, the modern Ottawa, is all the more interesting because it reveals something of the life of the *engagés.* Thus the "captain" who induces the voyageur to engage early and who produces writing materials to make the engagement certain was no small factor in the life of the ordinary canoeman. Probably the little scene here described between the lady and her lover was enacted frequently when it came time for the men to leave. The girl weeps and begs to be remembered when her lover is *en route* and reminds him of his promise to marry her. Thereupon he reminds her that she has refused him so often that now he has another sweetheart more to his taste.

The next song that La Rue gives shows the class-consciousness of the voyageurs, as well as some of their customs.[22]

PARMI LES VOYAGEURS

Parmi les voyageurs, lui y a de bons enfants,
Et qui ne mangent guère, mais qui boivent souvent;
Et la pipe à la bouche, et le verre à la main,
Ils disent: camarades, versez-moi du vin.

Lorsque nous faisons rout', la charge sur le dos,
En disant: camarades, ah! grand Dieu, qu'il fait chaud!
Que la chaleur est grande! il faut nous rafraîchir;
A la fin du voyage, on prendra du plaisir.

Ah! bonjour donc, Nannon, ma charmante Lison,
C'est-i toi, qui porte des souliers si mignons:
Garnis de rubans blancs, par derrièr' par devant,
Ce sont des voyageurs, qui t'en ont fait présent.

As one may see from the following literal translation, the song is strongly reminiscent of *"La Ronde"* given in the chapter on "Voyaging":

Among the voyageurs, there are some fine fellows, who seldom eat but often drink. Pipe in mouth, glass in hand, we say, "Comrades, pour me some wine." When we are marching pack on back, saying, "Comrades, Heavens! but it is hot! The heat is terrible!" it will be necessary to

refresh ourselves. At the end of the voyage we shall have
our fun. Then it will be, Nannon, my charming Lison,
there you are in your neat little shoes, decked front and
back with white ribbons, given you by the voyageurs.

The third of La Rue's songs is probably more accurately a shantyboy's song than a voyageur's and is omitted
here. The fourth, given below, shows the joy of the voyageur on returning to his home, where his mother greets
him tenderly, happy to have him again to solace her in
her old age.[23] The word *François* (Francis) might be
substituted for the *Français* (French) of this version of
the song to give it a more personal meaning.

Salut à mon pays

Salut à mon pays, après un' longue absence,
De mes anciens amis. O douce souvenance!
Dans ce désert affreux, où malgré moi je nage,
L'aurore des cieux vient bénir mon courage.

Salut, Français, salut,
Après un long séjour
Le laurier sur mon front
T'annonce mon retour.

Sur ses genoux tremblants, je vois ma bonne mère
Sortir de sa chaumière, venir en chansonnant;
Et elle a reconnu l'objet de sa tendresse,
Mon fils est revenu pour calmer ma vieillesse.

There were Enoch Ardens among the voyageurs, too,
if the next song is good evidence. The music and accompanying stanza are from *"Le retour du mari soldat,"*
from Barbeau and Sapir, although La Rue's slightly dif-

ferent version given below, beginning "voilà les voyageurs qu' arrivent," can be sung to the same tune. The
characters in La Rue's version are voyageurs and a hostess, instead of the hostess and the soldier of Mr. Barbeau's version. The voyageurs announce that men of their
class drink without paying, whereas the soldier pawns his
old hat, his belt, and his cloak. Otherwise the stanzas are
very similar.[24]

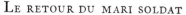

LE RETOUR DU MARI SOLDAT

Voilà les voyageurs qu'arrivent, (bis)
Bien mal chaussés, bien mal vêtus,
Pauvre soldat, d'où reviens-tu?

Madam', je reviens de la guerre (bis)
Madam', tirez-nous du vin blanc,
Les voyageurs boiv'nt sans argent.

Les voyageurs s' sont mi t'à table, (bis)
Ils s'sont mi t'à boire, à chanter,
Et l'hôtesses s'est mi t'à pleurer.

Ah! qu'avez-vous, jolie hôtesse? (bis)
Regrettez-vous votre vin blanc?
Les voyageurs boiv'nt sans argent.

145

THE VOYAGEUR

C' n'est pas mon vin que je regrette, (bis)
C'est la chanson que vous chantez,
Mon défunt mari la savait.

J'ai t'un mari dans le voyage, (bis)
Y a ben sept ans qu'il est parti,
Je crois que c'est lui qu'est ici.

Ah! taisez-vous, méchante femme, (bis)
Je n'vous ai laissé qu'un enfant,
En voilà quatr' dès à présent.

J'ai donc reçu de fausses lettres (bis)
Que vous étiez mort, enterré,
Aussi je me suis mariée.

TRANSLATION *

The Return of the Soldier Husband

One day the soldier comes to town, (*repeat*)
His clothes in rags, his shoes are worn:
"Whence is it, soldier, you return?"

He sought him room within a tavern: (*repeat*)
"Hostess, have you wine to drink?"
"And have you silver, man, to clink?"

"And as for silver, I've little enough. (*repeat*)
Take my old hat to pay for wine
And take this belt and cloak of mine."

And when he'd sat him down to table, (*repeat*)
Filling glass and singing strong,
She wept to hear him sing the song.

"Oh, what is wrong, my little hostess? (*repeat*)
Is it your wine that you regret,
The soldier drinking in your debt?"

" 'Tis not my wine that I regret; (*repeat*)
It is the lusty song that you
Are singing and my husband knew.

"I have a husband traveling; (*repeat*)
He's been for seven years from me.
I well believe that you are he."

"Oh, wicked woman, be you still! (*repeat*)
I left two children in your care,
I see that four are playing there."

"Lying letters came to me (*repeat*)
To say that you were in the ground;
Another husband I have found."

"In Paris there's a mighty war, (*repeat*)
And all the torturings of Hell.
My wife and children, fare you well!"

* From *Folk Songs of French Canada,* by Marius Barbeau and Edward Sapir, by permission of the publishers, Yale University Press.

La Rue gives a version of the song of the famous voyageur Cadieux, who, during the French régime, saved his party from the Iroquois near the Grand Calumet on the Ottawa route. Separated from his party in performing this valorous deed, he became exhausted by hunger and fear. When a searching party returned to find him, he was so overjoyed that he could not cry out to them from where he lay, and so the men passed on up the river. When they returned, a few days later, they found his body lying in a grave which he himself had dug. In his hands, crossed over his chest, was a piece of birch bark, on which were written the words of the song which was so popular thereafter among the voyageurs. Whenever a brigade of canoes passed the spot, one of the older *engagés* always told the story of Cadieux to the pork-eaters. The version La Rue gives is slightly different from Gagnon's, which follows: [25]

Petit rocher

Pe-tit ro - cher de la hau-te mon-ta - gne,

Je viens i - ci fi-nir cet-te cam-pa - gne!

Ah! doux é - chos, en-ten-dez mes sou-pirs;

En lan-guis-sant je vais bien-tôt mou-rir!

Petit rocher de la haute montagne,
Je viens ici finir cette campagne.
Ah! doux échos, entendez mes soupirs,
En languissant je vais bientôt mourir.

Petits oiseaux, vos douces harmonies,
Quand vous chantez, me rattach' à la vie:
Ah! si j'avais des ailes comme vous,
Je s'rais heureux avant qu'il fût deux jours!

Seul en ces bois, que j'ai eu de soucis!
Pensant toujours à mes si chers amis,
Je demandais: Hélas! sont-ils noyés?
Les Iroquois les auraient-ils tués?

Un de ces jours que, m'étant éloigné,
En revenant je vis une fumée;
Je me suis dit: Ah! grand Dieu, qu'est ceci?
Les Iroquois m'ont-ils pris mon logis?

Je me suis mis un peu à l'ambassade,
Afin de voir si c'était embuscade;
Alors je vis trois visages français! . . .
M'ont mis le cœur d'une trop grande joie!

VOYAGEUR SONGS

Mes genoux plient, ma faible voix s'arrête,
Je tombe . . . Hélas! à partir ils s'apprêtent:
Je reste seul . . . Pas un qui me console,
Quand la mort vient par un si grand désole!

Un loup hurlant vint près de ma cabane
Voir si mon feu n'avait plus de boucane;
Je lui ai dit: Retire-toi d'ici;
Car, par ma foi, je perc'rai ton habit!

Un noir corbeau, volant à l'aventure,
Vient se percher tout près de ma toiture:
Je lui ai dit: Mangeur de chair humaine,
Va-t'en chercher autre viande que mienne.

Va-t'en là-bas, dans ces bois et marais,
Tu trouveras plusieurs corps iroquois;
Tu trouveras des chairs, aussi des os;
Va-t'en plus loin, laisse-moi en repos!

Rossignolet, va dire à ma maîtresse,
A mes enfants qu'un adieu je leur laisse;
Que j'ai gardé mon amour et ma foi,
Et désormais faut renoncer à moi!

C'est donc ici que le mond' m'abandonne! . . .
Mais j'ai secours en vous, Sauveur des hommes!
Très-Sainte Vierge, ah! m'abandonnez pas,
Permettez-moi d'mourir entre vos bras!

TRANSLATION *

O LITTLE ROCK

O little rock of the mountain I stand on,
I venture here my campaign to abandon.
    Ah! echoes sweet, give ear unto my sigh,
    Languid with wounds I come here but to die.

O little birds, with your sweet sounds of harmony,
Bring in your song all my life once again to me.
    Ah! would that I had only wings like you!
    Happy I'd fly ere another day were due.

THE VOYAGEUR

In yonder woods have I harboured a lonely fear,
Thinking the while of my friends all I hold so dear.
   This was my doubt: "Alas! if drowned are they,
   Or Iroquois should have ended their day!"

Not long ago on a far trail I dared to roam,
And coming back there was smoke rising from my home.
   This I have thought: "Great God! What does it mean?
   Do Iroquois hold my humble demesne?"

I then prepared myself as if for an embassy,
So as to find if in ambush the Indian lay.
   Then I espy French faces as I peep—
   With wondrous joy all my pulses do leap.

My knees succumb, nor can I any voice retrieve,
I fall—alas! they are now just about to leave.
   Lone I remain, not one left to console
   When death shall come with his desolate toll.

Howling a wolf round my shanty is turning,
Looking for smoke, if the fire still is burning.
   I said to him, "You'd better leave this spot,
   Or, by my faith, I shall shoot through your coat."

One black old crow, flying round at a venture,
Perched on a branch just close to my shelter;
   I said, "Oh, you, who feed on human flesh,
   Begone, nor think my blood will you refresh.

"Go over yonder in these woods and marshes,
There you will find more than one Indian corpse is,
   There you will find their flesh as well as bones.
   Get farther off and let me have repose."

Say, nightingale, to the wife I'm bereaving,
Just an adieu to my children I'm leaving,
   Still I have kept my love and loyalty,
   And from this time she must give up hope of me.

Here then it is that the world me abandons,
But I seek aid in the Saviour of mankind.
   Most Holy Maid! ah, do not me forsake,
   Let me but die in your arms I refuge take.

* From *Canadian Folk Songs: Old and New* by J. Murray Gibbon, by permission of the publishers, J. M. Dent & Sons, Ltd., London, Toronto and Vancouver, and E. P. Dutton & Company, New York.

Another voyageur song that La Rue has preserved is
very similar to the one already quoted in describing *la
ronde* which occupied one of the first evenings on the
lower Ottawa. Since La Rue's version differs considerably
from Taché's, it may be well to give it here.[26]

QUAND UN CHRÉTIEN SE DÉTERMINE À VOYAGER

Quand un chrétien se détermine
  A voyager,
Faut bien penser qu'il se destine
  A des dangers.
Mille fois à ses yeux la mort
  Par son image,
Mille fois il maudit son sort
  Dans le cours du voyage.

Ami, veux-tu voyager sur l'onde
  De tous les vents?
Les flots et la tempête grondent
  Cruellement.
Les vagues changent tous les jours,
  Et il est écrit:
Que l'image de ton retour
  Est l'image de ta vie.

Quand tu seras sur ces traverses,
  Pauvre affligé,
Un coup de vent vient qui t'exerce
  Avec danger.
Prenant et poussant ton aviron
  Contre la lame,
Tu es ici près du démon,
  Qui guette ta pauvre âme.

Quand tu seras sur le rivage,
  Las de nager,
Si tu veux faire un bon usage
  De ce danger,

THE VOYAGEUR

Va prier Dieu dévotement,
  Avec Marie.
Mais promets—lui sincèrement
  De réformer ta vie.

Si, le soir, l'essaim de mouches
  Pique trop fort,
Dans un berceau tu te couches,
  Pense à la mort.
Apprends que ce petit berceau
  Te fait comprendre
Que c'est l'image du tombeau,
  Où ton corps doit se rendre.

Si les maringouins te réveillent
  De leurs chansons,
Ou te chatouillent l'oreille
  De leurs aiguillons.
Apprends, cher voyageur, alors,
  Que c'est le diable
Qui chante tout autour de ton corps
  Pour avoir ta pauvre âme.

Quand tu seras dans ces rapides
  Très-dangereux,
Ah! prie la Vierge Marie,
  Fais-lui des vœux.
Alors lance-toi dans ces flots
  Avec hardiesse,
Et puis dirige ton canot
  Avec beaucoup d'adresse.

Quand tu seras dans les portages,
  Pauvre engagé,
Les sueurs te couleront du visage,
  Pauvre affligé.
Loin de jurer, si tu me crois,
  Dans ta colère,
Pense à Jésus portant sa croix,
  Il a monté au Calvaire.

VOYAGEUR SONGS

Ami, veux-tu marcher par terre,
  Dans ces grands bois,
Les sauvages te feront la guerre,
  En vrais sournois.
Si tu veux braver leur fureur,
  Sans plus attendre,
Prie alors de tout ton cœur,
  Ton ange de te défendre.

As a translation will show, this extremely moralizing piece was prepared by one thoroughly conversant with the technicalities of voyaging. The voyageurs' own terms are employed—traverses, voyaging, portages, rapids, marching, the great woods, etc. It suggests the priest giving advice to his voyageur flock about to start on a trip to the *pays d'en haut*, perhaps a priest who has accompanied a brigade and learned at first hand to sympathize with the men. "When a Christian decides to voyage," he warns, "he must think of the dangers that will beset him. A thousand times Death will approach him, a thousand times he will curse his lot during the trip. Friend, do you plan to travel on the water amid the winds and where the waves and tempest menace cruelly? The waves are different every day, and it is written that the appearance of your return is that of your life. When you are on traverses, poor soul, the wind will come up suddenly, seizing your oar and breaking it and putting you in grave danger. You then are close to the demon, who is lying in wait for your soul. When you have reached the shore, exhausted from swimming [after your canoe has been broken in the traverse], if you wish to profit from this experience, go, pray God devoutly, and Mary also. But promise them sincerely that you will reform. In the evening if the swarms of mosquitoes assail you unbearably as you lie in your narrow bed, think how this couch is the likeness of the grave where your body will be placed. If the mosquitoes waken you with their buzzing and tickle your ears with their stings, think, dear voyageur, how like to the Devil they are, who is singing about your body, ready to seize your soul. When you are in those very dangerous rapids, pray to the Virgin, make your vow to her. Then take the waves boldly and guide your canoe with skill. When you are on portages, poor soul, sweat will drip from your brow, poor *engagé*. Then do not swear in your wrath, rather think of Jesus bearing his cross. He mounted to Calvary. When you are traveling in the great forests, the Indians will attack you from ambuscade. If you wish to brave their fury, wait no longer, but pray to your guardian angel to protect you."

Examples of voyageurs' songs might be multiplied. It is enough here to cite some of the most common *chansons* that illustrate the various types. The manner of singing needs to be mentioned in more detail. Sometimes all sang in unison. Again, one of the voyageurs, usually the steersman, sang a solo part and his companions joined him in the chorus. The effect in general seems to have been good. Long's companion, Keating, wrote of them in 1823: "As we proceeded along these rapids our canoe-men entertained us with songs more remarkable for the wildness and originality of their notes than for the skill and method with which they were sung. It is one of the delights of these men to sing in unison as they proceed, and the effect is very fine." [27] Dr. Bigsby mentions the method of ending the song: "Thus commanded, Mr. M—— sang it as only the true *voyageur* can do, imitating the action of the paddle, and in their high, resounding, and yet musical tones. His practised voice enabled him to give us the various swells and falls of sounds upon the waters, driven about by the winds, dispersed and softened in the wide expanses, or brought close again to the ear by neighboring rocks. He finished, as is usual, with the piercing Indian shriek." [28]

One traveler mentions that the voyageur who could sing had a greater economic value than the average man: "This done, he called for a song; and many were gleefully carolled—each verse in solo, and then repeated in chorus, north-west fashion. Of such use is singing, in enabling the men to work eighteen and nineteen hours a-day (at a pinch), through forests and across great bays, that a good singer has additional pay." [29] McKenney, like the Norwegian trader of the far Northwest, W. F. Wentzel, mentions the indecorous quality of some of their songs. It is a great pity, nevertheless, that Wentzel's large collection of these songs has not survived. His musical gifts added to his unusual command of languages would surely have made the collection invaluable. [30]

C. BERTSCH

VII

AMONG the services rendered by voyageurs was that of the soldier. During the American Revolution it is certain that they played a not inconsiderable rôle in the country lying between the Appalachians and St. Louis and about the Great Lakes. As they were usually mentioned by some other epithet than that of their calling, however, it is difficult to single them out from the "French," "Canadians," "traders," and others for whom many contemporary references can be found. It is especially difficult to distinguish them from the *habitants* of such settlements as Detroit, Vincennes, Green Bay, and Prairie du Chien. Some voyageurs were doubtless recruited from these settlements every year.

The editor of a well-known book depicting the Revolution in the Northwest includes voyageurs, apparently, in a statement concerning the general attitude of westerners during the war. She says: "The news of the French alliance, which reached Pittsburgh on May 26, 1778, heartened the defenders of the frontier, and gave them hope of relief from hostile attacks. The little clusters of French-Canadian settlers scattered throughout the Indian country and the French-Canadian traders and half-breeds in the Indian villages had unbounded influence over the red men, and the news that their French 'father' was giving aid and comfort to the American colonists tended to check the inimical propensities of our fiercest enemies. That this influence was not more effective, however, was due to the counteracting efforts of the American Loyalists whom General Hand had allowed to escape from Pittsburgh in the spring of 1778, and who had established themselves in the more important villages of the Ohio tribesmen." [1]

Thus many of the voyageurs gave their support to the Americans. From the correspondence of such frontiersmen as David Zeisberger and Daniel Boone, on the other hand, it seems perfectly apparent that a great many adhered to the British. Thus Zeisberger on June 9, 1778, sent Colonel George Morgan the following information: "There is a small army of French 150 or 200 men that is for the frontiers, commanded by one Mr Lemot [Guillaume LaMothe]. I imagine he is for his old hunting ground on Red Stone." Boone in the same year addressed Colonel Arthur Campbell in a dispatch telling of a Mr. Hancock "who arrived here Yesterday and informed us of both French and Indians coming against us to the number of near 400 which I expect in 12 days from this." [2]

A trader by the name of Jean Marie Ducharme, who had traded through the Illinois and Wisconsin countries prior to the outbreak of the war, seems to have held an important position in the British expedition against St. Louis in 1780. Other voyageurs also are known to have taken part in this important campaign. As a brother and a cousin of Ducharme's were voyageurs, it may be assumed that he was also in that category. His services to the British cause, however, seem to be in doubt. At the outset of the war he was suspected by the British of furnishing provisions to the colonists. In 1780 he was accused of sympathy with the Americans and of causing the expedition to miscarry.[3]

The numerous references made by British partisans to disloyalty among various persons in the Indian country who purported to be pro-British provide further evidence that many of the voyageurs must have upheld the American cause. Even at Grand Portage disaffection was rampant, and in 1778 Lieutenant Thomas Bennett was detailed to take a force thither to protect the British merchants there, and incidentally to secure their loyalty, which was in some cases considered doubtful.[4]

Both sides evidently relied again and again on the information that only traders and voyageurs could offer concerning the topography of the country and the Indians. It is difficult in many cases to distinguish between the trader and the voyageur. Thus the man sent by the British to the upper Mississippi to prevent the Sioux from attaching themselves to the Spanish, Augustin Rocque, was not far removed, if at all, from the voyageur ranks.[5]

In this contest, as later in the War of 1812, both sides were to discover that voyageurs were not always to be relied upon when the odds seemed going against them. Like so many effervescent, fun-loving natures, they lacked stamina. Thus Colonel A. S. De Peyster wrote to General Haldimand on August 23, 1779, that Lieutenant Bennett's "Canadians" and Indians had grown homesick and were desirous of turning back from a certain expedition.[6] Indeed, as a soldier the voyageur, it must be ad-

mitted at the outset, had his disqualifications. He must
have been the despair of officers accustomed to implicit
obedience, and to a deliberate assumption of fearlessness
on the part of their men, whatever the threatening danger. The voyageurs were as naïve in war time as in peace
and presumed the same easy tolerance on the part of
their army superiors as on that of their trading *bourgeois*.
Moreover, when danger threatened, they were afraid and
said so as unmistakably as they expressed their joys in
their *chansons*. And they positively could not accustom
themselves to doing without their pipes for sometimes as
many as three or four hours! Yet they served well and
won distinction in the War of 1812.

In the fall of 1812 the Northwest Company patriotic-
ally offered their *engagés* to Canada and their king.[7] The
offer was accepted, and in October the Corps of Canadian
Voyageurs came into existence. It served in at least two
engagements and was disbanded at Lachine on March 14,
1813. A translation of the essential portions of the governor-general's proclamation ordering this corps to be
enrolled is as follows:[8] "It has pleased His Excellence,
the Governor-General, to order John M'Donell, Esquire,
to enroll the names of all residents of the parishes of
La Pointe Claire, &c.; and Messrs. A. N. M'Leod and
James Hughes, Esquires, to enroll the names of voyageurs in the parishes of St. Ours, &c., &c.; and Mr.
William M'Kay, Esquire, to enroll the voyageurs in the
parishes of La Norraye, &c.; and Mr. Pierre de Roche-
blave, Esquire, to enroll the names of the voyageurs in
the parishes of La Prairie, &c.; Those who are now or
have been voyageurs, and to see that they are in Mont-

real on the first day of October in order to form a corps, which shall be named the Voyageur Corps, under the command of William M'Gillivray, Esquire."

A uniform was adopted, and twenty-seven officers were appointed, among whom one recognizes many of the men who opened up the Northwest.[9] William M'Gillivray was lieutenant-colonel and in command. His is such an outstanding figure in the fur trade in the period of the Northwest Company's greatest activity that no account of his life need be given here. It is sufficient to mention that he had served for years with voyageurs in the region beyond Grand Portage and knew them intimately. Fort William is named for him.

Angus Shaw was made a major, and so also was Archibald Norman McLeod. Both were experienced fur-traders whose exploits in the Northwest are well known. The reader has already become acquainted with McLeod through his diary, kept on the Assiniboine River in what is now Saskatchewan. It is a remarkably intimate picture of the voyageur at home. A man who had directed the life of such a post could be relied on not to be shocked when Private Jean-Baptiste appeared on parade with his pipe in his mouth.

Among the six captains were Alexander Mackenzie, Kenneth Mackenzie, and John McDonell. The last is known to the reader ere this, for not a little of the description of the voyageur in this book has been derived from McDonell's unpublished diary. The two Mackenzies were outstanding figures in the fur trade and in the exploration of western Canada.

James Stanley Goddard's name among the six lieutenants recalls that famous expedition up the Mississippi to Grand Portage in 1767 for which Jonathan Carver has claimed all the glory, but of which Captain James Tute was the leader and Goddard second in command. Surely Goddard learned much of voyageur temperament on that ill-fated journey.

M'Gillivray's son Joseph was one of eight ensigns. To him we are indebted for an insight into the temperament and morale of soldiering voyageurs: [10]

"When on duty in company with the regular forces or the militia they were guilty of much insubordination, and it was quite impossible to make them amenable to military law. They generally came on parade with a pipe in their mouths and their rations of pork and bread stuck on their bayonets. On seeing an officer, whether general, colonel, or subaltern, they took off their hats and made a low bow, with the common saluation of *Bon jour, Monsieur le Général*, or *le Colonel*, as the case might be, and, if they happened to know that the officer was married, never failed to inquire after the health of *Madame et les enfans*. On parade they talked incessantly, called each other 'pork eaters,' quarrelled about their rations, wished they were back in the Indian country again, &c., and when called to order by their officers and told to hold their tongues, one or more would reply, 'Ah, dear captain, let us off as quick as you can; some of us have not yet breakfasted, and it's upwards of an hour since I had a smoke.' If the officer was a North-Wester, he generally told them to have patience, and he would give them their *congé tout de suite*. In moments when danger ought to have produced a little steadiness, they completely set discipline at defiance, and the volatile volunteer broke out into all the unrestrained mirth and anti-military familiarity of the thoughtless *voyageur*. In vain the subaltern winked, in vain the captain threatened, in vain the colonel frowned; neither winks, threats, or frowns, could restrain the vivacious laugh, silence the noisy tongue, or compose the ever changing features into any thing like military seriousness.

"These repeated infractions of the *code militaire* subjected many of them to temporary confinement; but as night approached, if the sentinel was a *voyageur*, he told the prisoner to *'aller coucher avec sa femme, et retourner le lendemain de bonne heure.'* This friendly advice was immediately followed, and they had always the honour to return according to promise. They could not be got to wear stocks; and such as did not use cravats came on parade with naked necks, and very often with rough beards. In this condition they presented a curious contrast to the unchangeable countenances and well-drilled movements of the British soldiery, with whom they occasionally did duty. Notwithstanding these peculiarities the *voyageurs* were excellent partisans, and, from their superior knowledge of the country, were able to render material service during the war. They had great confidence in their officers, particularly their colonel, Mr. M'Gillivray, whose influence frequently saved them from the punishment to which their repeated breaches of discipline subjected them."

The first Canadian to lose his life in defence of his country was a voyageur, Pierre Rototte, of the Corps of Canadian Voyageurs, who fell at St. Regis, October 23,

1812.[11] Captain McDonell, one of his lieutenants, and thirty-five of his men were taken prisoners.[12] On November 5 of the same year voyageurs took part in the fight at Chrysler's Farm. On November 10 the Corps participated in the battle of La Colle. There may well have been other organizations of voyageurs within the British troops at this time. Dr. Bigsby refers to "three regiments of hardy *voyageurs*, of eight hundred or one thousand men each, which the Northwest Company sent into the field." [13]

The unique services of the voyageurs, however, were performed on the western front. The first engagement of the war was largely a voyageur victory. Michilimackinac was the great inland fur post, chiefly because of its strategic position on the trade route to the West and Northwest. The fur-traders as well as the Canadian Government were directly concerned in its fate. Should the Americans retain control, most of the fur trade of Canada would be intercepted and the western Indians would become the allies of the United States. Ruin faced Montreal merchants. Accordingly, on the outbreak of hostilities, steps were taken at once to secure British control of this fort. On July 15 Captain Charles Roberts, who commanded the nearest British post at St. Joseph's Island, received an order from his superior, Major-General Brock, authorizing an attack on Michilimackinac. On the following day Roberts and his "army" set out on their journey of fifty miles. His force consisted of some three hundred Indians, for whose presence Robert Dickson, a famous fur-trader of the Red River Valley, and his voyageurs were responsible; one hundred and eighty voyageurs; and forty-five men of the Tenth Royal Veterans. The Indians as effective soldiery can be discounted largely, for their influence was felt mainly in instilling in the Americans the fear of massacre. Two pieces of artillery were carried, which were unwieldy and caused the voyageurs much labor. "By the almost unparalleled exertions of the Canadians who manned the boats we arrived at the place of Rendezvous at 3 o'clock the following morning." [14] These are the words in which their commander, when reporting the affair, describes their services. The Americans, who numbered but fifty-nine effectives, saw the uselessness of an engagement and surrendered when they discovered a gun on an eminence commanding their garrison. This had been dragged thither with much difficulty "by the exertions of the Canadians." [15] Well had the voyageurs been trained for such herculean feats in the course of their canoe journeys. Incidentally one learns that of the fifty-nine in the American garrison, eighteen were voyageurs who after the capitulation of the post took the oath of allegiance to Great Britain and "after much solicitation, volunteered to serve for a limited period." [16]

It may be interesting to learn of further patriotic activities of voyageurs in this campaign. An eyewitness of events in this far corner, Toussaint Pothier, an agent of the Southwest Company, tells us that Captain Roberts consulted him on the deficiencies of men and provisions in his garrison as soon as he learned of the outbreak of war and that he, Pothier, sent an express canoe to Fort William, the great rendezvous of the Northwest Company's men, asking for assistance. "Those Gentlemen with great alacrity came down with a strong party to Cooperate; bringing to St Maries Several Carryage Guns and other arms. And altho the distance between St Josephs and Fort William is about 500 Miles they arrived at Michilimackinac the ninth day from the date of the Express." [17] And who but voyageurs made Captain William McKay's express canoe speed over the bosom of Lake Superior to Fort William with the request, and who if not voyageurs constituted the "strong party" that came down in the little schooner, *The Beaver?* Indeed, McKenzie at Fort William wrote: "Our agents ordered a general muster, which amounted to 1200, exclusive of several hundred of the natives. We are now equal in all to 1600 or 1700 strong . . . I have not the least doubt but our force will, in ten days hence, amount to at least five thousand effective men. Our young gentlemen and engagees offered most handsomely to march immediately for Michilimackinac." [18]

The fall of Michilimackinac had a direct effect on Hull's surrender of Detroit. In his trial the disgraced American officer referred to the four thousand *engagés* of the British traders as likely to be used against him and thus influencing him in his decision to yield the post.

Late in the war another victory in the West was due largely to voyageurs. This was the capture of Fort Shelby at Prairie du Chien. One corps, known locally as the Canadian Voyageurs, had already taken part in the campaign against Michilimackinac in 1812. Five other units took part, practically every man of which was either a trader or a voyageur. The official names of

168

these units were: Michigan Fencibles, Mississippi Volunteers, Mississippi Volunteer Artillery, Dease's Mississippi Volunteers, and Green Bay Militia.[19]

Prairie du Chien was only less essential to the British fur-traders than Michilimackinac, for it controlled the entrance to the Sioux country where Robert Dickson, James Aird, John Lawe, and others had been building up an immense trade during the thirty years since the close of the Revolution. Montreal and London firms were deeply involved in this trade; hence, when the Americans under General Clark took Prairie du Chien in 1814 and proceeded to build a fort, the situation called for a drastic remedy. Accordingly Colonel McDouall, the British commander at Michilimackinac, sent forces under Captain William McKay to take possession. Among his officers one reads such names as Porlier, Rolette, Honoré, Grignon, Brisbois, Renville, Nolin, Lacroix, and Biron. In their scarlet uniforms they made a great showing when they arrived at the Prairie after a long journey by way of Green Bay and the portage between the Fox and Wisconsin rivers. The single gun, for which Wabasha and La Tête de Chien, chiefs of neighboring bands, had pleaded, was trained on the Americans' gunboat in the Mississippi and succeeded in hitting it. Its commander was obliged to cut the cable and get out of range, thus leaving the fort without assistance. Doubtless the red uniforms had their effect in persuading the little force that their opponents could more than equal them, and so the fort was surrendered. Prairie du Chien with its numerous voyageur residents thus became a British post and remained so till the end of the war. Many of the voyageurs who took part in this campaign also served during the next month, August, 1814, in the defence of Michilimackinac, when it was attacked by American forces. This again was a victory for the voyageurs. Among them were nearly a hundred armed and fitted out by John Johnston, the trader at Sault Ste. Marie.[20] We shall meet him again in the next chapter.

The voyageurs not only served with the land forces, but certain members of the craft very nearly had naval experience as well. In 1813 the *Isaac Todd*, on its way to Astoria, the new American post at the mouth of the Columbia River, was docked in Portsmouth, England. "We had on board half a dozen good Canadian *Voyageurs* . . . to make and man a canoe," writes John McDonald of Garth. "The Canadians [who] had been some time on board," asked and received shore leave. "Messrs. Ellice, McGillivray, McTavish and myself were dining at the principal hotel when the waiter came in and told us some men wished to see us. We knew immediately who they were . . . accordingly all made for the wharf, where they found a couple of the Canadians waiting. They had all made a little free with wine and women, and took a shore boat. They had not proceeded far when a press gang boarded them and were taking them all off to the hulk, an old 74, lying as a recruiting ship. Mr. McTavish made some resistance, . . . the midshipman took all except Mr. McTavish . . . and one of the clerks. We were still at table when McTavish came in all in a fury . . . blaming me for allowing the men to come ashore. Mr. Ellice winked at me and said: 'Never mind.' He was brother-in-law to

Earl Gray, and the Port Admiral was Earl Gray's brother. Next morning at breakfast, Mr. Ellice handed me an order from the Admiral for the release of our men, upon which I steered my course on board the hulk. The poor fellows had been put in close quarters all night for fear of escape. They were in a sad state of mind indeed, with the fear of being made sailors for the rest of their lives and of never seeing their fatherland again. . . . I returned with them to the Isaac Todd, all safe after what they believed a narrow escape."

Nor was this the last of their troubles. McDonald goes on with the narrative. "One evening while at Sancta Cruz, Tenerif, I had hardly gone to bed, when Mc-Tavish . . . came rushing into my cabin roaring out: 'McDonald, you allowed the Canadians to go ashore again! they have had a dust with the Spanish guard and half of them are taken prisoners and we will lose our men.' The fact was that the Spanish guard thought they were some of the French prisoners making their escape. . . . A scuffle ensued in which the *voyageurs* were wounded and locked up, but they were soon after released on their identity being made out." [21]

Something should be said, also, of the voyageurs in the party that founded Astoria, just at the outbreak of the war. On board the *Tonquin* were thirteen voyageurs. "An instance of the buoyant temperament and the professional pride of these people was furnished in the gay and braggart style in which they arrived at New York to join the enterprise. They were determined to regale and astonish the people of the 'States' with the sight of a Canadian boat and a Canadian crew. They accordingly

171

fitted up a large but light bark canoe, such as is used in
the fur trade; transported it in a wagon from the banks
of the St. Lawrence to the shores of Lake Champlain;
traversed the lake in it, from end to end; hoisted it again
in a wagon and wheeled it off to Lansingburgh, and there
launched it upon the waters of the Hudson. Down this
river they plied their course merrily on a fine summer's
day, making its banks resound for the first time with
their old French boat songs; passing by the villages with
whoop and halloo, so as to make the honest Dutch
farmers mistake them for a crew of savages. In this way
they swept, in full song, and with regular flourish of the
paddle, round New York, in a still summer evening, to
the wonder and admiration of its inhabitants, who had
never before witnessed on their waters, a nautical appari-
tion of the kind." [22]

They were told of the dangers that lay ahead of them
in the storms of the Horn and the impressing ships of the
British which might overtake them, but they replied that
they were Nor'westers and that they could live hard,
lie hard, sleep hard, eat dogs! Yet they were very lub-
berly on the *Tonquin* and excited the disgust of Captain
Thorn. David Stuart, however, "had made various expeditions with voyageurs. He was accustomed, therefore,
to the familiarity which prevails between that class and
their superiors, and the gossipings which take place
among them when seated round a fire at their encampments. Stuart was never so happy as when he could seat
himself on the deck with a number of these men round
him, in camping style, smoke together, passing the pipe
from mouth to mouth, after the manner of the Indians,

sing old Canadian boat-songs, and tell stories about their hardships and adventures."

The Astorians have been famous in American history for over a century. Ramsay Crooks, W. P. Hunt, Robert McLellan, Gabriel Franchere, and the two Stuarts, Robert and David—who does not know of their heroic adventures in crossing the great West and navigating around the Horn to found near the mouth of the Columbia an American trading post named in honor of the master spirit of the enterprise, John Jacob Astor? It is not generally recalled, however, that voyageurs were responsible to no inconsiderable extent for the success of the land expeditions. The canoes were propelled by them; by their sixth sense they detected rapids and falls in unfamiliar streams in time to avoid them; they knew the West from actual experience in many instances; and they were versed in wood lore and in making friendly contacts with Indians. Because they were inarticulate they should not be overlooked when history awards the glory for the planting of the American flag on the Pacific and for discovery of South Pass soon to be the gateway for an army of settlers on their way to Oregon and California.

C. BERTSCH

VIII

OUR picture of the voyageur would be incomplete without a representation of him in the rôle of a member of a frontier community. Many a voyageur lost his life in his hazardous calling; others remained about wilderness posts till death overtook them; not a few returned to spend the twilight of life in their native hamlets on the great St. Lawrence; but a large proportion of them in the later period of the fur-trade era became settlers on the frontier. As the frontier moved inexorably westward, the story of the voyageur as the first settler repeated itself at Sault Ste. Marie, Chicago, Milwaukee, Green Bay, Prairie du Chien, St. Paul, St. Louis, and Winnipeg, not to mention fur-trading posts of lesser rank. First the voyageurs lived at the trading forts of these regions; a little later they took up land, on which they resided during the portion of the year when they were not employed in paddling traders' canoes or absent on trading expeditions to the Indians. Finally the frontier reached their little cabins and they became one with the new town which sprang up almost overnight.

In certain localities, notably at Detroit, St. Louis, and the French hamlets in the Illinois country, it is difficult to distinguish in many cases between *habitants*, or actual colonists, and voyageurs. Frequently the *habitant* engaged himself for a trading voyage or made his livelihood as a small trapper. He is often referred to in the annals of the period as a "voyageur," a "Canadian," or a "Frenchman"—names by which the *engagé* of the fur trade, the true voyageur, is also mentioned. Thus it is difficult to distinguish the one from the other. Hence, it is necessary in studying the voyageurs to go to other frontier settlements where there were no *habitants* to be confused with them. The hamlets chosen for this study are Sault Ste. Marie, St. Peter's, and the Red River Settlement.

* * *

Sault Ste. Marie had been a mission station and fort during the French regime, but it came into its own after the fur trade was thrown open early in the British period. Thereafter for almost a hundred years it was known, alas too well, to voyageurs; for it was necessary to make a long and hard portage around the rapids that gave the place its name. In 1750 a plan had been afoot to establish a seigniory at "a place called the Sault Ste. Marie." [1] Settlements in that place "would be most useful, as voyageurs from the neighboring posts and those from the Western Sea would there find a safe retreat, and by . . . care and precaution . . . would destroy in those parts the trade of the Indians with the English." At least one Frenchman, probably a voyageur, settled there and began farming; but the struggle was soon on between France and Great Britain, and the voyageurs, instead of settling at frontier posts, accompanied Charles Langlade in his expedition against the British at Fort Duquesne. [2]

When the smoke of battle cleared away, Jean Baptiste Cadotte was found by Alexander Henry at the Sault, a

French Canadian there on sufferance by the new rulers.[3] Whether others of his compatriots remained, or whether there were accessions in the next ten years, is uncertain, but another traveler to that region in 1777, John Long, describes the place thus: "Here is a small picketted fort . . . and about ten log houses for the residence of English and French traders." [4]

In 1789 a still more famous traveler visited the Sault, Alexander Mackenzie. He writes: "Upon the South shore, there is a village . . . [of] about thirty families of the Algonquin Nation, who are one half the year starving and the other half intoxicated, and ten to twelve Canadians who have been in the Indian country from an early period of life and intermarried with the natives who have brought them families." [5]

Here, then, is a distinct allusion to a voyageur community. About 1800 a trading establishment of the Northwest Company which had grown up there, and possibly some of the voyageurs, moved to the north side of the strait to be on British soil. In May, 1800, Daniel W. Harmon, later a famous trader in the far West, found "on the opposite shore [the American side] . . . a few Americans, Scotch and Canadians, who carry on a small traffic with the natives and also till the ground a little." [6]

One of the most famous residents of the Sault was the Irishman, John Johnston, long a trader on Lake Superior. The romantic story of his protracted courtship of a chief's daughter, of their happy marriage and long residence at the Sault, of his royal hospitality to travelers passing that way, and of the marriage of his half-breed daughters to white men of respectability and even fame

179

should be read by all Americans and Canadians.[7] He
enters the story of the voyageurs because it was he who
gathered them under the British flag in the War of 1812
and assisted in the capture of Michilimackinac. The
fortunes of war were his, for while he was winning glory
on the battlefield, the enemy reached Sault Ste. Marie
and "plundered and destroyed" his property.[8]

At least one voyageur of Sault Ste. Marie emerges
from obscurity in the attack on Mackinac. This was
Augustin Nolin, who had retired before the war and
built for himself a house at Sault Ste. Marie. It is said
that at the siege he was of great assistance in restraining
the Indians and thus prevented such a catastrophe as followed the surrender of Fort Dearborn not long after.
It is likewise reported that in 1815 he warned the American officers at the Sault of an intended Indian attack.
Later he sold his home at the Sault and removed to
Pembina, on the Red River of the North.[9]

Franchere, the Astorian, tells in his narrative how over
three hundred voyageurs and traders evaded the Americans who had just burned Sault Ste. Marie, and slipped
by with an immensely valuable cargo of furs bound for
Montreal:[10] "The value of the furs which they carried
could not be estimated at less than a million of dollars:
an important prize for the Americans, if they could have
laid their hands upon it. We were three hundred and
thirty-five men, all well armed; a large camp was formed,
with a breast-work of fur-packs, and we kept watch all
night." Since the forty-seven canoes that carried this
valuable freight must have been propelled by voyageurs,
we have here another instance of the manner in which

these men served their country in time of need. What the loss of these furs would have meant to Canada at this time is partially revealed by the lengths to which the Northwest Company were willing to go to get them safely to Montreal. The course they proposed to take was none other than an appeal to their hated rivals, the Hudson's Bay Company, to allow their furs to go to England by way of Hudson Bay.

Franchere as he passed noted the appearance and character of the people living about the Sault. He mentions Charles Ermatinger, who was just finishing a grist mill. "He thought," says Franchere, "that . . . would lead the inhabitants to sow more grain than they did. These inhabitants are principally old Canadians, boatmen married to half-breed or Indian women. The fish afford them subsistence during the greater part of the year, and provided they secure potatoes enough to carry them through the remainder, they are content. It is to be regretted that these people are not more industrious, for the land is very fertile." [11]

In 1816 General McComb visited the Sault and expressed a desire to go up as far as the open lake. Accordingly John Johnston equipped him with a light canoe and nine of his most experienced voyageurs. When Point aux Pins was reached, a large camp of Indians came into view. Being drunk, they took offense at the American flag flying at the prow of the canoe and came rushing down to the river with war whoops and malicious intentions. One Indian aimed his gun at the General but fortunately missed his aim. Thereupon the leader of the *engagés*, Le Clair, rushed to the Indian, now priming his gun for further action, wrested it from him, and "with the butt end of it, laid him flat upon the ground." But Le Clair was sufficiently well versed in Indian tactics to warn against a further advance, and so the visit to Lake Superior was abandoned.[12]

And now the second act in the drama of occupation was about to begin. First always came the traders, who picked out the best site for a principal fort. Here in the course of time gathered, little by little, a hamlet of voyageurs. Then came the military. A post was erected, the first evidence of the advance of the settler's frontier as distinguished from that of the trader. In June, 1820, Governor Cass of Michigan came to Sault Ste. Marie accompanied by "ten Canadian *voyageurs* . . . to manage the canoes, ten United States soldiers to serve as an escort, and ten Ottawa, Chippewa, and Shawnee Indians to act as hunters," and others, the total numbering sixty-four persons.[13] After a stormy session with the Indians, who at first refused to grant land for a military post, the Indian woman, Mrs. Johnston, and others succeeded in bringing them to the point, and a treaty was finally signed. By it the Chippewa ceded four square miles of land, reserving a perpetual right to fish in the rapids. Fort Brady was soon erected at the Sault.

Close on the heels of the military came the missionary. Father Richard arrived in 1825 from his place of residence at Detroit. In his report of March 21, 1826, published in the *Annales de la Propagation de la Foi*, he mentions the six hundred and more Canadian voyageurs who were in the habit of assembling at Mackinac every year between the first of May and the first of October.

THE VOYAGEUR AS SETTLER

He then goes on to enumerate the heads of families
"originally from Canada" who lived at this time at
numerous frontier hamlets. Sault Ste. Marie is credited
with twenty families numbering 120 individuals. Other
Catholic missionaries and some Protestant ministers
served the inhabitants from time to time, notably the
priests *en route* to or from Fort William and the Red
River Settlement after 1818, including Fathers Tabeau,
Dumoulin, and Belcourt.[14] In 1836 Father Pierz began
his labors at the Sault. Thereafter the French Canadians
were not destitute of the consolations of their faith. In
1846 the Catholic mission was taken over by the Jesuits,
and Father J. B. Menet was appointed the first active
pastor. By this time the Catholic families are listed as
126, with such typical voyageur names as Benoît, Belanger, Brunette, Durocher, Des Jardins, Gauthier, La
Roche, Nolin, and Rouleau.[15]

After 1834 a new industry was opened to the voyageurs of Sault Ste. Marie. This was the fishing industry
inaugurated by the recently reorganized American Fur
Company. From the first records penned by explorers
down to the present day the rapids of Sault Ste. Marie
have been famous for their white fish. The new president
of the American Fur Company, Ramsay Crooks, believed
that he could make the fish of the upper lakes redound to
the profit of his firm. Moreover, he wished to dispense
with sixty-five of his voyageurs (who were too numerous
to be employed profitably as traders during the winter
and spring) by building sailing vessels on Lake Superior.
But sixty-five men, all conversant with the fur trade and
more or less acquainted with the American Fur Com-

pany's policies, could be engaged by rivals to the great detriment of the Company. Therefore they were to be employed in catching fish.[16]

For almost a decade hooks, twine, salt, and other articles were supplied to agents at Mackinac, Sault Ste. Marie, and La Pointe. These men engaged voyageurs, Indians, and half-breeds to take the fish, pack them, and ship them in barrels to market.

No part of the story of early Sault Ste. Marie is more picturesque than accounts of the manner of taking fish in the rapids. The Canadians learned the difficult art from the Indians, whose canoes, bobbing about like eggshells on the boiling water, have been mentioned in nearly every visitor's narrative. Each canoe was manned by two men, each supplied with a push-pole, *pique de fond* in the voyageur's vocabulary. The man standing at the bow had by his side a scoop net with the opening four feet or so in diameter and with a handle some twelve or fourteen feet in length. With push-poles the canoe was forced against the stream while the eyes of the bowsman scanned the depths of the rushing waters until he saw his prey and brought the net into position. Then the canoe was allowed to drop suddenly down stream dragging the net with it. With a dextrous movement the bowsman brought the net out of the water, and the fish was flipped into the canoe.

Crooks' fisheries were eminently successful, and hundreds of barrels of fish were salted and sent to the Ohio Valley, down the Mississippi, and even to New York. But the crisis of 1837 and the bad times which followed for half a decade prevented them from reaching a satisfactory market, and so the plan was abandoned in the forties.

A description of a neighboring fishing hamlet of voyageurs has survived. It is representative of life at Sault Ste. Marie at this period no less than of La Pointe, about which it was written. Even after discounting some of the glamorous haze which the lapse of time enabled the author to throw about these inhabitants of Madeline Island, the reader will still see a village of charming, idyllic, grown-up children.[17]

"The town proper consisted of clusters of houses built on each side of a road-way running east and west, close to the lake shore, terminating on the west [at] Pointe De Fret, and on the east at Middle Fort, which was either an episcopalian or a presbyterian mission, but at which no missionary was stationed during my time. Still farther to the east was what was called Old Fort, consisting of a clearing on the eastern side of the island, from which all of the buildings had been removed, but which had grown up to grass and second growth timber.

"There were about three or four white families on the island; the people were mostly half-breeds, the descendants of intermarriage between the old voyageurs and the Indian woman, and nearly all the men of middle or beyond middle life were Canadian French and had been voyageurs or *coureurs des bois*, and had evidently settled upon the island to pass their old age there with their families. In addition to the groups of houses at La Pointe proper and Middle Fort, there was a settlement upon the western side of the island, at a distance of one or two miles.

"The people were a most innocent, affectionate and happy people. They made their own boats and nets, and the barrels, half-barrels and quarter-barrels in which they packed their fish. During the winter they were out trapping. They raised potatoes and other root crops, and one or two of the white men occasionally raised wheat and oats, but very little of it. There were only two or three horses in the entire settlement, and one or two cows. In winter nearly all the hauling was done with dog teams; nearly every family owning from three to four dogs. These animals were fed upon fish heads taken from the fish in the fall, filled frozen into barrels and kept during the winter for dog food. During the entire time of my residence on the island I never knew of a case of larceny but one, and that was committed by a negro who had been left there by some steamboat. I remember the thrill of horror that went through the entire community at the idea of such a crime being committed. Drunkenness was rare.

"The great events were the arrival of the first steamboat in the spring. Payment time in the fall, when everybody went to Bad River on the Reservation to attend the payment. Christmas day, when we had midnight Mass, and New Year's day, when visits were exchanged, and everybody who had a house kept it open.

"In the spring and fall great flights of migratory birds used to light upon the island and were killed for food; in June pigeons were particularly numerous. The berry season included strawberries, raspberries, and altogether the life, while perhaps monotonous, was of great simplicity and singular beauty.

186

"From the time navigation ceased until it opened, we were an isolated community. Provisions were stored and provided for in the fall, precisely as if one were going on a voyage, and the first boats used to bring small packages of meat and sausages in their ice-chests, which were sold to such of the inhabitants as could pay for them, and were considered rare delicacies.

"A more simple, hospitable, honest community could not exist anywhere, and there was an element of cheerfulness and good nature that permeated the entire community which I have never seen since.

"The old voyageurs were a singularly interesting class of men; uneducated, perhaps, but of a singular dignity of manner and speech and of the utmost morality: scrupulous in the performance of their duties both to God and man. On Sundays, in the little old church, the head of the family always sat with stately dignity on the outside of the pew, and while they indulged in chewing tobacco during the service to a very large extent, yet the habit was conducted in such a simple and dignified way that it ceased to surprise or annoy anybody. The choir in the church included four or five of these old men who sat within the chancel and sang the responses and all of the hymns. I can almost see them now, clad in their white surplices and red shirts, intoning with the utmost dignity all of the responses."

Copper mining began to attract immigration to the southern shore of Lake Superior in the middle forties; steamboats appeared on the lake; and Sault Ste. Marie soon ceased to be a voyageurs' hamlet. Yet even today one finds there names and faces reminiscent of the days when red caps, plumes, sashes, and pipes were the fashion at the Sault.

*   *   *

Just when voyageurs began to settle around "the Entry," or "St. Peter's," that is, the mouth of the St. Peter's, now the Minnesota, River, is somewhat uncertain. There is good reason to suppose that it was not till the establishment of Fort St. Anthony, later Fort Snelling, in 1819 that a real hamlet existed in the neighborhood. From that year, however, until 1848 the region became increasingly popular among this class of men. For many years prior to 1834 Alexis Bailly was the principal trader. In 1817 he brought sixty voyageurs from Montreal, eighty in 1818, and fifty-nine in 1827. Probably these figures are indicative of the average yearly accession of new hands. His successor brought fifty in 1836 and thirty-three in 1837.[18] When Henry H. Sibley came in the fall of 1834 to succeed Bailly, he found in "the amphitheater where the hamlet was situated," to use his own language, "only a group of log huts, the most pretentious of which was the home of . . . Mr. Bailly."[19] He further describes the hamlet as consisting of "dwellings for the blacksmith, carpenter, and common voyageurs in the vicinity of Mr. Bailly's quarters." This was the beginning of Mendota, Minnesota.

Since the voyageur followed his own tradition in so many phases of his existence, it should be stated here that he had also his own peculiar method of building his house. Perhaps the best description of it is by a missionary who himself was a skillful carpenter. In the following extract from his letter of September 30, 1832, Sherman

Hall is describing the voyageurs' homes at Lac du Flambeau in western Wisconsin.[20]

"A few buildings are reared nearly in the old Yankee
manner of building log houses, that is, of round timbers
locked together at the ends. The most common method,
however, is to build with hewed timber. There is a great
abundance of good building timber almost everywhere in
this country. When a building is to be put up, the timber
of the sills, beams & posts is cut and squared into suitable sticks, usually with a common axe, for a hewing
broad axe is seldom seen here, and no body knows how to
use it. The sills & beams are generally locked, or halfed
together at the corners of the building, for few can frame
them together with tenant and mortice. A mortice is made
in the sill for a post wherever it is needed & an other in
the beam. A groove is made in each post from top to
bottom about 2 inches in width, and three or four inches
deep. Timbers are then hewed six or seven inches thick
and the ends cut till they are fitted to the groove in the
post, and of sufficient length to reach from one post to
another. They are then introduced one after another till
the walls of the building are completed. These timbers
answer every purpose answered by studs, braces, and
boarding in the English mode of building. Wherever a
window or a door is required, posts are erected, into
which the ends of the timbers are introduced, instead of
the main posts, and thus the required hole is made in the
wall. A post is placed at the centre of each end of the
building which is continued above the beam as high as
the top of the roof is intended to be. A stick of timber is
then laid on the top of these posts reaching from one end

of the building to the other, and forms the ridge pole. The roof is then formed by laying one end of timbers on this ridge pole and the other on the plate till the whole is covered. These timbers answer the purpose of boards on the roofs of English buildings. For shingling cedar barks are used. These barks are taken from the white cedar which is plenty in this part of the country, in the early part of summer. A single piece about 4 to 5 feet in length is pealed from each tree which is left standing. It is a smooth bark, not thick, rather stringy, and not brittle when dry. These barks are put upon the timbers of the roof in the manner of shingles, and are secured by narrow strips of boards which are laid across them and spiked to the timbers. A roof of this kind will last several years. The cracks between the timbers in the walls are plastered with a hard clay which abounds in this country and are then covered with cedar bark in the manner of the roof, if the building is intended for a house. We have now completed the body of our building without the use of boards. Windows are made of the same materials and in the same manner here as in N England, that is, a sash and glass makes a window, excep[t] occasionally a dried deer skin is used in the stead thereof.

"Sashes are made here; glass, nails, and all other foreign materials for building are imported as other foreign goods are. To this post they are brought more than 50 miles of the way *on men's backs*. We come now to the inside of our building where boards are at least convenient. These are all made by hand. The log is cut and hewed on two opposite sides to the thickness of 9 inches or a foot. It is then raised to the height of 6 or 7 feet from the ground and rests upon timbers. Lines are then struck as near to each other as the thickness of the board requires, which the saw is made to follow. One man stands upon the sticks to be sawed, and manages one end of a saw 5 or six feet in length . . . while a second . . . manages the other. The saw operates nearly in the same manner as that of a common saw mill. It is not however confined in a frame like [*manuscript torn*] The timber is cut only with the downward stroke which both the men contribute to produce. Two men will saw from a dozen to 20 of these boards per day, which are usually 10 or 12 feet in length. After our boards are made, floors, partitions, doors &c. can [be] made in this country as well as any other. For purposes of plastering, cementing, &c. clay is used instead of lime. . . . Chimneys are made of stones and clay, the art of brick making not having travelled so high up yet. The manner I cannot now describe. It is not howev[er] like the Yankee manner of building stone chimneys."

Unfortunately he nowhere in his letters describes just how these chimneys were constructed. A contemporary picture of such a chimney is in existence, however, and a reproduction of it incorporated in the wood-cut at the beginning of Chapter V will afford some idea of how it was made.[21]

In 1837 a rough census of the "white inhabitants" on the military reserve and about Fort Snelling was taken by Lieutenant E. K. Smith, who records a "total of 157 souls in no way connected with the military." [22] The fort itself was located in the angle between the Minnesota River (still the St. Peter's at this time) and the Mississippi, on the northern bank of the Minnesota. Just north of the fort, on the west bank of the Mississippi, was "Camp Coldwater," where the troops had been quartered for a time shortly after their arrival in 1819. Here and in its vicinity Smith found eighty-two persons. Across from the fort on the south bank of the Minnesota he found twenty-five residents about Sibley's trading post. Fifty others dwelt in the neighborhood, probably across the Mississippi on the Wisconsin side at "Le Clerc's."

The following year a famous English author, Captain Frederick Marryat, visited Fort Snelling. In the book he published later, *A Diary in America, with Remarks on Its Institutions*, he refers to the voyageur hamlet:[23] "The French Canadians, who are here employed by the Fur Company, are a strange set of people. There is no law here, or appeal to law; yet they submit to authority, and are managed with very little trouble. They bind themselves for three years, and during that time . . . they work diligently and faithfully; ready at all seasons and at all hours, and never complaining, although the work is often extremely hard. Occasionally they return to Canada with their earnings, but the major part have connected themselves with Indian women and have numerous families; for children in this fine climate are so numerous, that they almost appear to spring from the earth."

Who these early dwellers at St. Peter's were can be determined to a considerable extent by consulting the baptismal register in the cathedral at Dubuque, Iowa. In the year 1839 the good Bishop of Dubuque, Mathias Loras, was informed, probably by the great scientist Joseph N. Nicollet, who had been spending some years about the upper reaches of the Mississippi, that there were members of his flock at St. Peter's. Accordingly, early that summer he went up by steamboat to St. Peter's to make a visitation. Writing to his sister on July 26, he mentioned that "the Catholics of St. Peter's amounted to one hundred and eighty-five." [24] His list of baptisms, confirmations, and marriages reveals the fact that nearly every patronymic was French. Some of them were Brunelle, Prévot, Rèché, Dejarlat, Rondeau, Brissette, Papin, Le Claire, and Bouiderot. A study of these families shows that most of them were of voyageur origin.[25]

One of the best-known residents was Michel Le Claire, or Le Clere in the spelling of Americans with but a slender knowledge of French. To him is ascribed the honor of having been the first settler of the "Grand Marais," now within the limits of St. Paul, and probably thus the first settler on the site of the future capital of the state of Minnesota. When not employed as a voyageur, he was a carpenter, for it is recorded that he built a house for Alexander Faribault, a famous trader of the region, and that he made the doors and sashes for the home of another settler, Vetal Guerin.

Guerin was another voyageur, like his father before him. Born in Saint Rémi, Canada, in 1812, in 1832 he engaged himself to the American Fur Company for three years. After his term had expired, he settled near the trading post at St. Peter's and did odd jobs there and at Traverse des Sioux, another hamlet of voyageurs near the site of St. Peter, Minnesota, for three or four more years. Then he moved across the Mississippi and became one of the earliest residents of St. Paul.

Another early settler east of the Mississippi at the Entry was Joseph Turpin, a native of Montreal. His voyaging habits had taken him to Prairie du Chien, to the Red River Settlement for several years, and finally to Fort Snelling about 1831. With him on the long trek across the prairies had come in all probability another Canadian voyageur by the name of Chorette. Shortly after came another migration, among whom was Joseph Rondo or, probably, Rondeau. Rondeau's career had been that of the typical voyageur. He was born near Montreal in 1797. As a lad of seventeen or eighteen he had entered the fur trade as an employee of the Hudson's Bay Company, which in 1821 had coalesced with the great employer of voyageurs, the Northwest Company. Rondeau had paddled canoes across the breadth of the North American continent; had wintered on Fraser River, at Great Slave Lake, at Fort Edmonton, and elsewhere; and at last had settled at that favorite haven of voyageurs, the Red River Settlement. There he had married Josephine Boileau, a Kutenai half-breed, and had settled on a farm. Doubtless he would have continued there to the end of the story if plagues of mice, drought, grasshoppers, and floods, not to mention the onerous restrictions of the Hudson's Bay Company, had not beset the little colony and forced the numerous treks to St. Peter's and the "States." In 1835 he left, in company with many others, for St. Peter's. Some of the names of his companions are interesting—Gervais, Labissionère, Beaumette, and Dufeni. Rondeau, like others, settled under the walls of the fort and, like them, was ejected in the spring of 1840.

For tragedy found its way even to voyageur communities. Among the idyllic conditions at the Entry was one that brought disaster. The voyageurs had learned from their *bourgeois* how to traffic in fire water, and they were not long settled in their Eden, where land cost them nothing and where a benign government protected them with a stout fort, when they began to eke out their slender incomes by selling whiskey. It was not only to the great bands of Sioux and Chippewa that came often to visit the agent at the fort, but, alas, to the military also, that they offered their wares.

One of the worst offenders was a voyageur by the name of Pierre Parrant. Like the brethren of his profession, he had seen much of the continent, for he had been born in Canada and had lived at Sault Ste. Marie, at St. Louis, and at Prairie du Chien. From these points he had doubtless gone on extensive canoe trips. About 1832 he settled at the Entry, where he acquired among his fellows the sobriquet, *L'Œil de Cochon*, or "Pig's Eye," because of the ill-favored aspect of his single eye.

In 1837 the pressure of the frontier forced the United States Government to conclude treaties with the Sioux and Chippewa for the purchase of their lands east of the Mississippi as far north as the mouth of the Crow Wing River. In anticipation of these treaties, which would allow settlers to take up land, and because the authorities at the fort were obliging the settlers on the reserve to move, Parrant established himself across from the fort on the east bank of the Mississippi. Here, at Fountain Cave, within the present limits of the city of St. Paul, he built his cabin, close enough to the fort to attract its occupants, yet just outside the lines of the military reserve, as he believed. Indians and soldiers were not slow in finding him, and he and others became a great stench in the nostrils of the army officers at the fort. Accordingly the lines of the reserve were arbitrarily extended to take in the claims of Parrant and others who had settled near by, and in May, 1840, the poor settlers saw their cherished homes demolished by troops from the fort, when resistance was offered to the order to remove from the reserve. Parrant himself did not suffer with the others, for he had already lost his claim by another turn of Fortune's wheel. He had signed (with a cross) a note promising to pay Guillaume Beaumette ninety dollars. As security he had given his claim. The document itself is interesting:[26] "Know all men by these presents, that I, Pierre Parrant, residing near the entry of the Saint Peter's River, and in Wisconsin Territory, do hereby make over, transfer and quit-claim to Guillaume Beaumette, of said Saint Peter's, all my right, title, and interest in and to all that tract or portion of land which I, the said Parrant, now reside upon and occupy, at the cave, so-called, about four miles below Fort Snelling. . . ." Beaumette was also a voyageur who had migrated to the Red River about 1819. He was a stone mason and helped build the stone fort there.

Having lost his claim, Parrant moved down the river a little way and set up his grog shop once more, in the heart of the present business district of St. Paul. Still later he moved to the present Pig's Eye, then known as "Grand Marais." His notoriety may be judged from the fact that thereafter the place took his name. Here was

THE VOYAGEUR AS SETTLER

quite a community of voyageurs: the Le Claire already mentioned; Amable Turpin, whose voyaging had taken him from Montreal to Mackinac, thence to Green Bay, and finally to St. Peter's before he settled near Fort Snelling and became the man who was always sent by the American Fur Company on its most difficult and hazardous trips; Charles Mousseau, born in Canada in 1807; Denis Cherrier, whose violin enlivened many an early dance in St. Paul; and a number of other voyageurs.

As a result of Bishop Loras' pastoral call of 1839, Father Lucian Galtier was sent to care for the little flock of voyageurs that had been so recently discovered by the Church. His residence was established at Mendota, but it was not long before he discovered the little settlements on the other side of the river. "I deemed it my duty," he wrote later, "to visit occasionally those families, and set to work to choose a suitable spot for a church. Three different points were offered, one called La Point Basse, or Point Le Claire . . . but I objected because that locality was the very extreme end of the new settlement, and in high water, was exposed to inundation. . . . Two miles and a half further up on his elevated claim, . . . Mr. Charles Mousseau offered me an acre of his ground, but the place did not suit my purpose. I was truly looking ahead, thinking of the future as well as of the present. Steamboats could not stop there; the bank was too steep, the place on the summit of the hill too restricted; communication difficult with the other parts of the settlement up and down the river. After mature deliberation, I resolved to put up the church at the nearest possible point to the cave. . . . I accepted the extreme eastern part of Mr. Vetal's claim, and the extreme west of Mr. Gervais'. . . . I had, previously to this time, fixed my residence at Saint Peter's and as the name of Paul is generally connected with that of Peter . . . I called it Saint Paul." [27] The church's name soon attached itself to the hamlet. When the land had been surveyed and opened to settlement in 1848, the hoards of incoming settlers took up land near or in the hamlet. Thus was a great city born. Thus, too, it was named, because of voyageurs and their need of religious instruction.

Sibley has left us some indication of the quaintness and fun-loving qualities of his voyageur neighbors. In his reminiscences he tells how they looked to him as the serfs of old England looked to their lords. He was consulted on all matters of importance. Thus in 1848, when the land upon which St. Paul has arisen was offered for sale by the United States Land Office, the squatters there realized that they must attend the sale at Stillwater if they were to keep possession of their lands. But who could accomplish such a weighty matter for them so well as Monsieur Sibley? Accordingly it was Sibley who did the bidding, surrounded by the squatters, each provided with a big stick with which to wreak vengeance on any speculator who should dare to bid higher than their chosen representative. After the sale was over, Sibley presented each man with a deed to his land. It was only after a long delay and much persuasion that he could induce them to take their deeds. Ignorant of American ways, they felt that their homes would be more secure in the hands of Monsieur Sibley than in their own.[28]

Sibley enjoyed contacts with these light-hearted, polite, vivacious French Canadians. In his reminiscences he devotes considerable space to them. The following extract will show something of his own fun-loving personality as well as that of the men whom he mentions: [29]

"Joseph Laframboise who died several years since, was a capital mimic, spoke with fluency four or five different languages and he was withal an inveterate practical joker. He and Alex. Faribault were wont to amuse themselves at the expense of Labathe, who was simple minded, honest sort of a man, and by no means a match for his tormentors.

"A standing jest at his cost, was his experience at a tea party at Fort Snelling. The trio mentioned was invited by Capt. G. of the army to take tea and spend the evening at his quarters, and the invitation was accepted. It was in the month of July, and the weather intensely warm. The party in due time were seated around the table, and the cups and saucers were of the generous proportions ignored in these modern and more fashionable days. It should be premised that Indian etiquette demands on all festive occasions, that the visitor shall leave nothing unconsumed of the meat or drink placed before him. The large cup filled with tea was handed to Labathe and the contents disposed of. The poor fellow at that time could speak nothing more of English than the imperfect sentence 'Tank you.' When his cup was empty, Mrs. G., who was at the head of the table, said in her suave and gentle manner, 'Mr. Labathe, please take some more tea.' Labathe responded, 'Tank you, madam,' which being interpreted by the waiter to mean an assent, he took the cup and handed it to the hostess, and Mr. Labathe was forthwith freshly supplied with the hot liquid. Labathe managed to swallow it, sweltering meanwhile with the fervent heat of the evening, and again he was requested to permit his cup to be replenished. 'Tank you, madam,' was the only reply the victim could give. Seven great vessels full of the boiling tea were thus successively poured down his throat, Laframboise and Faribault meantime almost choking with suppressed laughter. For the eighth time the waiter approached to seize the cup, when the aboriginal politeness which had enabled Labathe to bear up amid his sufferings gave way entirely, and rising from his seat to the amazement of the company, he exclaimed frantically, 'Laframboise, pour l'amour de bon Dieu, pourquoi ne dites vous pas a madame, que je n'en veut point davantage.' (Laframboise, for the love of God, why do you not tell madame that I do not wish for any more tea.) Labathe never heard the last of that scene while he lived.

"The old man Roque, mentioned as residing near Lake Pepin, afforded another instance of the inconvenience of not being able to speak English. He knew one compound word only, and that was roast beef, which he called 'Ros-bif.' He accompanied a Dakota delegation to Washington City on one occasion, and when asked at the public houses what he would be helped to, he could only say Ros-bif! So that the unhappy old gentleman, although longing for a chance at the many good things that he would have preferred, performed the round trip on 'Ros-bif.' "

*   *   *

The story of the Red River Settlement is not only the most unique chapter in the account of the voyageurs; it is also the explanation, in large measure, of their disappearance. It centers about that grim struggle between the Hudson's Bay Company and the Northwest Company which deluged the Northwest with blood, destroyed a peaceful community twice, and ended in the consolidation of the two great monopolies. The bitterness of that contest can hardly be imagined today.

From the days of Pierre Esprit Radisson and the founding of the Honourable Company of Adventurers of England Trading into Hudson's Bay until towards the close of the War of American Independence there had been little serious opposition to the Company's monopoly of the fur-trading areas about the frozen sea. Even after the founding of the Canadian concern, the Northwest Company, there was a period of some thirty years before it became obvious that the furs of the central portion of the continent were rapidly being depleted and that both companies must find new areas for exploitation. Then commenced the struggle. At first the advantage was all with the Montreal traders, despite their long line of unbelievably difficult transportation. Indeed, this very line of communication was a source of strength to the Northwest Company, for in order to maintain it they had developed a class of servants who proved the finest kind of weapon in the warfare with the "English," as their rivals were known locally. The latter had made use of Orkney men for the most part, but, excellent as they were, they were no match for French-Canadian voyageurs in withstanding the rigors of trade in the far North, especially in the wooded areas, and in establishing happy contacts with the natives.

When, therefore, the odds seemed going against the Honourable Company in its struggle to expand into the wooded valley of the Churchill River, hitherto regarded by the Northwesters as their sacred precinct, the members took stock in thorough, English fashion and reached certain revolutionary conclusions. One was that voyageurs should be pitted against voyageurs. This meant, however, more men and hence more provisions. Cheaper food and supplies than those hitherto brought by way of the Bay from England must be secured for these tried voyageurs from Montreal. Hence the conception of a colony near enough to the scene of warfare to be the source of supply.

Thus it came about that the noble Earl of Selkirk, the largest stockholder in the Hudson's Bay Company, was granted the District of Assiniboia in 1811 for another of his many philanthropic schemes. Probably philanthropic motives *were* mixed with other purposes in His Lordship's mind, but the correspondence of the Company at this time leaves no room to doubt what *its* aim was. One of the provisions of the grant is interesting in a study of the voyageur. Lord Selkirk was to set apart one-tenth of the district "to the use of such person or persons being or having been in the service or employ of the said Governor and Company for a term of not less than three years immediately preceding." Of this A. S. Morton says: "The first intention of this condition was that the settlement should be reinforced by such retiring servants as should choose to settle in it with their squaws and their dusky families. We may infer that as the company was contemplating employing French Canadians they thought of the Red River Settlement as becoming a retiring ground for them also and in the more distant future offering a reserve of the sort of servants that had contributed so much to the success of the rival traders from Montreal." [30] This long look into the future revealed half-breed voyageurs from the colony in places which, but for this scheme, might have been occupied by their cousins from the little hamlets on the mighty St. Lawrence.

So it came to pass that the Hudson's Bay Company took to heart the lesson that canny John Jacob Astor, the president of the American Fur Company, had learned early in his struggle with the same rivals, the Northwest Company. Until the American Fur Company passed out of existence in the forties, Astor, and later his pupil and successor, Ramsay Crooks, recruited their canoemen and winterers from Montreal. It may not be amiss here to quote Crooks' convincing argument to his chief when the latter was getting Congress to legislate the Northwest Company out of the upper Mississippi Valley just after the War of 1812. Crooks, being then an agent at Mackinac and in close touch with the actual trade, perceived that Congress must make an exception in the case of voyageurs when passing a law excluding all foreigners from the American fur trade. He therefore wrote: "It will still be good policy to admit freely & without the least restraint the Canadian Boatmen. these people are indispensable to the successful prosecution of the trade, their places cannot be supplied by Americans, who are for the most part are [*sic*] too independent to submit quietly to a proper controul, and who can gain any where a subsistence much superior to a man of the interior and although the body of the Yankee can resist as much hardship as any man, tis only in the Canadian we find that temper of mind, to render him patient docile and perserving. in short they are a people harmless in themselves whose habits of submission fit them peculiarly for our business and if guided as it is my wish they should be, will never give just cause of alarm to the Government of the Union it is of course your object to exclude every foreigner except those for whom you obtain licenses." [31]

Crooks' advice was followed, and the American Fur Company employed Canadian voyageurs for twenty years and more after the coalition of the Northwest Company and the Hudson's Bay Company brought about the practical abandonment by English and Canadian traders of the long canoe route which was one of the chief *raisons d'être* of the voyageur. Then the failure of the American Fur Company, the advance of the frontier into Wisconsin, Minnesota, and neighboring regions, and the consequent abandonment by Americans of the old canoe route from Montreal in favor of steamboats and railroads sounded the final death knell of the voyageurs as a class. As a class they were gone by 1850. The Hudson's Bay Company still employed boatmen and canoemen, but they were Orkney men, half-breeds, and Iroquois now in the main, recruited largely from the Red River area.

To return to Selkirk's scheme and what came of it. His twofold plan of settling needy Europeans in his colony and making it the haven of refuge for the "great body of vagabond Canadians" he mentions in one of his letters was succeeding even at the time of his death in 1820.

One writer estimates the number of "supernumeraries" of the two companies there as fifteen hundred, "far exceeding all the settlers ever brought 'under the auspices of the Earl of Selkirk.' " [32]

In the years of famine, drought, floods, and pestilence that the little colony endured during the first two decades of its existence, many of the Europeans and some of the voyageurs migrated to St. Peter's and the "States." Yet it lived and eventually prospered. After one of the largest migrations, the Roman Catholic bishop wrote to his superior in Quebec that the loss had been more than offset by the providential arrival of a large body of voyageurs from the far Northwest.[33] It is not necessary here to go into the sordid warfare against the colony that was waged by the Northwest Company from 1811 till coalition. Twice the settlement was destroyed, in 1815 and 1816. In this warfare the companies relied to no slight degree on their voyageurs. Under the grim relentlessness of their *bourgeois* they did their hideous work thoroughly. *La Grenouillère* was the name by which they knew the famous battle of Seven Oaks, when Governor Semple and others were killed by them in 1816. Finally came peace with coalition. The expanded Company found itself embarrassed with servants, of both *bourgeois* and voyageur rank. Arrangements were made with both groups to settle in the colony. The voyageurs were given lands on the east bank of the Red River, and their expenses to the colony from the interior forts were defrayed. With them, of course, came their squaws and numerous half-breed children.

It is our good fortune that a contemporary noted and

wrote down how certain of these voyageurs made their way to their new home and the type of men they were. Alexander Ross, who likewise settled in the colony and became its historian, was on his way thither soon after the coalition.[34] At Norway House, one of the chief northern posts, he found a company of "infirm and superannuated servants of the Company," of whom a large percentage were destined for the same haven of refuge as himself. "Hearing that I was on my way thither," he writes, "rather than wait the Company's regular conveyance they applied for a passage with me, and promised to work their way." He surveyed them and found that "as far as appearances went they seemed to be worthless." But they assured him that they were experienced hands and, indeed, boasted of their ability in handling boats. He finally took six and started out. Of these six he has left a detailed picture:

"And as it may be interesting to the reader to know something of the character of these superannuated sons of the wilderness, we shall sketch them. In the first place, then, three of them were able to help themselves, if not others; but as for the other three, their day was gone by: all of them were poor, more or less mutilated, infirm, and clogged with large families. But they were, nevertheless, very talkative, and independent in their way—North-Westers to the backbone; they had long yarns to tell of their past lives, as all voyageurs have, and were full of life and spirits.

"Of this motley crew, we shall notice some striking peculiarities in the more aged and experienced of them: one was blind of an eye, and lame from having been

THE VOYAGEUR AS SETTLER

frost-bitten; another was a cripple from the same cause; and a third had lost his thumb by accident. The last of this trio, the patriarchal head, had reached the wrong side of seventy years; and his wife, from infirmity, walked on crutches; but the froward old man, still active for his age, was as waggish and thoughtless as a youth of fifteen.

"One day, while in a jocular mood, the old man began to talk over his past life: it was full of adventure, and may appear amusing to others, as it did to us. I shall give it, as nearly as I can, in his own words.

" 'I have now,' said he, 'been forty-two years in this country. For twenty-four I was a light canoe-man; I required but little sleep, but sometimes got less than I required. No portage was too long for me; all portages were alike. My end of the canoe never touched the ground till I saw the end of it. Fifty songs a day were nothing to me. I could carry, paddle, walk, and sing with any man I ever saw. During that period, I saved the lives of ten Bourgeois, and was always the favourite, because when others stopped to carry at a bad step, and lost time, I pushed on—over rapids, over cascades, over chutes; all were the same to me. No water, no weather, ever stopped the paddle or the song. I had twelve wives in the country; and was once possessed of fifty horses, and six running dogs, trimmed in the first style. I was then like a Bourgeois, rich and happy: no Bourgeois had better-dressed wives than I; no Indian chief finer horses; no white man better-harnessed or swifter dogs. I beat all Indians at the race, and no white man ever passed me in the chase. I wanted for nothing; and I spent all my earnings in the enjoyment of pleasure. Five hundred pounds, twice told, have passed through my hands; although now I have not a spare shirt to my back, nor a penny to buy one. Yet, were I young again, I should glory in commencing the same career again, I would willing spend another half-century in the same fields of enjoyment. There is no life so happy as a voyageur's life; none so independent; no place where a man enjoys so much variety and freedom as in the Indian country. Huzza! Huzza! pour le pays sauvage!'" Clearly Baker in the opening quotation of this volume had this passage in mind.

Despite these voyageurs' protestations of expertness in handling a boat, the sequence of events proved them very awkward and incompetent. Indeed, says Ross, they were as awkward in managing a boat as they were adroit in handling a canoe. A storm arose on Lake Winnipeg which nearly ended the careers of all in the boat. "They lost all presence of mind, and in their confusion, let go the sail!" says Ross of his companions. "Those men who had but a short time before boasted so much of their skill and prowess among lakes, now abandoned their posts and began to count their beads and cross themselves: only one man stood at his duty; yet Providence favoured us, and we reached the island in safety." It took another storm, however, to teach the voyageurs that *traverses* made in boats in fine weather were one thing, and in foul weather quite another. Thereafter they were content to take the more tedious but safer route along the shore. In so doing they passed a small island on which "a fine tall pine, trimmed into a maypole, with its broom head, was conspicuous at a distance." One of the men pointed to it, remarking, "That's a lop-stick I trimmed eighteen years ago."

En route the men showed some of their characteristic traits. One of these was building air castles for the future. When it became obvious that they had been saved from a great peril, they became gay and voluble. The next evening at the encampment "they passed the evening cracking their jokes and forming new plans and projects for enjoying life in Red River. One observed, 'I will have my house built with double rooms'; another, 'I will have my rooms ceiled and painted.' It was really amusing to hear men without a shilling in the world enjoying life in their airy dreams, where nothing was real."

One of the stories told that evening related to a trip taken by the narrator from Fort Alexander to Jack River a few years before. A fearful storm arose, and it seemed almost impossible to reach the nearest shore. "Some baled out the water, while others kept a sharp look-out, which amounted to nothing; for except the lightning flashed, no one could see another in the boat, and we every moment fancied we heard the rush of waves dashing on the rocks ahead of us. Some said they saw the rocks, and called to prepare for the danger: death stared us in the face." Then an unusual phenomenon occurred. "In the midst of this confusion a . . . meteor of fire, resembling a lighted candle, settled on the left end of the yard-arm. Supposing it to have been fire communicated by the lightening, we secured our guns under the covering; this done, another light settled on the right end of the yard, and immediately afterwards another showed itself on the top of the mast. The lights were rather pale, and of a reddish hue. All the three continued bright and steady for more than half an hour, without shifting. . . . At length they dropped off and disappeared." Of course the voyageurs were terrified. Soon, however, they were aware of bushes and realized they were safe near some shore away from the fury of the storm. Then, in characteristic fashion, they set about linking the fires with their deliverance. "Some said it was two of the Apostles, Peter and Paul, guarding the Virgin Mary; others, that the appearance was ominous, and presaged that three of us would be drowned; while some said that only three out of the nine who were in the boat would survive the storm. We then knelt down, took our rosaries, and ran over our Ave-Marias and Pater-nosters; praying, some to one saint, some to another: I prayed to the Virgin Mary. This done, we made a solemn vow, that if we lived to see a priest we would have a grand mass offered up as a thanksgiving to the Virgin Mary for our miraculous deliverance." Ross goes on to remark that these vows, so often made by voyageurs in moments of peril, were always religiously observed.

For years the dusky families of the voyageurs, inhabitants of the posts, had been regarded as an ever-increasing menace to the Hudson's Bay and Northwest companies. Now they were collected at Red River and formed a nation no less picturesque than, though notably different from, their French-Canadian fathers. They were known as *gens libre* ("freemen"), as *métis*, and as *bois brulés*. From their ranks in future years the Hudson's Bay Company was to recruit its canoe- and boatmen, who proved no less fitted for their work than their fathers be-for them. Instead of being hired by the year, however, the half-breeds were usually engaged for specific journeys or to carry the freight to the distant posts by contract lot. They were characterized by the same light-heartedness and the same lack of responsibility that had endeared their fathers to all who traveled with them. From their mothers they inherited a love of the buffalo chase. Their journeys onto the Dakota plains to hunt the buffalo have been described many times.

Major Samuel Woods, who was sent by the Secretary of War in 1849 to inspect the valley of the Red River of the North preparatory to establishing a military post there, found these half-breeds worthy of several pages of his report on the expedition. "The greater part of these people," he writes, "are descendants of the Cana-dian French. They speak the French language, are nearly all Catholics, with mild and gentle manners, great vi-vacity, generous and honest in their transactions, and disposed to be a civil and orderly community. They are hale and hearty, robust men, evidently accustomed to hardships and exposure, to which they submit cheer-fully. . . . They now devote themselves entirely to fur hunting and the chase. . . . They go to the plains in the Spring and Fall, in parties of from 300 to 500 hunters. They appoint, before going out, a captain who controls and directs their hunts, which assume rather the character of an expedition than the unregulated ex-cursions of Indians or whites when abroad with such objects. Their families go with them, and each family has from one to ten carts."

Accompanying his report is a letter from the Reverend Georges Antoine Belcourt, a French-Canadian priest who labored for years among the Red River *métis*. It describes in great detail the manner in which one of these chases was conducted. Belcourt accompanied the hunters and their families and watched how they formed their 213 carts into three long columns, one of ox-drawn vehicles, the other two of *charrettes* drawn by horses. These carts, a Red River product, were made entirely of wood and rent the air with the squeaks of their ungreased axles as they moved out onto the prairies. At night they were formed into a corral and served as protection against the Indians.

When scouts reported that herds had been sighted, cries of *"la vache, la vache!"* were heard through the encampment, and riders mounted and departed "beaming with the keenest joy," as Belcourt writes in French words that sparkle in remembrance of that lively scene. But no words can describe adequately the confusion and danger when the herd was charged by the hunters. These, on horses trained to respond to the slightest pressure or even to pursue the buffalo without guidance, came up with streaming sashes and mouths full of shot, and fired round after round from their awkward guns. No one but a *métis*, or perhaps an Indian, could have used these weapons with such speed and accuracy while charging at full tilt. Then came the work of cutting up the slaughtered animals, the selection of only the finer portions, and the transportation to the encampment. There the women took charge of the work of drying, pounding, and otherwise preparing the meat for future use. After weeks of this nomadic life the train wound its slow way back to Pembina laden with the remains of 1,776 *vaches*, that is to say, 228 *taureaux*, or leather bags of pemmican; 1,213 rolls of dried meat; 166 *boskoyas*, or bags of grease; and 556 bladders of marrow grease.[35]

Though at first entirely unlettered and pagan, these *métis* were soon supplied with schools and priests. As in the case of St. Peter's, voyageurs and their religious needs called the attention of the Church to this region far beyond her most distant outpost. On April 4, 1816, Lord Selkirk wrote the following in a letter to the Bishop of Quebec:[36]

"I have been informed by Mr. McDonell, late governor of the settlement on Red River that he had some Conversation with your Lordship last autumn, to recommend that a missionary should be sent into that country, to give spiritual aid to a great number of Canadians who have established themselves there, & who lead a wandering life in the manner of the savages, with whose women they have formed irregular connections. . . . I have been lately informed . . . that your Lordship has it in contemplation to send two ecclesiastics this summer to pay a visit to Lake Superior & Lake La Pluie [Rainy Lake] during the season when the voyageurs in the service of the North West Company resort there from the interior. As these people also are very much in want of wholesome advice, I am happy to hear of such a plan being in agitation . . . but on the other hand, a Missionary sent from Canada on a summer visit to these posts, would have no intercourse with the great body of the vagabond Canadians, to whom I have alluded, who are not in the service of the North West nor any other company, & who having renounced all idea of returning to their native places are more particularly in want of spiritual aid. . . . Mr. McDonell is to set out as soon as the ice will permit, in a light canoe, with which he expects to reach Red River about the end of May, or in the very beginning of June. He would be happy to have the company of the Missionary, who would thus have an opportunity of being for several weeks among the wandering Canadians of Red River before the period when any great number of the Northwest Company's voyageurs can be expected at Lake La Pluie or Lake Superior."

Some say that it was a voyageur, Jean Baptiste Lagimonière, who won the Earl's interest in sending missionaries to the settlement. This maternal grandfather of Louis Riel was born at Maskinongé. After some experience as a voyageur in the Northwest, he, unlike most of his fellows, returned to Canada for a bride. Their child, born in 1808 at Pembina, was probably the second (and the first legitimate) white child born on the banks of the Red River. In 1815, when the little colony was suffering from the horrors of warfare, a courier was needed to carry dispatches to Lord Selkirk, who had just arrived in the East on his first visit to his colony. An experienced and responsible man was needed, one who would make the trip in the shortest possible time and evade all efforts of the opposition to intercept his messages. For this hazardous undertaking Lagimonière was chosen.[37]

For years voyageurs had been used to carry the mail from the interior posts to Canada, and from one post to another. Probably Lagimonière had come to the atten-

tion of his superiors as expressman. Roderick Mackenzie
tells us that "the first winter Express from the Interior
for the Lake Superior, which was in 1798, left Fort
Chipewean on the 1st Octr and arrived at the Sault St.
Marie's on the 17th May following—229 days." Even
more famous was the "Inland Packet." [38] These were
perilous and lonely enterprises. Storms must be braved,
nights must be spent in the open when spirit thermom-
eters registered as low as sixty degrees below zero, hazardous rapids must be run, wild beasts must be warded
off or killed, and Indians must be treated in just the
way to ensure their friendship. Usually the messenger
visited most of the posts, carrying mail to winterbound
and lonesome *bourgeois* and *commis* and taking their
replies, for which he waited. The importance of the dispatches must not be overlooked, for on them the chiefs
of the trade based their calculations for the next year's
operations. If great speed were necessary, the record of
the first courier *could* be reduced by two-thirds. Thus in
1834, when Captain Back, the Arctic explorer who was
searching for Captain Ross, wished to know the fate of
his friend, a courier bearing news of Ross' safe arrival
in England passed from Lake Superior to Fort Chipewyan in only seventy-four days.

Lagimonière's journey took him eighteen hundred
miles from the colony in the dead of winter. Thirty-six
days after his departure from Fort Douglas he handed
over the precious dispatches to the Earl, having slipped
by all the opposition's men. "The Scotch lord was so
touched by this act of devotion that he could not help
asking what favor he wished in return. 'Priests: give us

priests,' said the humble Canadian. Then Selkirk asked Plessis." [39]

That summer Father Pierre Antoine Tabeau set forth. Though his instructions were to do as Lord Selkirk had suggested, he reached Rainy Lake just when the reports of the battle of Seven Oaks arrived and contented himself with a mission to the voyageurs there and at Fort William. His report of his summer's work did not favor the permanent mission at Red River that the bishop, as well as the Earl, wished to see established there. For his partiality to the known viewpoint of the Northwest Company, which saw a menace in anything permanent at Red River, he was soundly berated by his ordinary in a letter revealing much indignation.[40] In 1818 Father Joseph Norbert Provencher, accompanied by Father Sévère Dumoulin and a school teacher, William Edge, traveled the long canoe route with a body of voyageurs and arrived finally at Red River. On their journey they had ministered to the needs of several groups of voyageurs whom they had encountered.

The story of Father, later Bishop, Provencher and his several assistants at Red River is one of heroic self-sacrifice, discouragement, and final success. It was at "The Forks," as the junction of the Red and Assiniboine rivers was known locally, that Provencher worked, almost entirely with the Catholic voyageurs, their Indian or half-breed wives, and their children. Dumoulin and Edge and a number of their associates and successors labored at Pembina, a number of miles up the river and nearer the plains. This was a favorite gathering place for voyageurs and *métis* because of the nearness of the buffaloes. Among the Protestant colonists from Europe other clergymen worked, but they seldom attempted to interfere with the priests' work among the Canadians and half-breeds.

One of Bishop Provencher's hopes was to build a stone cathedral. Early in the thirties it became possible to erect this building. It is this church of which the poet Whittier sings in his well-known poem.

THE RED RIVER VOYAGEUR

Out and in the river is winding
 The links of its long, red chain,
Through belts of dusky pine-land
 And gusty leagues of plain.

Only, at times, a smoke-wreath
 With the drifting cloud-rack joins,—
The smoke of the hunting-lodges
 Of the wild Assiniboins!

Drearily blows the north-wind
 From the land of ice and snow;
The eyes that look are weary
 And heavy the hands that row.

And with one foot on the water,
 And one upon the shore,
The Angel of Shadow gives warning
 That day shall be no more.

Is it the clang of wild-geese?
 Is it the Indian's yell,
That lends to the voice of the north-wind
 The tones of a far-off bell?

The voyageur smiles as he listens
 To the sound that grows apace;
Well he knows the vesper ringing
 Of the bells of St. Boniface.

The bells of the Roman Mission,
That call from their turrets twain,
To the boatman on the river,
To the hunter on the plain!

For his mason, Provencher selected an erstwhile voyageur, Jean Baptiste Charbonneau. Since it is very seldom that a voyageur's life can be outlined throughout its entire course, for voyageurs were men without education or other means of leaving a record of their careers, it may be well to take this opportunity to tell the full life history of one member of the class whose record has been preserved.[41]

Charbonneau was born at Boucherville in the province of Quebec on December 25, 1795. His father, a simple farmer, was Joseph Charbonneau; his mother's maiden name was Marguerite Lamoureux. There were ten other children in the family. When Jean Baptiste was twelve years of age, he was apprenticed to a master mason in Montreal, and there he remained for four years. Then, the War of 1812 breaking out, he enlisted and fought in the engagement at Châteauguay. He also served on the River Raisin campaign and at Chambly. After the war he was discontented and dreamed of following in the footsteps of his grandfather, a voyageur. It was with Colin Robertson's famous brigade of voyageurs which left Montreal in the spring of 1815 to fight for the Hudson's Bay Company against their rivals that Jean Baptiste departed for the *pays d'en haut*. After the usual "march" he reached Lake Winnipeg, fifty days from Montreal. But he was not destined to remain with those whose business it was to resuscitate the colony and pro-

tect it from the Northwest Company. He was sent first
to Jack River. On this trip he was left on a peninsula
far from any post while his companions went on a day's
trip to another spot to trade with the Indians. He had
no firearms or other means of supplying himself with
food. After a little it became apparent that something
had happened to his comrades. Days passed. Famine and
its attendant calamities threatened what his fate might
be. Only by great good fortune did a canoe carrying
some *bourgeois* pass and discover him, almost dead with
hunger. He never learned the fate of his comrades. His
next assignment was to York Factory on Hudson Bay.
A month later he was sent to Isle-à-la-Crosse, in the heart
of the area so hotly contested at this time by the two companies. Most of the remainder of his service of many
years was spent at this post.

Since Charbonneau was not of the great stature and
force that were required for the battles fought between
the servants of the two companies, he was used as a
courier. This, however, was nearly as dangerous a service
as that of his comrades of more heroic proportions, for
it was to the advantage of the enemy to intercept messages and imprison and mistreat couriers of the opposition. Once he returned to his post to find it in the hands
of the enemy, who at once seized him and placed him
with the rest of the prisoners. But too much food and too
many guards were necessary to keep these prisoners, and
so they were removed to a desolate post, La Ronge, two
hundred miles distant. Here, on a large island in the lake,
the prisoners were left with only a few hatchets, fish-
hooks, and firearms. For them the outlook was not happy

when the little game and few hooks should be gone. Fortunately a truce was arranged between the two companies, and after two weeks canoes were sent to rescue them.

On one of his long journeys Charbonneau and his companion were visited in their encampment by an Indian who begged for powder. After a little had been given him, he opened his sack and proceeded to make a meal of the meat it contained. It did not take the two whites long to see that it was human flesh. Nor was the realization long in reaching them that with the powder they had given him they were more or less in his power. Next morning, after a sleepless night, they slipped away before he awakened. He followed them for three days, trying to ambush them, but in the end they escaped to a post.

Like most voyageurs, Charbonneau had his experiences in blizzards on the prairies. Safety lay in remaining encamped. Once he lay three days in a blizzard waiting for a respite, while his dogs became more and more ravenous and he himself was almost without food. At another time his dogs gave out on a long trip, and he and his companions were obliged to harness themselves to the sled and drag it for three weeks across the wilderness.

After fifteen years of this life he had a great desire to settle at Red River, especially since he had not seen a priest in all this time and many things lay sore on his conscience. He settled in the little village of St. Boniface and began to cultivate his land. But this was not the life for him, and so, in 1832, he became Provencher's mason for building the cathedral. Of a somewhat explosive and very proud nature, he resented the tall Bishop's efforts to aid his small mason. Once he lost his temper completely and offered to fight when the Bishop made some pleasantry on the subject.

Red River did not hold him long. Like so many of his fellows, he trekked to Minnesota. Here he lived as best he could and where he could, as hunter, fisher, and even as mail-carrier. When the great uprising of the Sioux occurred in 1862, it found him at the mouth of the Redwood River, on the upper waters of the Minnesota River. He and a companion were overtaken by the Sioux as they attempted to escape and were taken prisoners. He was thus a witness of the fiendish work of the savages in massacring the settlers. When General Henry H. Sibley's army arrived and effected the release of the prisoners, Charbonneau returned to St. Boniface to spend the evening of his life. In 1865 he became blind. He died in 1883 at the age of eighty-eight years.

It was characteristic of the voyageurs that they kept their respect for the Church and its ministers even when their work took them into regions where its priests were unknown and where they disobeyed nearly every rule of conduct inculcated by it. Sometimes it happened that a priest traveled part of the long canoe route with a brigade of canoes. In 1821 Father Tabeau, who has already been mentioned, accompanied the brigade that conveyed Dr. Bigsby, the physician and secretary to the British commissioners appointed under the convention of 1818 to survey the boundary between the United States and Canada from Grand Portage to Lake of the Woods. Dr. Bigsby relates how the good father, "a stout, rosy, happy-looking priest of middle age, of unaffected and even polished manners, fond of music, and reasonably so of good living," greeted each voyageur as the brigade started off, having a pleasant word for each.[42] "As soon as we were well settled down in our places, and the canoe began to feel the paddles, Mr. Tabeau, by way of asking a blessing on the voyage, pulled off his hat, and sounded forth a Latin invocation to the Deity, and to a long train of male and female saints, in a loud and full voice, while all the men, at the end of each versicle, made response, 'Qu'il me bénisse.' "

Of course, the priest held a service on Sundays. The description Dr. Bigsby gives of one such gathering affords no little insight into the fundamentals of the voyageur's character. "It being Sunday, Mr. Tabeau had the tent set up; and he dressed an altar within it with crucifix and candles, little pictures, and clean linen cloth. With his singing-boy and bell he performed a religious service, all the *voyageurs* kneeling round the tent door with great seriousness." With this seriousness was mixed a half-superstitious awe. This explains the voyageurs' respect for Latin, "it being the only language the Devil does not understand and cannot learn," according to David Thompson, a renowned trader, geographer, and explorer of the region west of Hudson Bay and Lake Superior.

*   *   *

In all these voyageur hamlets a charming, Arcadian simplicity prevailed. There was time for friendliness, politeness, the trinket or ribbon that added a note of picturesqueness to the attire, a simple faith, and a childlike objectivity. The background of this Norman stock had not prepared them for more endeavor than the immediate present demanded. Hence they kept the friendship of the Indians by taking only the land needed for poorly-kept gardens which American settlers derided. They accepted the Indian at his own valuation, which was not low, whereas the American frontiersman could scarcely find words for his contempt of what he considered a thieving, shiftless, dirty race. They had no social ambitions and accepted as a matter of course the superior standing of their traders. Their magistrates and their priests were all worthy of respect and homage in their eyes. It sometimes happened that their traders were scoundrels and their magistrates ignorant, but who were simple voyageurs to judge of men of such quality?

Many stories are told of one French-Canadian justice at Green Bay, Charles Reaume.[43] In this voyageur community he held an enviable position, though he could read and write but little. Acting under the laws of the territory of Indiana, he nevertheless administered the *coutume de Paris*, as a good descendant of Norman forbears should. Many a voyageur was told peremptorily by this arbitrary lawmaker to obey his *bourgeois* in all cases whatsoever. Before him came one day Boisvert and Crely. Reaume listened to the plaintiff and to the defendant, then rose in all the majesty of the law to pronounce judgement: "You are both wrong. You, Boisvert, you bring me one load of hay, and you, Crely, you bring me one load of wood; and now the matter is settled." Where but among voyageurs could such a justice long be held in awe?

Reaume, like other justices in the fur country, found himself faced again and again with the problem of frontier marriage and divorce. Since priests were seldom if ever seen in these early settlements, men and women lived together without formal marriage. When married under the provisions of the *coutume de Paris*, they were often divorced. Of course, the enormity of their sins was brought forcibly to their attention when a priest *did* come. Thus in 1817 a Catholic priest from St. Louis appeared at the voyageur hamlet of Prairie du Chien and disturbed many domestic arrangements. He found several women living with men other than their husbands, and these he required to return to their former mates. Likewise at the Red River Settlement, Provencher, Dumoulin, and others of the earliest priests were scandalized at the matrimonial arrangements in vogue among the voyageurs. But respect for the orders of the Church was ingrained in the voyageur, and accordingly resident priests seldom had to reprove their flock on this score. As long as a guide in morals was at hand, all went well; it was in his prolonged absence that the voyageur lapsed from grace.

Much more might be written of these three typical voyageur settlements, but it would be mainly but an elaboration of what has already been given. Stress has been laid on this colonizing aspect of the voyageurs because many western towns, even Sault Ste. Marie, St. Paul, and Winnipeg, do not appear to appreciate the rôle played by the voyageurs in locating and beginning them.

IX

PROBABLY the greatest contribution of the voyageur to the development of the continent was the knowledge of the wilderness and its ways that he put freely and with no hope of recognition at the disposal of the great explorers of the West and North. It may be said without fear of gainsay that practically every exploring trip in western Canada after the British conquest made use of voyageurs. The exact proportion of the success of those ventures that was due to them cannot be gauged, but it was great.

Voyageurs were useful in exploration even during the French period. Mention has been made of Radisson's recognition of them. La Vérendrye, Lahontan, Le Sueur, Du Lhut, St. Pierre, Perrot, La Salle, Nicolet, and others must have found them indispensable, since they are mentioned so freely in contemporary documents.

The first explorer of note after the conquest was Alexander Henry. His narrow escape from the general massacre at Mackinac during Pontiac's uprising, his captivity and trading adventures during the next years on Lake Superior, and finally his advance into western Canada by the well-marked route *via* Grand Portage are all described in his book of travels. Now and then he mentions his voyageurs, who must have been his guides, since this was *terra incognita* to him; but his remarks are not sufficient to enable us to gain any real knowledge of their services to him. In one brief passage he pauses in his narrative long enough to pay tribute to his subordinates: "And often, notwithstanding every exertion, the men went supperless to bed. In a situation like this the Canadians are the best men in the world; they rarely murmur at their lot, and their obedience is yielded cheerfully." [1]

Another early explorer was the Massachusetts Yankee, Jonathan Carver. Long maligned, because his plagiarisms ended in casting doubts on the authenticity of any part of his *Narrative*, he has come into his own since the discovery of his diary and the narrative based on it. These are now in the British Museum. We know from them and other documents that he was advance agent and draftsman of a party attempting to find the "Ouragan" River and a waterway to the Pacific in 1766 and 1767. Though his writings mention voyageurs, especially one who accompanied him from Prairie du Chien to the St. Peter's River, again the evidence is too slight to form any estimate of the servant's contribution to the success of his master's journey.

More unique and of more significance because of his explorations was another Yankee, Peter Pond. His description of voyageurs' customs has been given in part in an earlier chapter. His map of the Athabasca region and its environs, prepared, it is said, for the Empress of Russia, was admittedly drawn in part from the accounts of voyageurs. Since this map and Pond's accounts influenced Alexander Mackenzie to his two great exploring trips in the Northwest, the region especially mapped from the voyageurs' accounts, and because of the reputed use of this map by Benjamin Franklin and others in making the treaty of 1783, it is obvious that North America owes much to a number of unknown voyageurs.

Sir Alexander Mackenzie devotes a good deal of space to his voyageurs in the narrative of his explorations of 1789 and 1793. The naming of a mighty stream for him and a baronetcy were his rewards for these arduous adventures, but probably not one reader in a hundred remembers even the names of his voyageurs.

His first trip, down the Mackenzie River, did not require so much of his voyageurs as the second. The perils and the labor of that voyage of exploration are almost unbelievable. Mackenzie himself refers in one of his journal entries to the "inexpressible toil these people had endured, as well as the dangers they had encountered." [2] It must be added that on several occasions only the leader's grim determination to go on held his people to their tasks.

After a winter spent in the mountains on Peace River, Mackenzie with his six voyageurs, Alexander Mackay, and two Indians started on May 9, 1793, in a small birch canoe, twenty-five feet long and so light that "two men could carry her on a good road three or four miles without resting." [3] Two of his men, Joseph Landry and Charles Ducette, had accompanied him on his earlier voyage. His steersman had been with him for five years in that capacity. The pride that he had in his men comes out in the statement: "I had imagined that the Canadians who accompanied me were the most expert canoe-men in the world." [4]

Up the Peace River and over the divide into a small

229

stream, a branch of the Fraser River, running toward the Pacific, they journeyed. From the time they approached the Fraser, hazards, hostility of Indians, toil beyond words, discontent, desertions, and other embarrassments faced the little party. On the small stream already mentioned an unusual accident occurred: [5]

"At an early hour of this morning the men began to cut a road, in order to carry the canoe and lading beyond the rapid; and by seven they were ready. That business was soon effected, and the canoe reladen, to proceed with the current which ran with great rapidity. In order to lighten her, it was my intention to walk with some of the people; but those in the boat with great earnestness requested me to embark, declaring, at the same time, that, if they perished, I should perish with them. I did not then imagine in how short a period their apprehension would be justified. We accordingly pushed off, and had proceeded but a very short way when the canoe struck, and notwithstanding all our exertions, the violence of the current was so great as to drive her sideways down the river, and break her by the first bar, when I instantly jumped into the water, and the men followed my example; but before we could set her straight, or stop her, we came to deeper water, so that we were obliged to re-embark with the utmost precipitation. One of the men who was not sufficiently active, was left to get on shore in the best manner in his power. We had hardly regained our situations when we drove against a rock which shattered the stern of the canoe in such a manner, that it held only by the gunwales, so that the steersman could no longer keep his place. The violence of this stroke drove us to the opposite side of the river, which is but narrow, when the bow met with the same fate as the stern. At this moment the foreman seized on some branches of a small tree in the hope of bringing up the canoe, but such was their elasticity that, in a manner not easily described, he was jerked on shore in an instant, and with a degree of violence that threatened his destruction. But we had no time to turn from our own situation to enquire what had befallen him; for, in a few moments, we came across a cascade which broke several large holes in the bottom of the canoe, and started all the bars, except one behind the scooping seat. If this accident, however, had not happened, the vessel must have been irretrievably over-set. The wreck becoming flat on the water, we all jumped out, while the steersman, who had been compelled to abandon his place, and had not recovered from his fright, called out to his companions to save themselves. My peremptory commands superseded the effects of his fear, and they all held fast to the wreck; to which fortunate resolution we owed our safety, as we should otherwise have been dashed against the rocks by the force of the water, or driven over the cascades. In this condition we were forced several hundred yards, and every yard on the verge of destruction; but, at length, we most fortunately arrived in shallow water and a small eddy, where we were enabled to make a stand, from the weight of the canoe resting on the stones, rather than from any exertions of our exhausted strength. For though our efforts were short, they were pushed to the utmost, as life or death depended on them.

"This alarming scene, with all its terrors and dangers,

occupied only a few minutes; and in the present suspension of it, we called to the people on shore to come to our assistance, and they immediately obeyed the summons. The foreman, however, was the first with us; he had escaped unhurt from the extraordinary jerk with which he was thrown out of the boat, and just as we were beginning to take our effects out of the water, he appeared to give us his assistance."

This accident had such a dampening effect on Mackenzie's men that he was obliged to remind them of their engagement to go with him to the end of his journey: [6] "I also urged the honour of conquering disasters, and the disgrace that would attend them on their return home, without having attained the object of the expedition. Nor did I fail to mention the courage and resolution which was the peculiar boast of the North men; and that I depended on them, at that moment, for the maintenance of their character." Appeals of this sort were seldom made in vain to Northmen, and Mackenzie soon had the satisfaction of promises to go wherever he might lead. Appeals to them were always more effective than threats.

The canoe, repaired again and again, and only passably with the substances at hand, became more and more crazy as the journey progressed. Portages became a serious matter, [7] "for the canoe was now become so heavy, from the additional quantity of bark and gum necessary to patch her up, that two men could not carry her more than an hundred yards, without being relieved; and as their way lay through deep mud, was rendered more difficult by the roots and prostrate trunks of trees, they were every moment in danger of falling; and beneath such a weight, one false step might have been attended with fatal consequences."

Indians were encountered here and there, most of whom had never before seen a white man. Cajolery, threats, medicine, and apparent magic were expedients to which Mackenzie had to have recourse at times with these simple people. His men seem to have established amicable relations in a more effective fashion and one which was common with them throughout the Indian country:[8] "When the dawn appeared I had already quitted my bed, and was waiting with impatience for another conference with the natives. The sun, however, had risen before they left their leafy bowers, whither they had retired with their children, having most hospitably resigned their beds, and the partners of them, to the solicitations of my young men."

The large river on the west of the mountain ridge was entered with "inexpressible satisfaction." On the second day on this stream rapids were encountered which were deemed too boisterous for the canoe. Accordingly a portage had to be made. Of this task the leader writes: "The labour and fatigue of this undertaking, from eight till twelve, beggars all description . . . we at length conquered this afflicting passage, of about half a mile, over a rocky and most rugged hill."[9]

The next rapids were also dangerous, and Mackenzie ordered a portage, "but she was now become so heavy that the men preferred running the rapid to the carrying her overland. . . . Four of them undertook this hazardous expedition, and I hastened to the foot of the rapid with great anxiety, to wait the event, which turned out as I expected." [10] In other words, the canoe was wrecked, and the men "in an half-drowned condition arrived safe on shore." Three hours were required to mend the canoe and add even more to its already great weight. Indians were now encountered who were very hostile and suspicious at first and who later gave most discouraging accounts of the navigation and other Indians lower down. Such reports, acting on the lively imaginations of the voyageurs, filled them with dismay, and they began to evidence extreme discontent. Their leader, convinced now that he was not on a river which emptied "into the ocean to the North of what is called the river of the West," and realizing that though he might overcome the tremendous difficulties of navigation on the downward trip he would still have to return *against* them and the mighty current, resolved to go overland: "I now called those of my people about me, who had not been present at my consultation with the natives; and after passing a warm eulogium on their fortitude, patience, and perseverance, I stated the difficulties that threatened our continuing to navigate the river, the length of time it would require, and the scanty provision we had for such a voyage: I then proceeded for the foregoing reasons to propose a shorter route, by trying the overland road to the sea. . . . This proposition met with the most zealous return, and they unanimously assured me, that they were as willing now as they had ever been, to abide by my resolutions, whatever they might be, and to follow me wherever I should go." [11]

The retrograde movement that was necessary to take them to the beginning of the overland route, however,

excited the fears of the Indians, and considerable trouble
was experienced. "This alarm among the natives was a
very unexpected as well as perilous event, and my powers
of conjecture were exhausted in searching for the cause
of it. A general panic seized all around me, and any further prosecution of the voyage was now considered by
them as altogether hopeless and impracticable." [12] Mackenzie, however, held them to their course. "Throughout
the whole of this day the men had been in a state of extreme ill-humour, and as they did not choose openly to
vent it upon me, they disputed and quarreled among
themselves. About sun-set the canoe struck upon the
stump of a tree, which broke a large hole in her bottom;
a circumstance that gave them an opportunity to let loose
their discontents without reserve." [13] Next day it was evident that a new canoe must be constructed, and a halt
was made at an appropriate place. Parties were sent out,
some to get wood, some *wattape*, and others gum. Bark
had been obtained a number of days earlier. There in
the wilderness, thousands of miles from white habita-
tions, this little band of voyageurs constructed a totally
new craft. What other vehicle could have been so constructed, without nails or other substances than what the
forests afforded? Four days later all was ready. "She
proved a stronger and better boat than the old one, though
had it not been for the gum obtained from the latter, it
would have been a matter of great difficulty to have procured a sufficiency of that article to have prevented her
from leaking." [14]

Soon the bad rapid where misfortune had met the party
on its way down was reached. This time a curious and

very hazardous manner of getting by the obstruction was devised. "Two of the men . . . [took] the line, which was seventy fathoms in length, with a small roll of bark, and . . . [climbed] up the rocks, from whence they . . . [descended] on the other side of that which opposed our progress; they then . . . [fastened] the end of the line to the roll of bark, which the current . . . [brought] to us; this being effected, they . . . [drew] us up . . . though to get to the water's edge above, the men were obliged to let themselves down with the line, run round a tree, from the summit of the rock." [15]

Now the party struck westward, up a smaller stream. Soon they had to leave their canoe, cache their goods, and go forward on foot, each man carrying about ninety pounds besides his gun and some ammunition. For several days they traveled, meeting Indians, sleeping in their encampments, climbing mountains, and descending into valleys. Finally, "before us appeared a stupendous mountain, whose snow-clad summit was lost in the clouds; between it and our immediate course, flowed the river to which we were going." [16]

Here two canoes and seven natives took them down the river. In a few days the mouth of the stream and the sea came into sight. The great feat had been accomplished: North America had been crossed in northern latitudes from coast to coast for the first time.

On the return trip more Indian hostility was encountered, and part of the voyageurs refused to go on by water. So the party divided for a time, some going by land and the remainder in a canoe. The land party had its misfortunes, too, for one of the men was attacked by a female bear with two cubs. The opportune arrival of one of his mates, who shot the old bear, saved him, however. After great labor and many frights the divide was surmounted, and the cached provisions and the canoe were found intact. "We now pitched our tent, and made a blazing fire, and I treated myself, as well as the people, with a dram; but we had been so long without tasting any spirituous liquor, that we had lost all relish for it." [17] On August 17 they "began to glide along with the current of Peace River," and at four o'clock in the afternoon of August 24, they arrived at the Fort they had left on the ninth of May. "The men were in such spirits, and made such an active use of their paddles, that we arrived before the two men whom we left here in the spring, could recover their senses to answer us," is the entry in the leader's diary for a day long to be remembered by all of the group.[18]

*   *   *

Other thrilling adventures of an explorer of the first rank were those of Simon Fraser. His name still attaches to the river he explored in 1808 at the greatest hazard to himself, his nineteen voyageurs, and four other companions. For three or four years prior to this exploit he had been making reconnaissances in the far Northwest for his partners of the Northwest Company. This was practically an unknown country, and to Fraser goes the credit of having opened it to trade. In the autumn of 1807, Fraser, at Fort New Caledonia, about 55 degrees north latitude, received instructions from his company to descend the *"Grande Rivière"* then known by its Indian name, *Tacoutché Tesse*, and believed to be the Columbia

River. Lewis and Clarke's expedition had roused the Northwest Company to a sense of its danger from American competition in a region whose ownership was contested. Hence Fraser's mission was to explore and hold it for the British Crown.

In May, 1808, Fraser, accompanied by John Stuart, Jules-Maurice Quesnel, nineteen voyageurs, and two Indians, embarked in four canoes on a trip whose dangers could not have been foreseen at the start.[19] The upper stretches of the river, where Mackenzie had already explored, were passed without trouble. On June 1, however, the voyageurs had a foretaste of the experiences that were to be theirs almost continuously for many days. A narrow channel between high rocks forced the water through at terrific speed and with deafening noise. "Nevertheless, since it was considered as next to impossible to carry the canoes across the land on account of the height and steepness of the hills, it was resolved to venture them down this dangerous pass." As a test, one canoe manned by "the five best men out of the crews" was sent down. "Flying from one danger to another until the last cascade but one" was reached, the canoe at that point was wrecked on a low, projecting rock. Happily the men were able to save both themselves and their freight but found themselves stranded in a deep gorge. There was but one recourse. Steps were cut in the steep bank, and a line was fastened to the end of the canoe. Some of the voyageurs ascended with the line while others remained to push the canoe. Inch by inch the precious craft was lifted. "Our situation was most precarious; our lives hung, as it were, upon a thread, as the failure of the line or a false step of one of the men might have hurled the whole of us into Eternity." Before dark that night the top was reached.

Three days later another rapid nearly cost the lives of the party. "The nature of our situation . . . left us no choice, we were under the necessity, either of running down the canoes, or of abandoning them; we therefore unloaded and provided each of them with five men." It was a desperate undertaking. Between their efforts to keep away from the whirlpools on one hand and the rocks on the other the men nearly exhausted their strength. But again they were victorious. When bringing the baggage by land around this rapid, one of these men found himself in a perilous predicament. The voyageurs, carrying their heavy burdens, were "obliged to pass on a declivity which formed the border of a huge precipice, on loose stones and gravel which constantly gave way under their feet." One of them lost his way and with a large package on his back "got so engaged among the rocks that he could neither move forward nor backward, nor yet unload himself, without imminent danger." Finally the leader of the party himself crawled to the poor wretch's assistance and by cutting the load loose and allowing it to be lost over the precipice saved his canoeman's life.

Other challenges to the strength and coolness of the men followed now in quick succession till navigation finally had to be given up in favor of overland journeying. The leader of the expedition describes the worst of these dangers, the famous *rapide couvert*, where the channel of the great river contracts to about forty yards and is nearly enclosed by overhanging walls of stone: [20]

"Once engaged, the die was cast, our great difficulty consisted in keeping the canoes within the medium, or *fil d'eau*, that is, clear of the precipice on one side and from the gulfs formed by the waves on the other. Thus skimming along as fast as lightning, the crews, cool and determined, followed each other in awful silence, and when we arrived at the end, we stood gazing at each other in silent congratulation at our narrow escape from total destruction."

The Indians for most of the way were friendly, though very curious. Since most of them had never encountered white men before and were totally unacquainted with firearms, they were probably more overawed than genuinely friendly. Once, when a curious Indian took the interpreter's gun, one of the voyageurs saved the situation by knocking up the muzzle, which was aimed directly at some of the Indians, when the would-be investigator pulled the trigger. To have killed a native, however accidentally, would have brought down on the little party the wrath of all the Indians. The men had to be eternally vigilant, standing guard at night, keeping the natives from the luggage, and yet convincing them of the friendliness of the whites.

After the canoes had been abandoned, Indian trails were followed over the precipices. Native guides were employed who, monkey-fashion, climbed easily the twig ladders that formed the way up the faces of precipices and over yawning chasms. Trained as they were to face danger, the voyageurs had all they could do to follow their guides over these swaying bridges and up swinging ladders. On the return trip they were obliged at times to put their burdens on the shoulders of the Indians when descending by means of these ladders. When a voyageur yielded his gun to an Indian, it was indeed a hazardous trail.

The Indians on the lower river were not friendly, and the expedition started on their return trip without having actually been to the mouth. It was truly mortifying to the leader to be obliged to conclude that he had descended another stream than the Columbia. Yet his astronomical instruments showed him that he was nearly three degrees north of the mouth of that river and so had not accomplished what his company had desired. He did not realize, of course, that he had performed a more remarkable feat.

On the return trip the lower Indians became so menacing that the voyageurs refused to penetrate farther into their midst. Preferring even blistered feet and rocks that wore out a pair of moccasins a day, they showed how much their morale had been shattered by insisting upon abandoning the water route. Ordinarily a voyageur would face Death itself if thereby he saved himself a trip by land. Fraser and his friends had to remonstrate, cajole, and threaten. "After much debate on both sides, they yielded and we all shook hands, resolved not to separate during the voyage, which resolution was immediately confirmed by the following oath taken on the spot by each of the party. 'I solemnly swear before Almighty God that I shall sooner perish than forsake in distress any of our crew during the present voyage.'" Thereupon "all hands dressed in their best apparel and . . . decamped full of spirits, singing and making a great noise." [21] The Indians lost heart at so much confidence and eventually dropped back, allowing the whites to proceed unmolested. In due time they arrived at the point whence they had started. The river is known by the name of the leader, but not all the credit should go to him. Without his voyageurs the trip was unthinkable.

*   *   *

Another famous explorer of the Northwest who has left an account of the services rendered by his voyageurs was Sir John Franklin, whose story is entitled, *Narrative of a Journey to the Shores of the Polar Sea in the Years 1819-20-21-22.* Leaving Fort Chipewyan on Lake Athabasca, he started for the mouth of the Coppermine River assisted by fifteen Canadian voyageurs, an Italian canoeman, an Englishman, a Norwegian trader, two interpreters, an Iroquois Indian, and an Indian woman. The start was not auspicious, because of shortage of food and ammunition. Nevertheless, it lacked none of that picturesqueness with which voyageurs always enveloped their departures and arrivals. "It was gratifying . . . to perceive," writes the leader, "that this scarcity of food did not depress the spirits of our Canadian companions, who cheerfully loaded their canoes, and embarked in high glee after they had received the customary dram. . . . The crews commenced a lively paddling song on quitting the shore, which was continued until we had lost sight of the houses." [22]

Franklin was interested in the voyageur class and studied them. In his *Narrative* he tells of attending their New Year's dance, so much in favor among the squaws, who were the men's partners; of their marriages and morals, or perhaps more accurately, their lack of morals;

242

of the terrible Methye Portage, which was twelve miles in length and much of it so steep that it was descended by sliding, the voyageurs guiding their sledges as best they could at amazing speed; of their cruelty to their dogs, whom they beat incessantly and on whom they vented "the most dreadful and disgusting imprecations"; and of nightly encampments, where the men "stretch out before the fire and pass the evening recounting their former feats in traveling."

It had been a task of some magnitude to assemble a sufficient number of voyageurs for this trip, for in the Northwest encounters with the Esquimaux had made the men very fearful of further intercourse. These were, therefore, picked men, and accordingly they demanded unusually high wages. Their names are typical: Joseph Peltier, Matthew Pelonquin (*alias* Crédit), Solomon Belanger, Joseph Benoit, Joseph Gagné, Pierre Dumas, Joseph Forcier, Ignace Perrault, François Samandré, Gabriel Beauparlant, Registe Vaillant, Jean Baptiste Parent, Jean Baptiste Belanger, Jean Baptiste Belleau, and Emanuel Cournoyée. There is the usual proportion of Jean Baptistes. One wonders at times how many Jean Baptistes were scattered over the Canadian and American West at any given time during the eighteenth and early nineteenth centuries.

The journey had not progressed far before the leader realized what some of his trials were to be. The meagerness of the diet made the Canadians, "who had been for some days past murmuring . . . and striving to get the whole of our little provision to consume at once," break out into open rebellion.[23] Franklin was obliged to "address them in the strongest manner on the danger of insubordination," and to threaten with "the heaviest punishment . . . any that should persist in their refusal to go on, or in any other way attempt to retard the Expedition." He then explains his course to the reader: "I considered this decisive step necessary, having learned from the gentlemen, most intimately acquainted with the character of the Canadian voyageurs, that they invariably try how far they can impose upon every new master, and that they will continue to be disobedient and intractable if they gain any ascendancy over him." But the Englishman's sense of justice required him to add: "I must admit, however, that the present hardships of our companions were of a kind which few could support without murmuring, and no one could witness without a sincere pity for their sufferings." That night, to show how far these men were creatures of the moment, a little food was secured; it "instantly revived the spirits of our companions, and they immediately forgot all their cares."

A halt was made for the winter, and a house, Fort Enterprise, was erected by the voyageurs under W. F. Wentzel's direction. "It was merely a log-building, fifty feet long, and twenty-four wide, divided into a hall, three bed rooms and a kitchen. The walls and roof were plastered with clay, the floors laid with planks rudely squared with the hatchet, and the windows closed with parchment of deer-skin. . . . Having filled our capacious clay-built chimney with fagots, we spent a cheerful evening before the invigorating blaze." At first everyone lived on the floor, but the voyageurs soon proved their versatility. "Our working party, who had shown such skill as house carpenters, soon proved themselves to be, with the same tools (the hatchet and crooked knife), excellent cabinet makers, and daily added a table, chair, or bedstead, to the comforts of our establishment. The crooked knife generally made of an old file, bent and tempered by heat, serves an Indian or Canadian voyager for plane, chisel, and auger. With it the snow-shoe and canoe-timbers are fashioned, the deals of their sledges reduced to the requisite thinness and polish, and their wooden bowls and spoons hollowed out." [24] Besides this home for the officers the voyageurs built a storehouse and a house for themselves.

An expedition of voyageurs had to be sent back to Fort Providence in the dead of winter for supplies. When they returned, they were greeted with great joy. "They had been twenty-one days on their march from Slave Lake, and the labour they underwent was sufficiently evidenced by their sledge-collars having worn out the shoulders of their coats." [25] They carried about 180 pounds apiece when they started. But alas, they were typical voyageurs. Much of the provisions and liquor had disappeared down their voracious gullets. "As they were pretty well aware that such a circumstance could not long be concealed from us," writes Franklin, "one of them came the next morning with an artful apology for their conduct. He stated, that as they knew it was my intention to treat them with a dram on the commencement of the new year, they had helped themselves to a small[!] quantity on that day, trusting to my goodness for forgiveness." [26]

From this hospitable winter home one of the officers,

George Back, set out on one of the most extraordinary trips on record for this northwest country. He went on snowshoes and was accompanied as far as Great Slave Lake by Mr. Wentzel, two Canadians, and two Indians and their wives. Just before reaching Fort Providence they came to a river which was not frozen even at the edges. So the voyageurs had to make a raft. On this all the party crossed, ankle deep in water, each with a pine branch for a paddle. At the fort, supplies could not be obtained, and the party determined to go on, being now composed of Back, Wentzel, Beauparlant, and two other Canadians. Now they had dogs and sledges. At Moose-Deer Island Fort it was determined, because of inadequate supplies, to go on to Fort Chipewyan. This time Back, his faithful Beauparlant, a half-breed, and dog-sleds composed the party. The traveling was hazardous and fatiguing. Along the rapids of one of the rivers, Beauparlant, though an old Nor'wester, complained bitterly of the cold, from which even he received frost-bites. But no sooner had he reached the upper part of the river than he found the change of the temperature so great that he vented his indignation against the heat. "*Mais c'est terrible,*" said he, to be frozen and sunburnt in the same day. "The poor fellow," explains Franklin, "who had been a long time in the country, regarded it as the most severe punishment that could have been inflicted on him, and would willingly have given a part of his wages rather than this disgrace had happened; for there is a pride amongst 'Old Voyagers,' which makes them consider the state of being frost-bitten as effeminate, and only excusable in a 'Pork-eater.' " [27]

The astonishment of the men at Fort Chipewyan was great when this little party arrived from the great frozen North. After about five weeks at the fort they set out again with five sledges, four of which carried goods for Franklin's expedition. The outward route was followed substantially on the return, and on March 17, after nearly five months, Back and his party were back at Fort Enterprise after a walk of 1,104 miles on snowshoes, with "no other covering at night, in the woods, than a blanket and deer-skin, with the thermometer frequently at —40°, and once at —57°; and sometimes passing two or three days without tasting food." [28]

At Fort Enterprise the whole company, officers, voyageurs, and Indians, were amusing themselves sliding down the steep banks of the river and far out on the ice. It was uproarious fun and was encouraged by the officers to keep the men's minds off their scanty provisions. Games were also played, such as prison bars, of the sort with which the Canadians were wont to amuse themselves.

Then came the summer's rush to the shore of the frozen sea. Nothing more harrowing can be found in travel literature than the simple, restrained tale told by the officers of the end of this expedition. Food gave out, starvation and freezing took one after another, and insanity and murder finished the terrible work. Finally, when the outposts of civilization were reached, it was found that Hood, Beauparlant, Samandré, Peltier, J. B. Belanger, Perrault, Vaillant, and Crédit were dead, besides Michel, the Iroquois, and Fontano, the Italian canoeman. Possibly others were gone, for Cournoyée and Belleau are not mentioned among the survivors. As with most childlike natures, the harrowing circumstances in which they found themselves brought out the worst in the voyageurs. Thieving, lying, and shirking duties were recorded against them. Yet it is interesting to note that the only one to become so demoralized as to eat human flesh was the Indian, Michel.[29]

Most of these men become personalities to us as we read of them again and again in Franklin's account: Beauparlant, who had a horror of being thought a tenderfoot; Perrault, who saved his little store of food and distributed it when the others were starving; Solomon Belanger, considered the most trustworthy and conscientious of the lot, but who, under stress of starvation, proved otherwise, at least temporarily; and J. B. Belanger, who risked his life to hold a canoe in midstream in almost freezing water. These are a few of the men of the famous Franklin expedition.

*　　*　　*

Of quite another kind was a journey taken in 1828 by that famous traveler Sir George Simpson. As Governor of the Hudson's Bay Company from 1821 to 1860, he was accustomed to annual visitations of the corporation's far-flung domain. Before the days of railroads, automobiles, or airplanes he covered every year an area which would be considered great even for travelers of this day of easy and quick transportation. His canoes, his voyageurs, his dogs, his guides, and his horses were all of the best, and he was such an adept in the art of traveling that he literally sped from post to post with what seems, even today, incredible swiftness. George Bryce tells of hearing a story, current in the Red River country, of a stalwart voyageur in Simpson's canoe. Frenzied by the Governor's urging more speed, he seized his tormentor, who was small in stature, and dipped him in the lake to the accompaniment of an expressive French oath.[30]

Two light canoes carrying eighteen men, the Governor, a doctor, and Chief Factor Archibald McDonald, who kept a diary, composed the party of 1828. They left York Factory on Hudson Bay on July 12 with three cheers and a salute of seven guns from the fort and a paddling song from the voyageurs. The Governor's Scotch piper played a few strathspeys on the bagpipes as they advanced "on the line" up the river, low water necessitating this mode of travel. The diarist evidently found the Scotch music less appropriate for this labor than the men's paddling songs, for he remarked that it "as yet makes but a poor accordance with either the pole or the paddle." [31]

The crews of the two canoes soon began their usual rivalry, and the Governor's shot far ahead of the other and smaller craft. The crew of the latter argued that the vessel caused the difference. An exchange was thereupon effected, when, to the chagrin of the others, "the Governor's men with much ado, pushed the small canoe ahead." [32] Nevertheless, the winners conceded the superiority of the larger canoe, and the next day the Governor took two of the inferior crew and put two of his good hands in the smaller vessel.

A week's paddling and tracking brought them to the newly established Norway House. To make the impressive appearance that Simpson, not less than his voya-

geurs, loved, every man changed his clothes just before
the fort was sighted, and the paddlers mounted new
feathers. "As we wafted along under easy sail, . . . the
Highland bagpipes in the Governor's canoe, was echoed
by the bugle in mine!" writes McDonald. "Then these
were laid aside, on nearer approach to port, to give free
scope to the vocal organs of about eighteen Canadians
(French) to chant one of those voyageur airs peculiar to
them, and always so perfectly rendered. Our entry . . .
was certainly more imposing than anything hitherto seen
in this part of the Indian country." [33]

A boy who saw this impressive sight wrote his recol-
lections of it in his old age. Standing by his Scotch
trader father, who had just finished building the fine
new Norway House, the boy noted the flag flying from
"a tall Norway Pine shaft" on the "signal hill of rock,"
the skirl of the pipes with their "Campbell's are coming,
hourray! hourray!" or some such "music of our mountain land," and then, "as a *cadenza* of soothing, glad-
dening, exquisite charm—the deep and soft and so joy-
ously toned voices of those full throated *voyageurs*,
timed with a stroke—so quick—of glittering paddle
blade, singing with such heart their *'La Claire Fontaine'*
or some such loved air of *their* native land." Then he
saw "the Governor's canoe, with its grand high prow,
rounded, and brightly painted," coming into view.
"Never; never, had anything so grand and splendid, and
delightful withal, been seen in those primitive wilds." [34]

Only one evening and part of the next morning could
be spared for business and rest, and then the Lake Winnipeg journey was begun. The next day but one brought

the party to the mouth of the Saskatchewan. Up this stream now they labored, and on to Cumberland House, which they reached on the 27th. Here more provisions were taken on board, and after a very brief stop they were off once more "with fair weather, and a touch up of a favorite song chorused by both canoes." [35] On August 4 they were at the fort of Isle à la Crosse, where they met two important traders who brought the returns of the Mackenzie River District of the Company. On the 7th they were on the dreaded Methye Portage, the great watershed of this region. Twelve miles of the hardest kind of physical labor were accomplished, with the aid of ten Indians who met them there, in a single day. By seven in the evening they had gone on their way to still another portage. It is consoling to read that the men were rewarded for their toil of that strenuous day with "two or three extra glasses of spirits" at the night's encampment and two hours' extra sleep in the morning.

On August 11 they reached one of the most important posts, Fort Chipewyan, just a month from Hudson Bay. Here the Governor conducted a great amount of business and had an audience with a large number of Indians. On the 14th they were under way again with as imposing a departure "as the firing of guns, heavy cheers from master and men on the rocks, and the waving of flags, and songs in abundance on our part could make it." The next day they entered Peace River, and on the 20th Fort Vermilion was reached. The preceding day's entry in the diary contains the following sentence which says much of what was happening among the canoemen: "In the course of the day the foreman of the second canoe was called to account for not keeping up with the other, which seems to have had the effect of spurring them on the remainder of the day." On the 27th another landmark was reached, Fort Dunvegan, where the men were given a well-deserved rest. On September 2 the Rocky Mountains were reached—and a portage "about a mile of the worst road in Christendom." On the 5th they were all at the "upper end" of the portage, where the men repaired the canoes, washed and mended their shirts and trousers, and got almost an entire day for rest. On the 13th they left McLeod's Fort and their canoes, for the mountain divide made them useless, and continued overland, pack on back. On the 17th, as they neared Fort St. James, they changed their clothes, "and every arrangement was made to arrive . . . in the most imposing manner . . . for the sake of the Indians. . . . Accordingly, when within about a thousand yards of the establishment, descending a gentle hill, a gun was fired, the bugle sounded, and soon after, the piper commenced the celebrated march of the clans—'Si coma leum cogadh na shea.' . . . The guide, with the British ensign, led the van, followed by the band; then the Governor, on horseback, supported behind by Doctor Hamlyn and myself on our chargers, two deep; twenty men, with their burdens, next formed the line; then one loaded horse, and lastly, Mr. McGillivray closed the rear." Here they took to canoes again on the 24th, and now their way lay down a branch of that Fraser River which an intrepid trader and his voyageurs had opened to the fur-traders just twenty years earlier. On the 27th the party was at Fort Alexandria. On the 4th of October, after a trip partly by canoe, partly by horse, Kamloops Fort was reached in the usual impressive manner. Here a boat took most of the group, and on October 8 a meeting with another contingent of the party was successfully made. "This meeting is rendered still more interesting, from the circumstance of both parties descending rivers that were never ran before and that were always considered next to impossible."

The most thrilling part of the trip is told very unemotionally in the entry for October 10. It was the leaping of Simpson's Falls, under overhanging cliffs in the narrowest gorge of Fraser River Canyon. First went the guide in his bark canoe. When he had whizzed down the current past rocks and eddies to safety, the boat followed, and, finally, the second canoe. On that same day at eight in the evening, Fort Langley, the end of the diarist's trip, was reached. Of the remainder of the Governor's trip, to the Columbia and back to York Factory, we do not have the same detailed account. He and his men had crossed the continent from Hudson Bay to the Pacific in almost exactly three months.

*   *   *

Another Arctic expedition made use of Canadian voyageurs, but not to the extent that Franklin's had done. This was the undertaking of Chief Factor Peter Warren Dease and Thomas Simpson in the years from 1836 to 1839. Simpson, the leading spirit of this enterprise, was a relative of the famous Governor of the Hudson's Bay Company, which sponsored this expedition. His account of the discoveries that his party made west and east of the farthest limits of Franklin's travels, which appeared posthumously in 1843, furnished information which enabled cartographers to map thereafter most of the outline of the northern shores of North America from Point Barrow in the west to Hudson Bay. Of the twelve men who left Fort Norman on the Mackenzie River in July, 1837, two were Canadians, one of whom, François Felix, had accompanied Franklin in 1826. To him Simpson, not given to admiration of his race, pays a tribute in the latter part of his work:[36] "Our excellent assistant Ritch was left this summer, as usual, in charge of Fort Confidence, assisted by Felix and Morrison, two men specially selected for this important duty, on account of their steady, industrious habits."

Apparently, too, Ritch's assistants in building winter quarters on Great Bear Lake (Fort Confidence) were mainly Canadians, if one may judge by their names— John Norquay, Laurent Cartier, and François Framond. "This most important duty" of erecting buildings and providing stores of fish and other provisions with which to supply the entire party when it should be reunited after the first summer's expeditions was of outstanding significance for the success of the enterprise. It is interesting, also, to note that in the crew picked for the dangerous descent of the Coppermine River the bowsman was Laurent Cartier.

Simpson does not have much to say of any of his subordinates, in contrast to the full-length pictures that Franklin has left of his men. Occasionally, however, we catch a glimpse of them, as, for instance, when some native vehicles were found of a craftmanship which surprised the party. The large sledge with side rails was pro-

nounced made "comme à Montreal" by "our Canadians."
This remark led Simpson to an enlightening comment on
voyageur personality: [37] "French vanity has lost nothing
of its point in the New World. The largest sort of ducks
in the interior are called 'Canards de France'; English
tan-leather shoes, 'Souliers François'; the whites in general, 'les François'; as all Europeans of old were Franks:
and one old guide, talking of the place whence the Company's merchandise came, took it for granted that it was
from 'la vieille France de Londres!' "

The author also pays his tribute to voyageur appetites,
which he thought unreasonable, for their work was
"physically less severe than the compulsory tracking on
the rivers of Russia and China." He describes the daily
ration of twelve pounds of venison or four or five whitefish allotted to each person at Fort Confidence. "Yet,"
says he, "there was one of them who complained he had
not enough, and did not scruple to help himself to an
additional supply whenever the opportunity offered: it
would have taken twenty pounds of animal food daily to
satisfy him. This man, Framond, being in other respects
a very indifferent servant, was discharged the following
year." [38]

The voyageurs were admittedly a witty race, yet few
of their witticisms have come down to us. We are
obliged to take the word of traders and explorers, as in
poor novels we have to accept on faith the same quality
in heroes and heroines. It is pleasant, therefore, to find a
concrete illustration of voyageur humor in Simpson's
Narrative. To understand it, however, we must have in
mind that most of these men came originally from the

vicinity of Montreal, which is situated on an island of
the same name, and that the French word *taureau* ordinarily means "bull." With this explanation it is easy to
understand how delighted Simpson was when the discovery of a *cache* of Sir George Back's supplies on Montreal Island in the far north enabled him to record the
following incident: "The pemican, or 'taureau,' as the
voyageurs call it, was literally *alive;* and it was wittily
remarked, 'L'isle de Montreal sera bientôt peuplée de
jeunes *taureaux*' " [39] ("Montreal Island will soon be
stocked with young bulls").

Unlike Franklin's expedition, Simpson's travels were
attended with only one casualty, and that a natural
death. The leader himself was one of the most energetic
of travelers and explorers and outdid all the others in
mileage covered. When he took his long trips across the
plains with his dog trains, did he realize, we wonder, his
indebtedness to the men he understood so little and
affected to condemn on so many scores? Did he ever
think that the trails had been marked out, the ways
learned, the dogs trained, the places named, and the best
manner of withstanding winter's cold discovered by these
selfsame humble voyageurs, despite their gluttony, their
laziness, their boastfulness, and their filth? Probably not,
for Simpson was still in the full flush of youth's judg-
ment by appearances. Perhaps it was this very blindness
and intolerance of other ways of living that caused his
death at thirty-two at the hands of sons of this very class
of men. The story of his mysterious death is as follows.
He left the Red River Settlement for Fort Snelling in
June, 1840, accompanied by quite a large party, mostly

half-breeds. Finding the main body traveling too slowly to suit him, he and four men started ahead. On the 14th of June, so the survivors reported, he shot two of his men. Later he himself was found shot. No one seemed able or willing to tell what really happened. Some at the time believed he met his death at the hands of the half-breeds in retaliation for a severe chastisement he had given a half-breed at the Settlement a few years earlier.

*   *   *

It is impossible within the limits of a work of this scope to describe all the exploring trips and other important expeditions in Canada and western United States that made use of the services of voyageurs. The leaders of several of them have already been quoted in other chapters, as, for example, one of the boundary commissioners provided by the convention of 1818 between the United States and Great Britain, Long, Garry, McKenney, Kane, Kennicott, and Franklin. Among the others may be mentioned the overland Astorians like Robert Stuart, whose diary is soon to be published, and Ramsay Crooks; Lewis Cass, whose trip up the Great Lakes to the headwaters of the Mississippi in 1820 resulted in naming an important lake in Minnesota for him; Henry R. Schoolcraft, who in 1832 did what Cass had hoped to do, discover the source of the Mississippi; Joseph N. Nicollet, a French scientist, who with John C. Frémont explored the region between the Mississippi and the Missouri in the thirties and then published the first scientific map of that area; George Catlin, whose pictures of the Indian life of much of that same territory are so coveted today; Major John Pope, who explored the

257

valley of the Red River of the North in 1849 whilst it was still a wild, unsettled territory; and scores of others like the bishops of Juliopolis and Montreal, the priests and other missionaries that went in numbers to the Indians after Calhoun proclaimed a new Indian policy for the United States in 1817, Lord Selkirk, great traders like Daniel Harmon and David Thompson, British sportsmen like Lord Milton and the Earl of Southesk, artists like Manton Marble and Frank B. Mayer, railroad promoters like James J. Hill and Lord Mount Royal, scientists like Captain J. H. Lefroy and Captain John Palliser, and even women sightseers like Mrs. Jameson. In short, everyone who traveled in the Northwest before the days of the railroad sooner or later used French-Canadian voyageurs or their half-breed descendants to paddle their canoes, drive their dogs, lead their packhorses, choose their routes, or guide their York boats. Their services in opening up the West are incalculable.

Besides aiding travelers by conducting them through the fur country, the voyageurs rendered the very useful service of naming nearly every topographical feature, bird, animal, insect, fish, and reptile that the eye of the wayfarer encountered. At first glance this service may not seem to be extraordinarily valuable, because, one may say, the traveler could easily have supplied his own terminology. A traveler, Radisson, who explored the West before voyageurs had labeled all objects that came within his ken obviously must have thought otherwise. Read his account of travels in the country around Lake Superior about the year 1660. Had we some way of identifying "ye great river that divides itself in 2," or "the first landing Isle," or a certain "little lake," south of Lake Superior, how joyfully we should welcome it! As it is, we must forever wonder just where his route took him.

It is enlightening and amusing to note the geographic names supplied by the voyageurs. To be sure, they merely translated many of them from the Indian names, but who among the white men knew enough of the natives' speech to translate them? Few traders could deal with the Indians except through an interpreter, usually a voyageur or half-breed. As a sample of voyageur nomenclature, let us follow a part of Sir John Richardson's route from Lachine to Lake Winnipeg and on to the Arctic Ocean in 1848. The following names of places, flora, and fauna are supplied in both French and English quite as a matter of course, as though it was to be expected that both should be known: [40]

Sturgeon River	*La Rivière Maligne*
(Actaea alba)	*la racine d'ours*
Birch lightening-place	*Demi-charge du bouleau*
Pine Portage	*Portage des Epinettes*
Half-Moon Lake	*Lac Mi-rond*
Pelican lightening-place	*Demi-charge de chetauque*
Frog Portage	*Portage de Traite*
(root of the Sium lineare)	*Queue de rat*
(non-edible " ")	*carotte de moreau*
Steep Bank Portage	*Portage des Ecores*
Thicket Portage	*Portage des Haliers*
Angle Rapid	*Rapide de l'Equerre*
Noisy Rapid	*Rapide Sonnant*
Deep River	*Rivière Creuse*
Rapid of the Tomb	*Le Cimetière*
Methy River	*La Loche*
mink	*foutreau* or *foutereau*

(pinus banksiana)	*cyprès*
Nurse Portage	*Portage de Bonne*
dogbane	*herbe à la puce*
Rocky Islands	*Isles des Pierres*
Great Balsam Fir Island	*La Grande Isle des Epinettes*
Portage of the Drowned	*Portage des Noyés*

Besides these he mentions many French terms for which there were, apparently, no English equivalents.

Many of the place names of the voyageurs have remained, either in their original form or corrupted, sometimes beyond recognition. Consider as examples the following place names in the state of Minnesota: Grand Portage, Grand Marais, Fond du Lac, St. Croix River, Mille Lacs Lake, Lac Qui Parle, Lake Traverse, Zumbrota River (a corruption of Rivière aux Embarras), and Cannon River (a corruption of Canot, or Canoe River). Or take these in Wisconsin: Prairie du Chien, Eau Claire, La Crosse, Racine, Trempealeau, and Little Chute. Or the following in Michigan: Presque Isle, Au Sable County, Traverse City, Detroit, Bois Blanc Island, Point Seul, Isle Royal, Isle Chapeau, Grossepoint, Grosse Isle, Au Train Bay, Bete Grise Bay, Grand Sable Lake, Parisienne Island, and Point aux Barques. Almost without exception these places owe their names to voyageurs. Behind most of these place names is a story, more frequently a distressing tale than a humorous one. It was the difficulty of voyaging that accounts for the frequency of *Traverse*, *Portage*, and *Embarras* on our maps today. Sometimes the memory of the naming of a spot has triumphed over time. Thus, Miette's Rock in western Canada was named for a calm-nerved voyageur who mounted to its summit, fifteen hundred feet above a yawning abyss, and sat there, his legs hanging over the edge, while he contemplated the scenery and smoked his pipe. Such daring always struck a responsive chord in the innermost being of other voyageurs. The matter of geographic names in the United States deserves more study than has ever been accorded it. For example, when shall we have a map of the voyageur's habitat, showing the French names for topographical features?

*　　*　　*

The passing of the voyageur was so gradual that no one noticed, much less lamented, his loss. A few writers like Taché and Dugas realized his significance for the history of North America. Most historians have not even comprehended the meaning of the term *voyageur*. If this book has succeeded in giving him his proper place in history, its purpose has been fulfilled. One poet of modern times has honored him with a poem which catches not a little of his jauntiness, *naïveté*, and young-heartedness: [41]

The Voyageur

Dere's somet'ing stirrin' ma blood tonight,
　　On de night of de young new year,
W'ile de camp is warm an' de fire is bright,
　　An' de bottle is close at han'—
Out on de reever de nort' win' blow,
　　Down on de valley is pile de snow,
But w'at do we care so long we know
　　We're safe on de log cabane?

Drink to de healt' of your wife an' girl,
　　Anoder wan for your frien'
Den geev' me a chance, for on all de worl'
　　I've not many frien' to spare—

THE VOYAGEUR

I'm born, w'ere de mountain scrape de sky,
An' bone of ma fader an' moder lie,
  So I fill de glass an' I raise it high
An' drink to de Voyageur.

For dis is de night of de jour de l'an,
  W'en de man of de Grand Nor' Wes'
T'ink of hees home on de St. Laurent,
  An' frien' he may never see—
Gone he is now, an' de beeg canoe
  No more you'll see wit' de red-shirt crew,
But long as he leev' he was alway true,
  So we'll drink to hees memory.

Ax' heem de nort' win' w'at he see
  Of de Voyageur long ago,
An' he'll say to you w'at he say to me,
  So lissen hees story well—
"I see de track of hees botte sau-vage
  On many a hill an' long portage
Far far away from hees own vill-age
  An' soun' of de parish bell—

"I never can play on de Hudson Bay
  Or mountain dat lie between
But I meet heem singin' hees lonely way
  De happies' man I know—
I cool hees face as he's sleepin' dere
  Under de star of de Red Rivière,
An' off on de home of de great w'ite bear,
  I'm seein' hees dog traineau.

"De woman an' chil'ren's runnin' out
  Of de wigwam of de Cree—
De leetle papoose dey laugh an' shout
  W'en de soun of hees voice dey hear—
De oldes' warrior of de Sioux
  Kill hese'f dancin' de w'ole night t'roo,
An de Blackfoot girl remember too
  De ole tam Voyageur.

"De blaze of hees camp on de snow I see,
　An' I lissen hees 'En Roulant'
On de lan' w'ere de reindeer travel free,
　Ringin' out strong an' clear—
Offen de grey wolf sit before
　De light is come from hees open door,
An' caribou foller along de shore
　De song of de Voyageur.

"If he only kip goin', de red ceinture,
　I'd see it upon de Pole
Some mornin' I'm startin' upon de tour
　For blowin' de worl' aroun'—
But w'erever he sail an' w'erever he ride,
　De trail is long an' de trail is wide,
An' city an' town on ev'ry side
　Can tell of hees campin' groun'."

So dat's de reason I drink tonight
　To de man of de Grand Nor' Wes',
For hees heart was young, an' hees heart was light
　So long as he's leevin' dere—
I'm proud of de sam' blood in my vein
　I'm a son of de Nort' Win wance again—
So we'll fill her up till de bottle's drain
　An' drink to de Voyageur.

WILLIAM HENRY DRUMMOND *

* From *The Voyageur and Other Poems,* by permission of the publishers, G. P. Putnam's Sons.

NOTES

FRONT MATTER

vi. The quotation is from James H. Baker, "Lake Superior," *Minnesota Historical Collections,* 3: 342.

I

FURS AND FUR-TRADERS

1. Abstracts of these licenses have been made and indexed for the period from 1768 to 1776. Consolidated returns of licenses cover the years from 1777 to 1790. These also have been indexed. A copy of the abstracts and index is filed with the Minnesota Historical Society, and other copies may be found in several libraries in Canada and the United States. For those interested in the licenses for the French period the following references will prove useful: E. Z. Massicotte, "Répertoire des Engagements pour l'Ouest Conservés dans les Archives Judiciaires de Montréal" in *Rapport de l'Archiviste de la Province de Québec, 1929-1930,* pp. 191-466; "Congés et Permis Déposés ou Enrégistrés à Montréal sous le Régime Français," in *Rapport de l'Archiviste de la Province de Québec, 1921-1922;* and "Les Congés de Traite sous le Régime Français au Canada," in *ibid.,* 1922-1923.
2. Since this paragraph was written, Harold A. Innis' *The Fur Trade in Canada* (New Haven, 1930) has appeared. It emphasizes a number of the points mentioned.
3. For further data on these companies see Gordon C. Davidson, *The Northwest Company,* which is Volume 7 of the *University of California Publications in History* (Berkeley, 1918); George Bryce, *Remarkable History of the Hudson's Bay Company,* 3d ed. (New York, 1910); Hiram M. Chittenden, *The American Fur Trade of the Far West,* three volumes (New York, 1902); and Grace Lee Nute, "The Papers of the American Fur Company," in *American Historical Review,* April, 1927.
4. See Grace Lee Nute, "Posts in the Minnesota Fur-trading Area, 1660-1855," in *Minnesota History,* 11: 353-85.

NOTES

II

PORTRAIT OF THE VOYAGEUR

1. Sherman Hall's diary in the archives of the American Board of Commissioners for Foreign Missions in Boston, Volume 74, Number 44, entry for September 18, 1832.
2. Thomas L. McKenney, *Sketches of a Tour to the Lakes, of the Character and Customs of the Chippeway Indians and of Incidents Connected with the Treaty of Fond Du Lac*, 417, 418 (Baltimore, 1827).
3. John J. Bigsby, *The Shoe and Canoe or Pictures of Travel in the Canadas*, 1:132, 133 (London, 1850).
4. "Diary of Nicholas Garry," in *Proceedings and Transactions of the Royal Society of Canada*, 113 (Second Series, Volume 6, Section 2, 1900).
5. William H. Keating, *Narrative of an Expedition to the Source of St. Peter's River, Lake Winnepeek, Lake of the Woods, &c. Performed in the Year 1823*, 2:85 (London, 1825).
6. McKenney, *Tour to the Lakes*, 350, 351.
7. *Ibid.*, 199.
8. "Robert Kennicott," in *Transactions of the Chicago Academy of Sciences*, 1869. The references are to page 160 of Volume 1, Part 2.
9. *Ibid.*, 151, 152.
10. McKenney, *Tour to the Lakes*, 228.
11. "Robert Kennicott," 187.
12. *Ibid.*, 192, 194, 195.

III

THE VOYAGEUR'S CANOE

1. Merchants of Montreal to Simcoe, April 23, 1792, in *The Correspondence of Lieut. Governor John Graves Simcoe, with Allied Documents Relating to His Administration of the Government of Upper Canada*, ed. E. A. Cruikshank, 1:135, 136 (Toronto, 1923).
2. For canoes and their equipment consult the following: McKenney, *Tour to the Lakes*, 199, 200; "Robert Kennicott," 146, 148; Daniel W. Harmon, *A Journal of Voyages and Travels in the Interior of North America*, 1, 2 (Toronto, 1911); John McDonell's manuscript diary in the library of McGill University, Montreal, entry for May 25, 1793; and Innis, *Fur Trade in Canada*, 192-265.
3. McKenney, *Tour to the Lakes*, 382, 383.
4. "Robert Kennicott," 147.
5. McKenney, *Tour to the Lakes*, 211.

NOTES

6. From E. Z. Massicotte and C. M. Barbeau, "Chants populaires du Canada," in *Journal of American Folk-Lore*, 32: 78, 79 (January-March, 1919). The air accompanies the words.
7. Mrs. William Lewis to James R. Wright, May 29, 1844, in the possession of the Minnesota Historical Society.

IV

VOYAGING

1. See *ante*, p. 6.
2. Wages and equipment varied greatly in different periods and departments. A good summary of the details of engagements, wages, costs of transportation, and equipments may be found in Innis, *Fur Trade in Canada*, 242-245. This author also mentions a sort of insurance that was provided for disabled voyageurs by the deduction of one per cent of the wages of all the *engagés*. See p. 242.
3. Ramsay Crooks to John Jacob Astor, May 3, 1817, in a letterbook of the American Fur Company at Mackinac. Photostatic copies of this volume have been made by the State Historical Society of Wisconsin and the Minnesota Historical Society.
4. The remnant of Peter Pond's diary is reprinted in *Wisconsin Historical Collections*, 18: 326 (Madison, 1908).
5. Harmon, *Journal*, 10.
6. The account of this custom is drawn from J. C. Taché, *Forestiers et Voyageurs*, 158-164 (Montreal, 1884). A different version is given *post*, p. 151.
7. Keating, *Narrative of an Expedition to the Source of St. Peter's River*, 2: 85, 86.
8. The diary of Sherman Hall describes the forty-five mile portage to Lac du Flambeau from Lake Superior. See entries for September 11 and 18, 1832.
9. Manuscript diary of Boutwell, a copy made by J. Fletcher Williams from the original, in the possession of the Minnesota Historical Society. The entry was for September 18, 1833.
10. Hall's diary, entry for September 18, 1832.
11. Boutwell's diary, entry for September 12, 1833.
12. *The Journal of Duncan M'Gillivray of the North West Company at Fort George on the Saskatchewan, 1794-5, with Introduction, Notes and Appendix* by Arthur S. Morton, entry for August 3, p. 6 (Toronto, 1929).
13. See *post*, pp. 232, 234, 235, 241, 243.
14. Ross Cox, *The Columbia River*, 2: 253 (London, 1832).
15. Garry specifies that Indian corn was used. See his diary, p. 122.
16. "Personal Narrative of Capt. Thomas G. Anderson," in *Wisconsin Historical Collections*, 9: 140, 141 (Madison, 1882).
17. McKenney, *Tour to the Lakes*, 201.

18. Boutwell's diary, entry for June 12, 1832.
19. *Ibid.,* entry for June 27, 1832.
20. "Robert Kennicott," 154, 161, 162.
21. *Ibid.,* 177.
22. *Journal of the Reverend Peter Jacobs, Indian Wesleyan Missionary,* 72, 73 (New York, 1857).
23. McKenney, *Tour to the Lakes,* 351.
24. Bigsby, *Shoe and Canoe,* 2:92-94.
25. "Diary of Nicholas Garry," 130, 131.
26. Paul Kane, *Wanderings of an Artist among the Indians of North America* in *Master-Works of Canadian Authors,* ed. John W. Garvin, 114 (Toronto, 1925).
27. See a manuscript account of fur-trade methods by an erstwhile voyageur, Paul Beaulieu, in the possession of the Minnesota Historical Society; and Sir John Richardson, *Arctic Searching Expedition: A Journal of a Boat-Voyage Through Rupert's Land and the Arctic Sea in Search of the Discovery Ships Under Command of Sir John Franklin,* 1:92 (London, 1851).
28. "Voyages of Peter Esprit Radisson," ed. Gideon D. Scull, in *Prince Society Publications,* 192 (Boston, 1885).
29. Washington Irving, *Astoria,* 23, 24 (N. Y. and London, 1849).
30. Kane, *Wanderings of an Artist,* 235, 236.
31. *Journal of Duncan M'Gillivray,* 11, 12.
32. Diary of John McDonell, entry for August 11, 1793.
33. "Robert Kennicott," 155, 159; John Franklin, *Narrative of a Journey to the Shores of the Polar Sea, in the Years 1819-20-21-22,* 61 (London, 1824); Kane, *Wanderings of an Artist,* 236.
34. "Robert Kennicott," 155-159.
35. "Diary of Nicholas Garry," 129, 133.
36. *Ibid.,* 98.
37. *Ibid.,* 149.
38. *Ibid.,* 149, 150.
39. *Ibid.,* 150, 151.
40. *Ibid.,* 122; diary of John McDonell, entry for August 5, 1793.
41. Gabriel Franchere's letter to Valée, Boyer and Company, quoted in Otto Fowle, *Sault Ste. Marie and Its Great Waterway,* 387, 388 (New York, 1925).
42. Bigsby, *Shoe and Canoe,* 1:141, 143, 147, 151, 154.

V

FORT LIFE

1. See *post,* p. 189.
2. The diary is anonymous, but references in contemporary lists of traders seem to indicate that Thomas Connor was in charge of the Snake River post to which allusion is made. It is in the possession of the Canadian Archives, Ottawa.
3. Connor's diary, entry for October 10, 1804.

4. The diary of Archibald Norman McLeod, 1800-1801, is preserved in the library of McGill University. The entries to which reference is made are for March 3 and 4, 1801.

5. Connor's diary, entries for February 18 and 20, March 1 and 3, 1805.

6. Harmon, *Journal*, 60, 77; McLeod's diary, entry for December 7, 1800.

7. Harmon, *Journal*, 86.

8. Grace Lee Nute, "A Description of Northern Minnesota by a Fur-Trader in 1807," in *Minnesota History Bulletin*, 5: 36, 38, and notes 20 and 26; Joseph N. Provencher, "Notice sur la Rivière Rouge," in *Les cloches de Saint-Boniface*, 26: 90.

9. Issue of February 9, 1860.

10. Harmon, *Journal*, 94.

11. *Ibid.*, 73.

12. "Robert Kennicott," 195.

13. Franklin, *Journey to the Shores of the Polar Sea,* 1: 84.

14. Robert Michael Ballantyne, *Hudson's Bay: Or Every-Day Life in the Wilds of North America*, 167 (London, 1859).

15. "Mr. James McKenzie: Extracts from His Journal, 1799-1800," in L. R. Masson, *Les bourgeois de la compagnie de nord-ouest,* 2: 377, 378 (Quebec, 1890).

16. McLeod's diary, entry for November 30, 1800.

17. Harmon, *Journal*, 23, 57, 58.

18. "Diary of Nicholas Garry," 92, 93.

19. Kane, *Wanderings of an Artist*, 260, 261.

20. Ross Cox, *The Columbia River,* 2: 294.

21. Various manuscripts or copies of documents in the possession of the Minnesota Historical Society, such as Boutwell's diary, the reports of missionaries of the American Board of Commissioners for Foreign Missions, and notes on F. A. Larocque's diary, give information on the careers of these men. See also Harmon, *Journal,* 126, 130.

22. The diaries of McLeod, Harmon, and McDonell have already been cited. François Victoire Malhiot's "Journal du Fort Kamanaiti-quoya à la Rivière Montréal" is published in Masson, *Les bourgeois,* 1: 228-263, and is especially valuable for preserving the everyday language of the voyageurs.

23. Connor's diary, entry of April 25, 1805.

24. "Diary of Nicholas Garry," 135, 136.

25. Kane, *Wanderings of an Artist*, 260.

26. David Thompson's *Narrative,* in *Publications of the Champlain Society*, XII, 216.

27. An anonymous diary, perhaps written by Hugh Faries, in the possession of the Canadian Archives.

28. Egerton R. Young, *The Apostle of the North, Rev. James Evans*, 166 (New York, 1899).

29. "Robert Kennicott," 188.

NOTES

30. Frederick Ayer to students at Oberlin College, February 24, 1843, in the *Oberlin Evangelist*, May 10, 1843.
31. Kane, *Wanderings of an Artist*, 108, 109.
32. Harmon, *Journal*, 61.

VI

VOYAGEUR SONGS

1. "Robert Kennicott," 193. The words and music of practically all the songs given in this chapter can be found in Ernest Gagnon's work cited below.
2. James Lanman, "The American Fur Trade," in *Hunt's Merchants' Magazine*, 3:189 (September, 1840).
3. Ernest Gagnon, *Chansons populaires du Canada*, 178, 179 (Quebec, 1894).
4. Lanman's version may be found in "The American Fur Trade," 189.

> *Tous les printemps,*
> *Tant de nouvelle,*
> *Tous les amants*
> *Changent de maîtresses;*
> *Le bon vin m'endort,*
> *L'amour me réveille.*

> *Tous les amants*
> *Changent de maîtresses.*
> *Qu'ils changent qui voudront,*
> *Pour moi je garde la mienne;*
> *Le bon vin m'endort,*
> *L'amour me réveille.*

5. Bela Hubbard, *Memorials of a Half-Century*, 153 (New York, 1887).
6. Hubbard's version makes the girl resist as she remembers another jealous lover.

> *La jeune Sophie*
> *Chantait l'autre jour,*
> *Son echo lui repete,*
> *Que non pas d'amour*
> *N'est pas de bon jour.*

> *Je suis jeune et belle,*
> *Je vieux mé engagé*
> *Un amant fidele,*
> *Je suis jeune,* etc.

NOTES

Mais ce vous etre belle,
Ce n'est pas de jour;
Ce n'est que vos yeaux
Qui bris à la chandelle.
Mais ce vous, etc.

Unisons ensemble,—
Son cour et le mein,—
Pourquoi tant le defendre,
Puis qu'il s'amaient bien?
Unisons, etc.

Point temps de badinage,
Envers mon amant,
Car il est jaloux:
Tout lui port embrage.
Point temps, etc.

7. Bigsby, *Shoe and Canoe,* 2:81.
8. Gagnon, *Chansons populaires,* 82-86.
9. McKenney, *Tour to the Lakes,* 210.
10. Ballantyne, *Hudson's Bay,* 222.
11. Gagnon, *Chansons populaires,* 87-89.
12. "Diary of Nicholas Garry," 159, 160. The following is Garry's version:

Cueillons la, la belle Rose
Cueillons la, la belle Rose
Cueillons la, car il est tard, la belle Rose
Cueillons la, car il est tard.
   La belle Rose du Rosier blanc.
Cueillons la feuille et par feuille
Cueillons la feuille et par feuille.
Mise dans mon tableau [sic] *blanc*
   La belle Rose du Rosier blanc.
Je l'ai portée chez mon Père
Je l'ai portée chez mon Père
Entre Paris et Rouen
Entre Paris et Rouen
   La belle Rose du Rosier blanc.

Dans mon Chemin je récontrai [sic]
Dans mon Chemin je récontrai
Un Rossignol chantant la belle Rose
Un Rossignol chantant la belle Rose
   La belle Rose du Rosier blanc.
Qui m'a dit dans son Langage
Qui m'a dit dans son Langage

271

Mariez-toi—car il est temps, la belle Rose
Mariez-toi—car il est temps, la belle Rose
La belle Rose du Rosier blanc.

Eh! Comment me marierai je
Eh! Comment me marierai je?
Mon Père n'est pas content
Mon Père n'est pas content
Ni mon Père, ni ma Mère
Ni mon Père, ni ma Mère
Ni aucune de mes Parents
Ni aucune de mes Parents
Je m'en irai au Service
Je m'en irai au Service;
En Service pour un An
Et la belle Rose du Rosier blanc
En Service pour un An
Et la belle Rose du Rosier blanc.

Combien gagnez vous, la belle
Combien gagnez vous, la belle
Combien gagnez vous par An
Combien gagnez vous par An
Je ne gagne que cinq cent Livres
Je ne gagne que cinq cent Livres
Cinq cents Livres en Argent blanc
Cinq cents Livres en Argent blanc
La belle Rose du Rosier blanc.

13. Garry's version, given below, may be found in "Diary of Nicholas Garry," 160-161.

Quand j'étais chez mon Père,
Petite Janeton,
Il m'envoyait à la fontaine
Pour pêcher du poisson.
La Violette Dandon, oh! la Violette dondé.

Il m'envoyait à la fontaine
Pour pêcher du poisson.
La fontaine est profonde
Je suis coulée au fond.
La Violette, etc.

Il m'envoyait à la fontaine
Pour pêcher du poisson.
Par-ici ils passèrent trois
Trois Cavaliers barons.
La Violette, etc.

Par-ici ils passèrent trois
  Trois Cavaliers barons.
"Que donneriez vous, ma belle,
  Qui vous tireront du fond?"
La Violette, etc.

"Que donneriez vous, ma belle,
  Qui vous tireront du fond?"
"Tirez, tirez," dit elle;
  "Après ça, nous verrons."
La Violette, etc.

"Tirez, tirez," dit elle;
  "Après ça, nous verrons."
Quand la belle fût tirée
  Elle va à sa Maison.
La Violette, etc.

Quand la belle fût tirée
  Elle va à sa Maison.
S'asseyant sur un fenêtre
  Elle composait un Chanson.
La Violette, etc.

S'asseyant sur un fenêtre
  Elle composait un Chanson.
"Ce n'est pas ce, ma belle,
  Ce que nous demandons."
La Violette, etc.

"Ce n'est pas ce, ma belle,
  Ce que nous demandons.
Votre petit Cœur en gage
  Sçavoir si nous l'aurons."
La Violette Dandon, oh! la Violette dondé.

14. Marius Barbeau and Edward Sapir, *Folk Songs of French Canada*, 83, 84 (New Haven, 1925).
15. "Diary of Nicholas Garry," 194; Gagnon, *Chansons populaires*, 12-15.
16. Gagnon, *Chansons populaires*, 189, 190.
17. Mrs. Jameson, *Sketches in Canada, and Rambles Among the Red Men*, 299 (London, 1852).
18. Gagnon, *Chansons populaires*, 129, 130.
19. Mrs. Jameson, *Sketches in Canada*, 299.
20. F. A. H. La Rue, "Les chansons populaires et historiques du Canada," in *Le foyer canadien*, 1 : 360; Gagnon, *Chansons populaires*, 8, 9.
21. Gagnon, *Chansons populaires*, 68; La Rue, "Les chansons populaires," 365.

NOTES

22. La Rue, "Les chansons populaires," 365.
23. *Ibid.*, 365, 366.
24. *Ibid.*, 367. It is only fair to remark that the word *voyageur* here probably was used in the sense of traveler, though doubtless the canoemen believed it had reference to themselves. The French of the Barbeau and Sapir version of this song is as follows:

> *Quand le soldat arrive en ville* (bis)
> *Bien mal chaussé, bien mal vêtu:*
> *"Pauvre soldat, d'où reviens-tu?"*
>
> *S'en fut loger dans une auberge:*
> *"Hôtesse, avez-vous du vin blanc?"*
> *—"Voyageur, a'-vous de l'argent?"*
>
> *—"Pour de l'argent, je n'en ai guère;*
> *J'engagerai mon vieux chapeau,*
> *Ma ceinture, aussi mon manteau."*
>
> *Quand le voyageur fut à table,*
> *Il se mit à boire, à chanter;*
> *L'hôtess' ne fit plus que pleurer.*
>
> *"Oh! qu'avez-vous, petite hôtesse?*
> *Regrettez-vous votre vin blanc*
> *Qu'un voyageur boit sans argent?"*
>
> *—"N'est pas mon vin que je regrette;*
> *C'est la chanson que vous chantez:*
> *Mon défunt mari la savait.*
>
> *"J'ai un mari dans les voyages;*
> *Voilà sept ans qu'il est parti,*
> *Je crois bien que vous êtes lui."*
>
> *—"Ah! taisez-vous, méchante femme.*
> *Je vous ai laissé deux enfants,*
> *En voilà quatre ici présents!"*
>
> *—"J'ai tant reçu de fausses lettres,*
> *Que vous étiez mort, enterré.*
> *Et moi, je me suis marié'."*
>
> *—"Dedans Paris, il y-a grand guerre,*
> *Grand guerre rempli' de tourments.*
> *Adieu, ma femme et mes enfants!"*

274

25. La Rue, "Les chansons populaires," 371, 372; Gagnon, *Chansons populaires*, 200-208. La Rue's version is as follows:

> Petits oiseaux, dedans vos charmants nids,
> Vous qui chantez pendant que je gémis,
> Si j'avais des ailes comme vous,
> Je vivrais content avant qu'il fut jour.
>
> Rossignolet, va dire à ma maitresse,
> Que de mon cœur engagé je la laisse,
> Que de mon cœur engagé, je la laisse;
> Que désormais elle ne pense plus à moi.
>
> Par un beau jour m'en allant à la chasse,
> Pensant toujours à mes chers camarades,
> Je me suis dit, hélas! sont'ils noyés,
> Ou les Iroquois les ont-ils tués.
>
> Un autre jour, revenant de la chasse,
> J'ai aperçu une petite boucane;
> Je me suis dit: ah! Grand Dieu! qu'est-ce que ceci,
> Les Iroquois ont-ils pris mon logis?
>
> Tout aussitôt je fus en embuscade,
> Pour reconnaître ces visages;
> Je crus connaître trois visages français,
> Qui me causa une très-grande joie.
>
> Un loup hurlant tout près de ma cabane:
> Il me disait: je sens ton corps qui est malade;
> Je lui ai dit: retire-toi d'ici,
> Car sur ma foi, je percerai ton habit.
>
> Va-t-en là-haut, là-bas sur ces montagnes,
> Tu trouveras des tripes, aussi des os,
> Tu trouveras des tripes, aussi des os;
> Mange ton saoul, et laisse-moi en repos.
>
> Tous ces corbeaux qui vont à l'aventure,
> Toujours cherchant une herbe de nature,
> Je leur ai dit: mangeurs de chair humaine,
> Allez ailleurs chercher un autre corps que le mien.
>
> C'est aujourd'hui que le monde j'abandonne,
> Je n'ai recours qu'à vous, Sauveur des hommes;
> Ah! Sainte-Vierge, ne m'abandonnez pas,
> Permettez-moi que je me rende entre vos bras.

NOTES

26. La Rue, "Les chansons populaires," 372, 373.
27. Keating, *Narrative of an Expedition to the Source of St. Peter's River,* 2:92.
28. Bigsby, *Shoe and Canoe,* 1:119.
29. *Ibid.,* 1:134.
30. "Mr. W. F. Wentzel, Letters to the Hon. Roderic M°Kenzie, 1807-1824," in Masson, *Les bourgeois,* 1:71.

VII

THE VOYAGEUR AS SOLDIER

1. Louise P. Kellogg, *Frontier Advance on the Upper Ohio, 1778-1779,* 14, in *Wisconsin Historical Collections,* 23 (Madison, 1916).
2. *Ibid.,* 83, 92, 114, 115, 119.
3. *Wisconsin Historical Collections,* 18:161.
4. *Ibid.,* 18:375.
5. A. P. Nasatir, "The Anglo-Spanish Frontier in the Illinois Country during the American Revolution, 1779-1783," in the Illinois Historical Society *Journal,* 21:353 (October, 1928).
6. *Wisconsin Historical Collections,* 18:396, 397.
7. Lord Selkirk, the sworn enemy of the Northwest Company, tarnished the glory of their act by declaring that they had an eye to business in securing voyageurs, who would thus be ready for signing trade engagements in the spring without the usual difficulties incident to rounding up crews. See Thomas, Earl of Selkirk, *A Sketch of the British Fur Trade in North America,* 30-36 (London, 1816); and [John Halkett] *Statement Respecting the Earl of Selkirk's Settlement upon the Red River in North America,* 13-15, vi (London, 1817). In this work, the date of the discharge of the corps is given as March 12, 1813.
8. Selkirk, *Sketch of the British Fur Trade in North America,* 33, 34.
9. Halkett, *Statement Respecting the Earl of Selkirk's Settlement,* 13; L. Homfray Irving, *Officers of the British Forces in Canada during the War of 1812-15,* 103, 114 (Welland, 1908).
10. Ross Cox, *The Columbia River,* 2:294-297.
11. William Wood, *Select British Documents of the Canadian War of 1812,* in *Publications of the Champlain Society,* No. XIII, 1:669, 676 (Toronto, 1920).
12. A. G. Morice, *Histoire de l'église catholique dans l'ouest canadien du Lac Supérieur au Pacifique (1659-1915),* 1:390 (Winnipeg, 1928).
13. Bigsby, *Shoe and Canoe,* 1:124.
14. Wood, *Select British Documents,* 1:24.
15. *Ibid.,* 1:432.
16. *Ibid.,* 1:438.

NOTES

17. Wood, *Select British Documents*, 1:448-452.
18. *Ibid.*, 1:437.
19. Irving, *Officers of the British Forces in Canada*, 96-99.
20. James H. Lockwood, "Early Times and Events in Wisconsin," in *Wisconsin Historical Collections*, 2:124.
21. "John McDonald of Garth Autobiographical Notes," in Masson, *Les bourgeois*, 2:44, 45.
22. Irving, *Astoria*, 49, 50.

VIII

THE VOYAGUER AS SETTLER

1. See D. L. Crossman, "How the Last French Claim to a Michigan Farm was Extinguished," in *Michigan Pioneer and Historical Collections*, 14:644 (Lansing, ——) quoting a report of La Jonquière and Bigot, governor and intendant of New France, respectively, in a document dated October 18, 1750. The translator has used "travelers" for the French word *voyageurs*, without a doubt the word used in the original.
2. See La Jonquière to the Minister of Colonies, October 5, 1751, quoted in William W. Warren, *History of the Ojibway Nation*, 433-436 (*Minnesota Historical Collections*, Volume 5, St. Paul, 1885).
3. Henry, *Travels*, 60.
4. John Long, *Voyages and Travels of an Indian Interpreter and Trader*, ed. Reuben Gold Thwaites, 2:79 (Cleveland, 1904).
5. Alexander Mackenzie, *Voyages from Montreal through the Continent of North America to the Frozen and Pacific Oceans in 1789 and 1793*, ed. W. L. Grant, 47 (Toronto, 1911).
6. Harmon, *Journal*, entry for May 30, 1800.
7. See a brief biographical account of Johnston in Masson, *Les bourgeois*, 2:137-142, as an introduction to Johnston's "An Account of Lake Superior, 1792-1807."
8. "Memoir of John Johnston," in *Michigan Pioneer and Historical Collections*, 25:663 (Lansing, 1894).
9. "The Fur-Trade in Wisconsin, 1812-15," in *Wisconsin Historical Collections*, 20:155, note 18 (Madison, 1911).
10. Gabriel Franchere, *Narrative of a Voyage to the Northwest Coast of America*, 354 (New York, 1854).
11. *Ibid.*, 352.
12. George Johnstone's "Reminiscences of Sault Ste. Marie, 1815," in *Michigan Pioneer and Historical Collections*, 12:607, 608 (Lansing, 1888).
13. Henry R. Schoolcraft, *Summary Narrative of an Exploring Expedition to the Sources of the Mississippi River in 1820*, 48 (Philadelphia, 1855).

NOTES

14. Reports of these priests may be found among the archiepiscopal archives of Quebec.

15. Franz Pierz, *Die Indianer in Nord-Amerika,* 68-70 (St. Louis, 1855); *Annales de la propagation de la foi,* 3:326-328; Antoine Ivan Rezek, *History of the Diocese of Sault Ste. Marie,* 2:44-48 (Houghton, Michigan, 1907).

16. Grace Lee Nute, "The American Fur Company's Fishing Enterprises on Lake Superior," in the *Mississippi Valley Historical Review,* 12:483-503 (March, 1926).

17. A quotation from C. D. O'Brien in P. Chrysostomus Verwyst, *Life and Labors of Rt. Rev. Frederic Baraga,* 291-293 (Milwaukee, 1900).

18. A master's thesis by Rollo Keithahn entitled "The American Fur Company in the Upper Mississippi Valley," University of Minnesota, p. 57.

19. "The Unfinished Autobiography of Henry Hastings Sibley," in *Minnesota History,* 8:353, 354.

20. This letter is addressed to Aaron Hall, Jr.; a copy is in the possession of the Minnesota Historical Society.

21. The pencil sketch is to be found among the Frank B. Mayer papers in the possession of the Edward E. Ayer collection of the Newberry Library, Chicago, Volume 42, 64-65. Faintly discernible above the mantel is the word "mud," indicating the main substance of which the chimney was made.

22. E. K. Smith to Major J. Plympton, October 19, 1837, in *Sale of Fort Snelling Reservation,* 16 (40th Congress, 3rd session, *House Executive Documents,* No. 9—Serial 1372); M. M. Hoffmann, "New Light on Old St. Peter's and Early St. Paul," in *Minnesota History,* 8:38.

23. Volume 2, p. 98 (London, 1839).

24. *Annals of the Propagation of the Faith* (Dublin), 3:339 (September, 1840).

25. Information on the ensuing individuals may be found in Hoffmann, "New Light"; and in J. Fletcher Williams, *A History of the City of Saint Paul, and of the County of Ramsey* (*Minnesota Historical Collections,* Volume 4). For the "atmosphere" of life at the Entry about 1840, read Maud Hart Lovelace, *Early Candlelight, A Novel* (New York, 1929), in which many voyageurs appear under their own names.

26. Williams, *Saint Paul,* 75.

27. *Ibid.,* 111, 112.

28. *Ibid.,* 184, 185.

29. Henry H. Sibley, "Reminiscences of the Early Days of Minnesota," in *Minnesota Historical Collections,* 3:248, 249.

30. A. S. Morton, "The Place of the Red River Settlement in the Plans of the Hudson's Bay Co., 1812-1825," in the Canadian Historical Association, *Report of the Annual Meeting held at Ottawa . . . 1929,* 106.

NOTES

31. Ramsay Crooks to John Jacob Astor, about April, 1817 [the first portion of the letter is missing], in a letterbook of the American Fur Company preserved at Mackinac, p. 12. Crooks knew the voyageur thoroughly and comprehended his needs and modest requirements with a genuine concern for his wellbeing that is a credit to one of the busiest and acutest business men of his age. Thus in this same letter he writes: "The necessity of an Agent at this place [*Montreal*] is obvious . . . [a portion is missing relating to the payment of voyageurs at Montreal on their return from the interior] to pay punctually for duties faithfully performed is one of the strongest pillars of commerce, and in this trade perhaps of more moment than in any other, for the family of the *Voyageur* in his absence not unfrequently subsists in part on the credit of the voyage he is then performing. Independent of every other consideration it is only necessary to recollect that [a] servant once disappointed in his just expectations will not be very likely to put himself again into the power of his deceiver. I would therefore recommend that a person be appointed Agent here for the above purposes. And that funds be always placed in time at his disposal, to meet every engagement on the day appointed."

32. E. H. Oliver, *The Canadian Northwest,* 632, "Introductory Remarks upon the Minutes of the Council of the Northern Department of Rupert's Land, 1830 to 1843, supplementary to those of Professor Oliver, by Isaac Cowie, formerly a Commissioned Official of the Hudson's Bay Company." In this paragraph Cowie refers to "the old plan of the North Westers to form a settlement on the Rainy River for their retired servants." He suggests that this may have given the Earl his idea of such a colony.

33. J. N. Provencher to Bishop Plessis, July 19, 1824, in Quebec archiepiscopal archives; printed in "Lettres de Monseigneur Joseph-Norrert Provencher, premier evêque de Saint-Boniface," in *Bulletin de la société historique de Saint-Boniface,* Volume 3, p. 100 (St. Boniface, 1913).

34. The ensuing quotations are from Alexander Ross, *The Fur Hunters of the Far West,* 2: 234-247 *passim* (London, 1855).

35. *Report of Major Wood, relative to his expedition to Pembina Settlement, and the condition of affairs on the North-Western frontier of the Territory of Minnesota,* in 31st Congress, 1st session, *House Executive Documents,* No. 51—Serial 577.

36. Lord Selkirk to Bishop Plessis, Quebec archiepiscopal archives.

37. Morice, *Histoire de l'église catholique,* 1: 137, note 13. See also the testimony of William M'Gillivray in A. Amos, *Report of Trials in the Courts of Canada Relating to the Destruction of the Earl of Selkirk's Settlement,* 275, 303 (London, 1820). On the return trip Lagimonière was captured, beat "in a shocking manner, and plundered . . . of his dispatches, his canoe, and everything it contained." See Halkett, *Statement Respecting the Earl of Selkirk's Settlement,* 41, 42, note.

NOTES

38. A manuscript history of the Northwest Company by Roderic Mackenzie in Canadian Archives, p. 165.
39. Morice, *Histoire de l'église catholique*, 1:137.
40. Bishop Plessis to Tabeau, March 8, 1818.
41. The details of Charbonneau's life are based on G. Dugas, *Un voyageur des pays d'en haut* (Montreal, 1912).
42. Bigsby, *Shoe and Canoe*, 1:130, 134, 148.
43. James H. Lockwood, "Early Times and Events in Wisconsin," in *Wisconsin Historical Collections*, 2:105, 107, 121, 122.

IX

THE VOYAGEUR AS EXPLORER

1. *Alexander Henry's Travels and Adventures in the Years 1760-1776*, 306 (Chicago, 1921).
2. Mackenzie, *Voyages*, 2:73, 74.
3. *Ibid.*, 2:29.
4. *Ibid.*, 2:251.
5. *Ibid.*, 2:112-115.
6. *Ibid.*, 2:116.
7. *Ibid.*, 2:123.
8. *Ibid.*, 2:94, 95.
9. *Ibid.*, 2:133, 134.
10. *Ibid.*, 2:142.
11. *Ibid.*, 2:167, 168.
12. *Ibid.*, 2:173.
13. *Ibid.*, 2:184, 185.
14. *Ibid.*, 2:192.
15. *Ibid.*, 2:194, 195.
16. *Ibid.*, 2:240.
17. *Ibid.*, 2:319, 320.
18. *Ibid.*, 2:340.
19. The ensuing quotations are taken from "Mr. Simon Fraser, Journal of a Voyage from the Rocky Mountains to the Pacific Coast 1808," in Masson, *Les bourgeois*, 1:157-221. Page numbers are not given if the date is indicated.
20. *Ibid.*, 170, 171.
21. *Ibid.*, 207, 208.
22. John Franklin, *Narrative of a Journey to the Shores of the Polar Sea, in the Years 1819-20-21-22*, 1:301, 302 (London, 1824).
23. *Ibid.*, 1:339, 340.
24. *Ibid.*, 2:3, 4.
25. *Ibid.*, 2:36.
26. *Ibid.*, 2:37.
27. *Ibid.*, 2:69.
28. *Ibid.*, 2:75.

NOTES

29. Wentzel insinuates very broadly that some of the voyageurs were eaten by the officers. He also takes occasion to score the printed accounts for injustice to the voyageurs. See his letters to [Roderic] Mackenzie, especially that of March 1, 1824, in Masson, *Les bourgeois*, 1: 149.

30. George Bryce, *The Remarkable History of the Hudson's Bay Company*, 272, 273 (New York, 1910).

31. Archibald McDonald, *Journal of Canoe Voyage from Hudson's Bay to the Pacific. By the Late Sir George Simpson, Governor of the Honorable Hudson's Bay Company*, 2 (Ottawa, 1872).

32. *Ibid.*, 3.

33. *Ibid.*, 4.

34. *Ibid.*, 52.

35. *Ibid.*, 6.

36. Thomas Simpson, *Narrative of the Discoveries on the North Coast of America*, 342 (London, 1843).

37. *Ibid.*, 112.

38. *Ibid.*, 218, 219.

39. *Ibid.*, 370.

40. Sir John Richardson, *Arctic Searching Expedition: A Journal of a Boat-Voyage Through Rupert's Land and the Arctic Sea* (London, 1851).

41. William Henry Drummond, M.D., *The Voyageur and Other Poems* (New York, 1905).

INDEX

283

INDEX

286

INDEX

Richelieu River, residence of voyageurs, 35

Riel, Louis, 214

Roberts, Charles, in War of 1812, 166, 167

Robertson, Colin, with brigade of voyageurs, 218

Rocheblava, Pierre de, in War of 1812, 162

Rocque (Roque), Augustin, 161, 200

Rondeau, Joseph (Rondo), 194

Ross, Alexander, cited, 206-210

St. Anne's church, 39

St. Croix River, fort on, 78

St. Louis, 89, 177

St. Louis River, 63

St. Paul, Minn., 89, 193, 195, 197, 198. *See also* St. Peter's.

St. Peter's (Mendota, Minn.), 178; voyageur community, 188-201

St. Pierre, 227

Salut à mon pays, song, 144

Sandy Lake, 82

Sapir, Edward, cited, 128, 144, 147

Saskatchewan River, 63, 251

Sault Ste. Marie, 60, 72, 170; in War of 1812, 168; as voyageur community, 178-188

Schoolcraft, Henry R., 257

Selkirk, Thomas, Earl of, 202, 204, 214, 215, 258; cited, 213

Semple, Robert, 205

Seven Oaks, battle, 205, 216

Shaw, Angus, in War of 1812, 163

Sibley, Henry Hastings, 188, 192; cited, 198-200, 221

Simpson, Sir George, travels, 248-253

Simpson, Thomas, explorations, 253-257

Sioux uprising of 1862, 221

Smith, Donald, Lord Strathcona and Mount Royal, 258

Smith, Lieut. E. K., 191

Snowshoes, 97

Songs, of voyageur, 28, 29, 104-155; *la ronde,* 41-45

South Pass, voyageurs at, 173

Southesk, Earl of, 258

Southwest Company, 9

Spain, in American Revolution, 161

Stuart, David, 172 173

Stuart, John, 238

Stuart, Robert, 173, 257

Sturgeon Lake, 91

Tabeau, Pierre Antoine, 183, 216, 221

Taché, J. C., 151, 261

Thompson, David, 258; cited, 94, 222

Tracking, 40

Travel methods of voyageurs, 35-74

Traverse des Sioux, voyageur community, 193

Traverses, 61

Turpin, Amable, 197

Turpin, Joseph, 194

Tute, James, 164

Une perdriole, song, 114

Vermilion Lake, 91

Vincennes, 159

Voici le printemps, song, 110, 111

Voyageurs, meaning of term, 3, 5; family names, 6; characteristics, 7, 255; number of, 7; relation to fur trade, 8; im-

INDEX

Voyageurs (*continued*)
portance in history, 8; as settlers, 10, 177-224; place names given by, 10, 40. 258-261; costume, 13, 42, 74; described, 13-20; nicknames, 16; pride of profession, 17; boasting, 19, 100; superstitions, 26, 62, 209, 210; language of, 28, 48, 255; travel methods, 35-74; equipment, 36; trade engagements, 36; customs, 40, 50, 95, 96; *la ronde,* 41-45; food, 45, 51-56; mutinies, 49, 50, 243, 244; politeness, 59; appearance, 73; building methods, 77, 78, 188-191, 244, 245; individuals mentioned, 81, 83, 87-90, 138, 165, 169, 181-183, 192-197, 206-210, 223, 229, 243, 246, 247, 254; amusements, 83-87, 99, 100; at New Year's, 83; dances, 83, 84, 90, 242; marriages, 87, 224; occupations in fort, 89-91; illnesses, 91, 97; as soldiers, 159-173, 178; services in War of 1812, 162-170, 180; as fisher-

Voyageurs (*continued*)
men, 183-185; and Exclusion Act of 1816, 203; as couriers, 214, 215, 219; as explorers, 227-263; relations with Indians, 233, 240; songs, 350 (*See* Songs); wit, 255, 256

Wattape, described, 25, 70
Wentzel, 85, 155, 244, 246
Whittier, John G., cited, 217, 218
Winnipeg, 89. *See also* Red River Settlement.
Winnipeg River, 59, 63
Winterer. *See Hivernant.*
Wisconsin, voyageur place names in, 260
Wisconsin River, 63
Woods, Major Samuel, cited, 211

Yellow Lake, Wisconsin, 92
Young, Egerton R., cited, 95

Zeisberger, David, 160